BECOMING MATURE

Childhood Ghosts and Spirits in Adult Life

COMMUNICATION AND SOCIAL ORDER

An Aldine de Gruyter Series of Texts and Monographs

Series Editor

David R. Maines, *The Pennsylvania State University*

Advisory Editors

Bruce E. Gronbeck, *University of Iowa*
Peter K. Manning, *Michigan State University*
William K. Rawlins, *Purdue University*

Becoming Mature: Childhood Ghosts and Spirits in Adult Life
Valerie Malhotra Bentz

Life As Theater: A Dramaturgical Sourcebook, Second Edition
Dennis Brissett and Charles Edgley, Editors

BECOMING MATURE

Childhood Ghosts and Spirits in Adult Life

Valerie Malhotra Bentz

Aldine de Gruyter
New York

About the Author

Valerie Malhotra Bentz is Associate Professor of Sociology at the Texas Woman's University in Denton, Texas. Her areas of expertise include Sociological Theory, Social Psychology, Qualitative Research Methods, Sociology of the Arts, Social Psychology of Women, Social Work Practice, Sociology of Childhood, and Sociological Practice. She is a co-editor of *Visual Images of Women in the Arts and Mass Media* and the author of numerous journal articles. She has also served as a reviewer for the journals *Sociological Quarterly*, *Qualitative Sociology*, and *Social Science Quarterly*. Professor Bentz is founder and Vice-President for Education and Research, Institute on Communication and Mental Health Studies, Inc., Denton.

ALDINE DE GRUYTER
A Division of Walter de Gruyter, Inc.
200 Saw Mill River Road
Hawthorne, New York 10532

Library of Congress Cataloging-in-Publication Data

Bentz, Valerie Malhotra, 1942–
    Becoming mature : childhood ghosts and spirits in adult life / Valerie Malhotra Bentz.
        p.   cm. — (Communication and social order)
    Bibliography: p.
    Includes index.
    ISBN 0-202-30358-6.   ISBN 0-202-30359-4 (pbk.)
    1. Women—United States—Psychology—Case studies.
    2. Developmental psychology—United States—Case studies.
    I. Title.   II. Series.
    HQ1206.B36   1989
    155.6'33—dc20   89-34828
                                                                              CIP

Printed in the United States of America
10 9 8 7 6 5 4 3 2 1

To my daughter, Pamela Malhotra

Contents

1

2

⑥

⑦

⑧

⑨

10

Acknowledgements _____

I appreciate the assistance of the following persons in various aspects of this research: Jeffrey LaMar Deneen, Tamera Bryant, Ann Tidball, Margaret Maher, Carol Stabel, Shirley Rombough, Jan Marlow, Abderahmane Azzi, Ann Shea, Bobby Moodley, Askwin Vyas, Tim Nissen, Steven Kurtz, John Johannsen, Mike Burnidge, Clarice Allen, Dai-Na Sun, Jerian Stem and Joan Haase. There were many others who helped in ways too numerous to mention.

The following persons have read the manuscript and provided helpful commentary: Mary Jo Deegan, Leo Papa, Walter French, Tamera Bryant, and Joyce Williams. The commentary of Peter K. Manning, editoral advisor to Aldine de Gruyter, was exceedingly insightful and helpful. The encouragement of David Maines, editor of the Aldine de Gruyter "Communication and Social Order" series is greatly appreciated.

The late Helmut Wagner, mentor, teacher and friend, was also a reader of this manuscript. His scholarship, humanity and gentleness will always inspire me.

I am grateful for the financial support received from a source which must remain anonymous to protect the anonymity of the participants.

Most of all I am thankful to the fifty-three participants in the research who must remain anonymous.

Only I am responsible for the content of the book and the opinions expressed.

Valerie Malhotra Bentz

Foreword
Ghosts and Spirits _____

It is not easy to integrate emotions, thoughts and choices, and even more difficult to accept graciously the constraints and unexplicated burdens of the past. To do so requires an understanding of the way the past reappears repeatedly in the present. *On Becoming Mature* is an exciting and touching book that struggles with these themes.

The central question addressed by Valerie Malhotra Bentz in this book is the influence of childhood experience on normal development and maturation. This theme is traced in a group of fifty-three young women in order to identify and describe the pertinent early influences shaping the quality of adult lives. The young women participated in an intense, self-reflective research project designed to reveal the impact of their childhood experiences on their current life adaptations. The book features "ghosts and spirits," inner voices, and echoes from the past, that establish the context for decisions and animate the present. Ghosts and spirits sit with us, representing figures from the past. They hover, circle and dance around, only unexpectedly revealing themselves. The power of such ghosts, called many things in the literature such as "transference," "significant others," or "objects," is manifest in these women's lives. In a rich set of vivid life narratives, the book successfully renders a sensitive evocation of persons and their ghosts as well as a powerful description of grief and passion.

The framework Bentz expertly employs allows her to weave together ideas from the rather dense and difficult works of Heidegger, Habermas, Mead, and Schutz into a theoretic perspective. She skillfully draws together her materials, narratives, quotes from interviews, and snippets from diaries to question the prevalent "stage" theories of development. The book's argument unfolds in an effective manner, as the author employs first delicate and then didactic prose, moving from the lives at issue to quotes and summaries from theorists, to the author's own hopeful, almost utopian, asides (reminiscent of Fielding's asides to the reader in *Tom Jones*). In the final chapters, she advances a general perspective on adequate parenting using these lives to outline conditions under which intergenerational communication is likely to be effective.

It is perhaps valuable to insert a word at the outset about the role and limits of language which is fundamental to phenomenological and hermeneutic analyses. The featured women do not fully articulate the shape and content of their most fundamental experiences. They index them, allude to them, gesture toward them. Perhaps this allusory quality arises from editorial decisions made by the author; or perhaps they result from my selective perception and projection. In any case, one can never fully know another. As a result of reading these stories, I was made curious, struck with my desire to meet, speak and listen to these people, see the cast of their eyes as the sun shone on them, and to assess the angle of their heads, measure their postures and gestures.

The bits of lives, you will soon discover, fit and glow like freshly-laid tiles in a subtle mosaic. Think, for example, of the diary excerpt in which the woman writes about arising to a new day and seeing herself looking fleetingly into a mirror. This vignette is brilliantly conceived and is powerful in its resonance. It says to the reader as the writer said to herself upon viewing herself in the mirror: here I am. Look at the me looking at myself this morning, see this body of mine, in the here and now. Is it ready? Am I ready? Is the me I see the me I desire others to like? As I read that passage, I thought of the rather sad and sometimes vaguely distressed women in the elegant novels of Anita Brookner and Barbara Pym, and in the dazzling prose portraits of Margaret Drabble. In those pages, as in these, one captures oblique glimpses of one's self—as one often does in the social sciences and in the mass media.

What, after all, is "normal?" The author notes that "Most of these women did not experience 'ideal' or normal childhoods . . . ," but she is well aware that the concept of "normal" is not clear in the social science or psychiatric literature. What does a life mean? How is it shaped by experience, odd conversations, chance meetings, wrong turns, and physical encounters? In these pages one finds rich, varied, and complex cameos of womens' lives embedded in social structure. So often, it would seem, the subjects of the work dance in happiness when they recognize some outlines, the shapes of constraint, even previously unseen vicissitudes. Is life a series of snapshots, or a film? One might think of how pictures taken at ritual occasions (weddings, anniversaries, birthdays, funerals) evoke both individual and shared memories. How will such pictures, much like the snatches of lives here, evoke future memories? Who is missing from such pictures, and which ghosts are residing in whose experience? That a clear resolution of these questions is unlikely and rarely shared is beside the point. Reading aspects of these lives arouses a passion for such knowledge, and suggests the value of scrutinizing those images that populate the conscious mind, as well as the forces of sex and violence, fantasies and the defenses, that shape their expression. What compromises yield the kinds of "internal voices" that speak, day and night, dreaming and awake, and drive us to places we little understand? Ghosts speak to us, and we replay mental images, pictures of ourselves as we are, might have been, could be, and were. These are ghostly pictures.

We can distinguish the voices from the past that speak to us and act on them accordingly as the author suggests. Understanding the nature of these delineation, rather than focusing merely on the presence or absence of spirits and ghosts, is a key to normal maturity. Maturity is an elusive matter, and is organized not on the basis of stages but by what Jaspers called "axial events," or those that change a person's history and life course. Lives are patterned and ordered by such events as crises, turning points, broken commitments, new bonds, and by turning back to see oneself looking at oneself. Clusters of people with shared experiences form the chapters, and they move the narrative toward the notion that people are shaped not by life cycles but by epiphanies, orbits in outer social space, epistemic breaks and fissures.

Is the quality of social bonds gender-specific, and should theories of development be "gender-sensitive"? Fragile indeed are most human bonds. At times they seem as delicate as lace, yet enduring and resilient. It is clear that negotiating relationships is difficult, and that intimate relations are the most problematic and most relevant. Women perhaps more than men seem to spin and twist silently in their webs, seeking to be "free," yet desiring intimacy. Yesterday, as I left another dreary academic meeting and crossed the street, I observed two women, heavily encumbered with backpacks, heavy coats and bags, stop in the middle of a road to embrace and pat each other as they exchanged tearful looks and comments. This scene is an evocative conjunction, something that the cameos rendered here seem to imply is an often unfilled human need. And this need for intimacy combined with autonomy is surely a product (at least in part) of the past, the living-in-the-present-past. Many victims of incest, abuse, bereavement, poverty, and neglect, fill these pages. Yet, they have forged lives with almost amazing tenacity. They grope for that which they imagine others possess, the semblance of peace and order, the resident happiness, the abiding satisfaction derived from love, sex and work.

What produces satisfaction? There is a particular theme or core of rationality here; the notion that life should or can be orderly, progressive, satisfying, and fulfilling. Having read these pages with fascination, one is not sure whether the women portrayed are themselves certain what fulfillment might entail. Whatever their efforts to change and to understand, their lives are admirable. This clinging belief drives these women to spend long hours commuting and studying, seeking further education. Will education liberate and empower them? They struggle, very self-reflective and painfully self-conscious, toward some version of self-truth. These are not happy women; they seem to edge toward happiness and then move away, like someone fascinated by the view and dizziness produced by looking over the edge of a cliff. The struggle depicted here is palpable.

Why should one read this book as a kind of human document, indexing one's self? The reader sees aspects of his or her self here, as do the subjects. The author is mirrored in the text as well. The text, the reader, the author and the subjects of the research should be seen as constituting parts of a complex humanistic paradigm. The research approach of *On Becoming Mature* is reflexive and was intended not simply as an academic exercise, but to help others to understand their experiences in a somewhat more detached fashion. Lives, at least of most of these people, are not so much lived as endured. As a result of the meetings required by participation in the research, the subjects faced painful memories, still resonant images, and events they might rather have forgotten. Behind these quilted lives of real women is a sensitive writer who occasionally peeks around her words to gaze thoughtfully at the reader. Cool, luminous, appraising, a watchful gaze, a warm appreciative eye, Valerie Malhotra Bentz tentatively reveals herself. She is a part of the humanistic equation as are her subjects, readers, and her data.

There are men as well as women here. Much reported misery comes from the men who variously need and love the women of this text. Men seem unable to fulfill ghostly requirements. Thus, something of a truism emerges: gender roles are relational roles, men and women are locked together in fateful adagios, and much of what is considered meaningful or "real" experience is gender-based or sexual in character.

The final chapters weave together various slippery ideas such as adulthood, maturity, and achievement like strands in a rope. These are in part shaped by male notions dominant in the culture. The concept of maturity remains complex in spite of the author's efforts to explicate and exemplify it. Altering focus, 'hermeneutic turns,' or changes in interpretative contexts serve as a feature of the author's analytic framework. She moves the focus from self to other, and thence to institutions, and presents facets of very real people in roles coping variously with vaguely understood contingencies.

P.K. Manning
East Lansing, Michigan

Ghost of a Chance _____ 1

Maturity is a process rather than a state of being, a way of being rather than a property, a response to a gift rather than an object to be controlled. Maturity is a fascinating and awesome adventure, and a creature response to an over-whelming gift; it also a work.   Bernard J. Boelen
Personal Maturity

Becoming Mature

Introduction

This book is about the way we grow, change, and become who we are. It is about how parents and others important to us in childhood shape our being, thinking, feeling, and subsequent relationships. These inter-actions with others are similarly framed by neighborhoods, work orga-nizations, schools, and other institutions.

The book originates from three sources. The first is an empirical study of the life experiences of 53 women from childhood until the present. The second is my work which juxtaposes current sociological theory, developmental theory, and qualitative methodology. The third source is my own life experiences and observations. While the primary focus of this book is on the 53 women, I interpret and understand their experi-ences through the colored lenses of my life experiences. The voices of significant others I hear in the present are echoed through the voices of my remembered parents. My work as a sociological theorist, psycho-therapist, and qualitative researcher, provides anchorage for these un-derstandings. Others would view the same data differently. In no way can the actual lives of real human beings be fully understood within the limited scope of a single study. The case constructions and conclusions reached in this book represent my best effort to make the information presented by the fifty-three persons meaningful. Readers and critics are welcome to offer alternative interpretations.

The overall approach taken in this book is "hermeneutic phenome-

1

nology" (see Ricoeur, 1981). Hermeneutics is the theory of interpretation particularly of texts. "Texts" may be written narratives, such as the
diaries used in this study. One may also look upon conversations, gestures, styles of dress, and various cultural artifacts as similar to texts in
that they may be interpreted. The experiences of living human beings
are embodied and situated in a rich natural and social context. As such,
lived experiences go far beyond a text. The phenomenological approach
includes all aspects of experience—textual and nontextual. Phenomenology focuses on consciousness which is intentional and constitut-
ive—that is, it structures experience. The hermeneutic phenomenologist
insists that the premises, perceptions, and judgments of the researcher/
writer not be falsely "hidden" or objectified, but clarified. They are in-
terwoven throughout the research process. Research from this perspective is neither "objective" nor "subjective." Knowledge is the result of
a dialectical process between our experiences and our interactions with
others in the lifeworld.

The women who participated in the study were volunteers who were
members of five separate support groups. Thirty-one of the fifty-three
women were age 25 or older. Twelve of them were members of minority
groups (five black, three Mexican-American and four "other"). More
than half were married and/or had children. The women were involved
in a variety of occupational and educational pursuits in diverse fields.
Each of the women were currently full- or part-time university students.
(See Appendix II, Tables A1 through A6.)

In a strictly "scientific" sense, the study is only about these fifty-three
women and is not generalizable to all human beings, all women, or even
all women college students. However, on a phenomenological level, to
the extent that descriptions and interpretations of the life of any one
person are understandable to us, we may see a part of ourselves in
them. It is in this sense that I dare to write about "becoming mature"
at the same time that I report on the results of this particular research.
In a similar vein, this book is not about children, but about how the
women remembered their childhoods. The parents of these same children may have remembered the same events differently. Nevertheless,
it is our remembrances of childhood—the way we reconstruct the meaning of childhood events—which affects us as adults.

Changing Lives and Family Patterns

The empirical basis of this book rests on the life experiences from
childhood to adulthood as represented in the narratives and statements

of these fifty-three women. The narratives included autobiographies from early childhood to the present time, daily diaries, time/memory studies, four separate weekly time schedules, videotaped group discussions, and audiotaped home dinnertime discussions with family members and/or friends.

The study grew out of my direct observation and experience of a dramatic change that occurred in the lives of women and their families over the past 15 years. Increasingly, the college student population now consists of a greater proportion of women and older students. More of the women I counseled and taught were returning to the university after having left school to marry and have families and/or to work. This change is borne out by statistics (see Tittle and Denker, 1977; U.S. Department of Commerce, 1974, 1975).

This demographic change on college and university campuses reflects a significant change in social and cultural patterns. The college experience has made a profound difference in the lives of many of these women and their families as well. As a counselor or professor to hundreds of such women, I heard first hand their fears that they would fail. I listened to their stories about the difficulties they were having in adding the tasks of a student or employee to already loaded schedules as wives, and mothers. I saw many of them drop all their classes in the middle of a term or quit their jobs to deal with a serious family illness, to get a job, or a divorce. I was also convinced that successful coping with stress often involved reflecting upon and reworking what Helen Harris Perlman (1986) calls "the unfinished business of childhood." Roach (1976) found that attending college has made women less traditional and more feminist in their orientations. Women begin to realize the extent to which sexist institutions and attitudes, of fathers, mothers, husbands, and children, have adversely affected them.

There are widely divergent family responses to the new situation. Some husbands are supportive while others are resistant. Often, preexisting marital difficulties come to a head as a result (Cohen *et al.*, 1980). The women overwhelmingly report positive personal growth from the experience (Astin, 1976; Rappaport, 1984). While women and their families are adjusting to the changes, employers and universities began to adapt by offering more flexible schedules, and by providing day care and other supportive services. The existing literature does not contain research in which the overall life changes and experiences of these women are addressed. Prior research did not look at their development of the self from childhood in relation to current life experiences and adjustments. This research will begin to fill this gap.

"Ghosts" and "Spirits" of Childhood

I use the term "ghosts" to mean the internalized voices of significant others from childhood that haunt us to think and act in immature, negative ways. Often we do not even hear these voices as the ghosts they are. They have been with us for so long that when we do reflect on them they seem to be our own thoughts or feelings. Once recognized, these ghosts can be "exorcized" and replaced by "spirits." Spirits are voices from the significant others of our past that "inspire" us to be our best, most mature selves.

My interest in the "development" of self in childhood was first stimulated by a mystery movie that I saw on television as a child. Although unsure of its title, it may have been something like "The Dark at the Top of the Stairs." I do remember it was in black and white and was about a little girl in bed who saw the shadow of a man killing her mother with a knife. The killer remained in close proximity to the child, increasing the terror of the film. He was a family friend or relative. The child was unable to speak about this incident until she went through psychotherapy. Her psychotherapist helped her to remember what she saw, which led to the prosecution and conviction of the murderer. From that moment, I wanted to become a child psychotherapist.

This early experience set the tone for this book. I find this childhood experience to have been more predictive than I could have imagined. My research and teaching interests have carried me continually back into the study of childhood in relation to adult life.

Childhood experiences leave their imprint on us all. As a child I remember feeling fear and confusion as I heard the frequent shouting matches between my parents, who were then so powerful. Today they are both deceased. I have learned to understand their immaturity and to appreciate the ways in which they were mature and through which they cultivated my becoming.

I remember that my wish during the brownie scout "good night ring" was always: "Please let everyone get along tonight." My dedicated mother, also the brownie leader, would typically become angry and upset at home with either my older sister, or me, or my father. Her rages occurred with little or no provocation. When her temper flared up she would chase my sister and I around the dining room table, hitting us on the head and back. Yet, she was also a giving and loving mother, who did not hold back on hugs and kisses when we were small. I was always the peace maker in the family, the one who did the nurturing when my mother could not.

My father, on the other hand, did not hit us. Rather he withdrew.

When not at work, he was usually in his basement workshop, where his genius flowered. This remarkable man, with only a high school technical education, could make or fix anything. He could even make missing metal parts on his lathe. He received several government patents for his inventions which earned him a job as a research engineer after he retired from the Milwaukee police force. Shortly before he died of cancer ten years ago, I came to know him at a deeper level. I was working on my own family history, along the lines of Murray Bowen's theory of "differentiation of self." As part of this process, you interview your own parents, as if you were an anthropological historian, about their own childhoods, and about the ways they experienced their parents. My father found his childhood very painful to talk about, and did not reveal much. What he did say was that they lived in great poverty from the time his father had lost his arm on a factory assembly line before the days of "worker's compensation." His mother was the sole support of five children and his father. The father was embittered and did not hesitate to take his frustration out on his two sons with a belt. For a time, Grandpa and Grandma Sajeck separated and my father, little George, took on the nurturing role in the family. Having learned of my father's early experiences I now understand why he was so serious and reserved. In spite of this, I could judge, however, from his dedication to me and my daughter over the years that he loved us dearly.

I also learned more of my mother's childhood. When my mother was a young teenager, her father died in a railway accident while working on the Milwaukee Road. Again, no pension or social security were forthcoming. This left my grandmother, Ida Bentz, to support my mother and her younger brother, who suffered with a heart problem from the time he was a child. All of my maternal grandmother's time and energies must have gone into making a living, as a laundress and maid, and caring for her ailing son. As a result my mother lost her opportunity to be a child.

Recently, in the aftermath of my mother's death, my sister wrote to me: "Why can I remember no, or so few, happy times in our family?" Much of my work has been related to this question. Why do people who love each other find it so difficult to be happy? With the completion of the research reported in this book, I am closer to an answer than ever before. By studying the way the fifty-three women who participated in the study experienced their childhoods, and by seeing how "ghosts" and "spirits" from their childhood both haunt and inspire them, I have concluded that the answer lies in the blockages each of us faces in maturation.

Childhood Pain and Interpretive Sociology

Interpretive sociology is a process of research about human experience which seeks to empower those involved: researchers, participants, and readers. Based on principles of hermeneutics and phenomenology, interpretive sociology strips away the cloak of technocratic positivism that endeavors to predict and control its subjects. Research is no longer a disembodied, objectivistic presentation of reified conclusions, but a hermeneutic spiral of understanding and self-understanding. The reader is asked to step into the circle and thereby to be changed, to catch her own experiences of the past and the present, to present a different future. For, as Ricoeur (1981) and Godamer (1975) contend, in hermeneutics the being of the interpreter is changed. The interpreter is also becoming.

After I finished the quantitative part of the study, I felt that these results did not tell the whole story. A phenomenological process was necessary to recover the experiences "themselves." This necessitated that I examine the way my own consciousness effected the way I perceived and reflected upon the data. "Bracketing" (setting aside) (Husserl, 1970) the assumptions I was making about the study as a "social scientist," I began to examine and then bracket my presuppositions about the data. I then became aware of how my own childhood experiences colored the way I perceived this data. As I became more open to the pain within my own past I made a second and profound turn through the hermeneutic circle. I was then able to realize at a more profound level the meaning of what the participants were saying. The women had experienced adversities in childhood which still caused them difficulties. As I reread their narratives I became more deeply aware of the implications of living in a society where many persons, perhaps the majority, grow up experiencing childhoods which are far less than ideal.

For me to come to grips with the pain of these women's childhoods and the internalized ghosts they harbored, I had to come to grips with my own. For me to seriously face how the ghosts of significant relationships from their pasts were affecting the way they were as spouses and mothers, I had to face the way Mom and Dad as ghosts influenced the way I related to those close to me. Having done this, if I could speak directly to my parental ghosts, I would say the following:

> Mom and Dad, you are no longer ghosts to me, but spirits. I see that your ways of raising me as a child were the very best you could offer. You gave of your lives, as they were given to you. While children you faced death and disability of your fathers. You suffered poverty. You had no possibility

to attend college although you were both brilliant. "Maturity" as parents was not "presented" to you in all ways, for you did not always have it bestowed on you as children. Yet you were mature in the ways open to you, and you loved me and opened up the possibility for me to strive for maturity.

Although this was not initially intended to be a study of childhood misfortunes, most of the women told about having experienced childhood adversity. They described these experiences in their autobiographies and other narrative documents which they wrote for the project. They also discussed them in the support groups which met weekly for several months. They wrote and spoke about child abuse, incest, neglect, deprivation, and death or loss of a parent. These findings were indeed startling, so startling that I repressed them throughout the quantitative analysis. What makes this especially significant was that this was not a study of childhood trauma. Rather, it was a study of whatever these women felt was important enough from their childhood experiences to write about or to discuss in the groups. Voluntary disclosures of such events in the context of their lives and which were presented freely in their own words carries greater weight and validity then responses designed specifically to elicit information, for example, "about incest." It was startling to realize the extent of the childhood adversity reported by the women. This directed me to look at national statistics to see if this was a select group, or if childhood adversities affect a large percentage of women.

According to the National Center on Child Abuse and Neglect (1985), 72,000 cases of sexual molestation by a parent or family member were reported. The reported cases are thought by practitioners to be the "tip of the iceberg," since children are pressured by the perpetrators, on whom they depend for support, to remain silent. This is dramatically borne out by Russell's study (1984), which is the only study of sexual abuse and exploitation based on a large, random sample. Of Russell's sample of 930, 16% reported one or more instances of incestuous abuse before the age of 18 (12% before the age of 14); 31% reported at least one experience of extrafamilial sexual abuse by age 18 (20% by age 14). Combining incestuous with extrafamilial sexual abuse, 38% reported having been victimized at least once by age 18 and 28% by age 14. Only 2% of cases of incest and 6% of extrafamilial sexual abuse were reported to the police. Russell's study is corroborated by other studies, such as that of Herman (1982) which was based on five surveys. Herman found that one fifth to one third of all women had experienced some form of sexual encounter with an adult male prior to puberty.

Cases of physical abuse of children are also dramatically high. According to criminologist Professor Joyce Williams, 1.5 million cases of child abuse were reported in 1985. These resulted in the deaths of over 4000 children.

For many children, poverty will also be the condition of their existence. In 1981, over half of all children in the United States lived in families with incomes below poverty level (Zastrow and Kirst-Ashman, 1987:148). The vast majority of the poor in the United States are women and children, usually living together in single-parent households. According to the Christian Science Monitor (November 25, 1985:26), 70% of children born today will spend some time with a single parent by age 18. Children in single-parent families are more likely to be poor and to have suffered the loss of a parent through divorce. If one adds to these figures the numbers who experience other traumas such as neglect, verbal abuse, or loss of parent through death, it is clear that childhood abuses and misfortunes effect nearly all persons.

Misfortunes experienced by the women as children remain as "ghosts" in their lives. This is not to say that the women have not succeeded. Some of them have done so well in spite of these ghosts that their stories will motivate others. Some of these ghosts have become "spirits," functioning as sources of inspiration for the women. The persons in this book experienced extreme forms of devaluing—physical, sexual, and psychological abuse—from those closest to them. The abusing other exists as a ghost voice, haunting her[1] with such attributions as "you are only an object for my gratification," "you are no good," "you are unworthy of good treatment and kindness," "you are stupid." Often, these ghosts remain hidden. The words of these internal ghosts are powerful because their source seems to be from the deepest parts of the self. They haunt her to fulfill their imperatives.

The persons in this study were encouraged to exorcize these hidden "ghosts" by writing about and discussing their childhoods in relation to present-day experiences. For some, the ghosts are a part of a divided self, which drives them to act in ways they do not condone. The ghosts may exist as low self-esteem, leading some of them to choose physically and/or emotionally ill husbands. The specter of physical abuse haunts one woman in her inability to control her aggressiveness toward her stepson. The ghosts of incest experiences exist as one young woman chooses to renounce the companionship of men. One woman lost her

---

[1]Male and female pronouns are used at alternate times throughout this text as generic pronouns. The selection of whether or not they are male or female pronouns is based on my feeling for which emphasis is more appropriate at the time.

mother when she was 9 years old. The mother's "ghost" haunts her today as she continues to act as caretaker for her grown sons and husband as she did as a child for her father and brothers.

As the women began to recognize the silent voices that were speaking to them, hearing the ghosts allowed them to say "no" to their promptings and to laugh at their absurdities. For some, the ghosts are now vapors, which may befuddle and annoy, but do not inhibit or scare. For others, they have become "spirits" which serve as promptings for their achievements. They acted in a determined, courageous fashion to overcome the influence of their negative childhood experiences.

It would be absurd to leave the impression, however, that misfortunes in childhood are good because they strengthen the child. Indeed, there are many abuses not easily overcome. This is made evident by comparing those who were abused with those who had relatively "trauma-free" childhoods. The trauma-free exhibit more of a sense of happiness and a more positive outlook than those who experienced the misfortunes (see Chapter 10).

From Developmental Theory To Interpretive Sociology[2]

Sociological Critique

A sociology of knowledge approach to existing developmental theory finds it situated in a historical-cultural context. As such it reflects the biases of those with the power to produce such theory and research. It tends to reflect the perspective of male, white, middle to upper middle class, heterosexual, able-bodied, and age-conscious persons. In spite of these difficulties, developmental theorists, particularly Freud, Erikson, Vaillant, Piaget, and Kohlberg, provide us with deeper insights into the experiences of becoming and of the relationship between childhood and adult life.

It is only because of the powerful work of Freud that we can see the importance of improving child care practices. It has so often already been demonstrated that Freud's work contains sexist biases that it is almost a cliche. Bracketing these aspects of Freud's work, the power of his insight remains and is of key importance for this study. The work of Freud provides a foundation for this text in that childhood experi-

[2]In this book, "hermeneutic phenomenology" and "interpretive sociology" will be used interchangeably. Of course, there are other kinds of hermeneutics, phenomenology and interpretive sociology than that applied here. The approach taken here is that social reality can best be studied using an interpretive approach combining key concerns of phenomenology with hermeneutics.

ences are viewed as formative for adult life and as having continued impact upon it. Each of us must inquire into the particular nature of this for us. Ghosts must be found before they can be either exorcized or changed into spirits.

Theories of child development from Freud through Piaget have focused on development as "normal" or "pathological." For Freud (1960) normal development is already conflict-laden—between id, ego, and superego, and between cathected objects as loved and hated. The aggressiveness, narcissism, and selfishness of parents—their immaturity—is simply the natural result of their instincts.

To Erikson (1950), the self will be functioning in a socially acceptable manner, as long as each developmental task, such as industry vs. inferiority, is mastered. He does not fully clarify the way abuse, neglect, and other adversities interfere with successful mastery at each stage treating lack of successful mastery of a stage as deviant.

Many children (perhaps the majority) do not follow developmental patterns smoothly, but rather are afflicted with the misfortunes of physical abuse, mental cruelty, rejection, neglect, loss of a parent, poverty, or incest. When one is drawing a map of a road with few hills and bends, a straight line suffices to show one how to get from New York to Delaware. Should the hills be many and rugged, the potholes deep, and the bridges faulty, the line on the map is dangerously deceptive. If one looks at the map long enough, one forgets the road she has really traveled, does not fill the potholes and fix the bridges, and cannot adequately guide those who are embarking on a similar journey. Similarly, theories of the development of self in childhood that describe the straight path, may gloss and distort our understanding and ability to cope with injuries we received while on the journey. Childhood adversities and their effects must be an integral part of socialization theories, Otherwise, theory may contribute to a kind of social amnesia, which fortifies adverse child-rearing practices.

While hermeneutic phenomenology views the consciousness of persons as embodied, it rejects the determinism of stage theories. Stage theories serve well as models for assessing biological development and those mental faculties directly dependent upon it. However, when extended beyond the area of biological aspects of becoming into ethical, moral, and even intellectual aspects, developmental/stage theories have tended to be biased in ways which promulgated scientism, sexism, ageism, racism, and other characteristics of those in power. Developmental theory tends to decontextualize the life processes it studies, reifying what has been true of persons in particular social circumstances (see Garbarino, 1982; Karp and Yoels, 1982; Maas, 1984).

A major reason that child development theory has not adequately incorporated adverse experience is the quest of social psychology to be "scientific," which, according to the prevailing position of positivism, includes being "value neutral." Such a view of science often masks scientistic ideology. The troubles of existence continue, overwhelming some persons to the point that their performance is disrupted and they require help and/or control. Value neutrality is set then aside as psychology labels persons "schizophrenic," "paranoid," or "borderline" according to the DSMIII (American Psychiatric Association, 1980). Such a categorization system, whereby selves are divided into two groups, the "normal" and the "pathological," reinforces the hegemony of the paradigm of "normal" development. Insights such as those of Glass (1985) that schizophrenic delusion and the structures of thinking of political and religious fanatics are essentially alike are swallowed up by such dichotomizations.

Ageism as implied in stage theories is evident in its treatment of both cognitive and moral "development." Analyses of children's art (Luquet, 1964; Merleau-Ponty, 1964; Selfe, 1977) found that cognitive "development," according to Piaget's categories, means the child relinquishes more expressive and creative modes in favor of mathematized perspectival realism. Changes in artistic style reflect educational influences. When one is concerned with aspects more central to the essence of the human being, such as emotional and ethical becoming, stage theories are similarly difficult to support. Some 6 year olds respond in terms of morality of respect [Piaget's stage three—reserved for adolescents to adults (see Piaget, 1965) and Kohlberg's conventional or even postconventional morality]. Erikson's all-encompassing eight stages of social psychological development is widely accepted and taught. He (Erikson, 1950) points out that persons reach crucial crossroads at eight points in their lives. At adolescence, for example, the individual faces establishing an identity through career choice or "role confusion." If this person fails to successfully develop "initiative" at the third stage, a pervasive sense of guilt will result, making it more likely that this person would be marred at the "latency" stage by an abiding sense of inferiority. This lack of confidence would decrease the chances to successfully achieve "identity." While Erikson does attempt to relate his theory to social institutions, he says little about the effect of significant others and social institutions on each stage. It has never been demonstrated that a teenager may have any more role confusion than an 80-year-old widow, a 65-year-old retired police officer, or a 30-year-old insurance salesman. "Ego-integrity vs. despair" may be an existential problem for a 12 year old or a teenager (as indicated by the epidemic of teen suicides) as well as for a 70 year old. Yet Erikson's stages are taught to cohort after cohort of students in the fields of nursing, education, social work, psychology, and sociology as if these were simply genetic inevitabilities! Notions such as "identity crisis," or "mid-life crisis" have become self-fulfilling prophecies (Karp and Yoels, 1982). Angst or guilt due to real life situations are thereby trivialized and made into cliches. "I'm 35 now, I guess I am just having a mid-life crisis!"

Vaillant's extension of Erikson's stage theory into the realms of ethical and emotional behavior lends itself to class biases, which must be watched for in such approaches. Vaillant (1977) extends and expands Erikson's eight stages by relating them to the Freud's "defense mechanisms." He further contends that immature defense mechanisms are normal, functional, and appropriate for children and adolescents. For example, delusion, such as talking to an imaginary other, is normal child's play, but may indicate psychosis in an adult. "Acting out" (such as getting drunk) is a normal testing activity for an adolescent but is dysfunctional as a continual part of adult existence. Most adults necessarily employ a number of neurotic defenses, such as displacement and passive aggression. Suppression, sublimation, and altruism are used by the most mature, successful individuals. Vaillant supports this model through his interviews of privileged male Yale university graduates, preselected for their maturity and achievement. He found that life stresses cause individuals to revert to less mature defensive strategies. By the same token, relationships with more mature persons help one move to higher adaptive levels.

The economically privileged group which Vaillant studied (these were the cream of a Yale, male cohort) may have experienced few of life's stresses which are associated with adults using lower-level defenses. Within this elite group, Vaillant found that those who had advanced economically, received regular promotions, and had happy and stable marriages, also tended to employ mature defenses. A theory sensitive to the context of becoming would ask if one who had every reason to expect success, but who was not fortunate enough to find it, would not be likely to "act out," "repress," or "project." Whether these "mechanisms" are truly stage related or primarily dependent upon context remains to be demonstrated. Few attempts have been made to systematically study the extent to which children also exhibit mature defense mechanisms, such as altruism.

Further evidence for the effect of social contextual factors on development comes from Henry S. Maas (1984, 1986), who demonstrates that "development" depends upon the availability of social and economic supports and relationships. He points out, for example, that no one in a crashing airplane is "competent" enough to prevent disaster. Similarly, persons in deprived environments cannot be expected to develop "competencies" that are only useful and supported in an environment with abundant opportunities.

Sexist biases inherent in Kohlberg's famous theory of moral development are astutely demonstrated by Gilligan (1982). Kohlberg's methodology is divorced from actual ethical decisions, based rather on the questioning of subjects about hypothetical situations. To determine why women consistently scored "lower" on Kohlberg's scales, Gilligan studied women's reasoning processes in relation to moral judgments. Gilligan found that women were better able than men to imagine themselves in a real situation with all its complex relationships. Since women tended to think about the effect of their deviant acts upon those for whom they cared, they were less likely to risk "postconventional" ethics. The women Gilligan studied were facing the serious decision of whether or not to have an abortion. They showed ethical progression dependent upon the level of social supports they received.

Sexist biases are also evident in theories of social development. According to Levinson et al. (1978), adult development moves from a stage of career exploration in early adulthood to career consolidation in midlife. Applying this scale to many women who delay career development until their thirties or forties (when their children have become more independent), women appear "developmentally delayed." Gibbs (1987) found that when criteria of increasing adaptability are applied instead of Levinson's stages, the women are more advanced than men at that age, for the women have greater flexibility to cope with change.

In addition to its sexist biases, moral "development" theory is untenable because of its "Anglo" cultural bias. Chicano children are raised by their parents to love and revere their elders. The moral independence and autonomy of Kohlberg's scale reflects capitalist competitive ethics as compared with the more communal ethics found in Chicano, black, and other cultural groups (Cortese, 1984; Young, 1978). Cortese concluded that moral judgment is located in the social milieu, not the individual and recommends that studies of morality should focus on quality of life variables, not on individual judgments. Basic economic and social indicators in communities, such as levels of education, and availability of health and recreation services predict, facilitate, and allow moral development in individuals.

Coming to "Terms" with Becoming Mature

Given the extensive difficulties with stage theory, the cornerstone of developmentalism, the first meaning of "development" in Webster's dictionary (1979) must be rejected. This primary definition of development reads as follows: "To cause to grow gradually in some way, to become gradually fuller, larger, better." Similarly, the second meaning of "development" must be rejected because of an unwarranted assumption of continued expansion: "To expand, as in a business." These rejected aspects of the term tend to be based on its Latin root, *"voluntus,"* meaning "to roll from."

Some of the ancillary meanings of "development" are in keeping with the kind of human becoming intended in this book. These acceptable aspects of the term reflect the French root of "develop," that is "developer" which means "to unfold." These include the following: to unfold gradually, as a bud; to make visible (as in a photograph); to disclose— work out by degree, show; to explain more clearly, enlarge upon; to uncover, unravel, exhibit, disentangle; to come into being or activity; to elaborate upon a theme as in music through rhythms, melodies or harmonic changes. A hermeneutical aspect is located in each of these connotations. Development as disclosure may reveal more, or less, of any particular quality at any point in time. The meaning of a change can be understood only through relationship to context and structure of the persons' experience.

Some synonyms for development also help in ascertaining the meaning of "becoming" in this work. "Cultivation" is a good synonym for this topic, since, as Heidegger emphasized, one cultivates what one cares for, like a vine, so that it may better fulfill its own potentialities. Cultivation is also appealing because once a self exists, *self-cultivation* is crucial to becoming. Cultivation does not suffice for our main term, however, because altogether too much of the experience of women in this study was not caring or self-cultivating. Instead of being nurtured as children, many of the women in this study were expected to take on nurturing roles in their families. They learned the bitter lesson as children that they did not matter intrinsically. Rather, they were worthwhile only insofar as they met the needs of others. They were not allowed to develop and pass through the stage of primary infant narcissism which is essential for adequate self-respect.

"Elaboration" is a synonym suggestive of aspects of development, as is "drift," but neither term suffices for an overarching signifier. "To constitute" is a good verb synonym of "to develop" especially for a phenomenological approach. For phenomenology, consciousness actively "intends" or "constitutes" objects. Such constitution is a *social* process, resulting from the active involvement of participants in interaction. In spite of the acceptability of these secondary meanings and synonyms of "development" the word must be rejected for a hermeneutic phenomenology because of the pervasity of the misleading primary meanings. The term also has stage theory connotations for most persons.

The movement of human beings from birth to adulthood has also been called both "aging," and "socialization." Aging connotes the ending stages of a process, and makes a time line its underlying moving force. Socialization, the most common term used in sociology to describe the growth process, is inadequate to express the dimensions of this topic, for it means "to make social, adjust, or fit for cooperative living "to adapt to the common needs of a group "to subject to governmental ownership and control" or "to nationalize" (Webster, 1979). Such processes are ancillary or incidental, and are not central to this topic. The actual *phenomenon* of humans coming into being involves the constituting and intending consciousness of persons in interaction with constituting others—not simply the inducement of conformity.

The term "biography" occurred to me as perhaps being more appropriate to this work, especially since my case studies are biographies based on autobiographies and other documents. However, the purpose of my work goes beyond biography. I am seeking to describe and understand childhood experience and its impact on adult adaptation. My aim is to improve the theoretical foundations for social psychology. Biography does not encompass this scientific aim.

"Becoming" derives from the root word of "to be." It literally means to come into existence. Becoming implies nothing about stages, or necessary progressions. Yet it has an inherent structure and nature to be cultivated, and self-cultivated. Only "beings" may be cultivated and only self-conscious beings may self-cultivate. An interpretive sociology of becoming rejects the technology of development and the reification of the human life cycle into stage theories. It rejects the labeling and categorizing which results from such theories, and the tendencies of such theories to decontextualize experience. It rejects both biological and cultural determinism. Because it is hermeneutical, this approach to becoming seeks to understand the meaning of processes and experiences rather than to discover "causes" in the sense of physics. Because it is phenomenological as well, it seeks to describe the essential intentional and conscious structures of these experiences in addition to their meanings.

Human becoming as hermeneutic phenomenology is a description of the evolving of embodied consciousness. This consciousness is recognized as constituted by and with others as well as by and with oneself. Consciousness is meaning-endowing and meaning-experiencing. It exists in and through narratives; for the self comes into being as one is able to hear and tell stories about oneself and others. In this sense the self is a story line. Consciousness and the constituting ego are both the horizon and grounds of the self. The human being exists already in a lifeworld as he becomes. In becoming, one is intertwined in a culture rich in meanings and identities by and through which the self is realized.

I use the term "becoming mature" rather than "development" to describe the process I am concerned with in this book. "Becoming" is emphasized as of equal weight with "mature." To be mature (following Boelen, 1978) implies that one has come to grips with oneself and others. One can be thoroughly "developed" physically and even "cognitively" but still be "immature." Maturation means "to be ripe." This connotation is a good one for our purposes, for the mature person is ripe with authentic being. A second connotation of "maturation" is rejected for our purposes. This is the biological meaning of "mature" which means the "final stage of a process" (Webster, 1979). As Boelen (1978) says:

> Maturity" is precisely that dimension in the personality which prevents one from being completely "fixed" or "fixated" and which transcends any sort of causal determinism.
>
> For the mature personality is a "person incarnate," and essentially involved in a living dialogue with his own immaturity, with the child in himself, with the fixity of his character, and the fixation of some measure of disorder. Immaturity is an essential constituent of maturity. We have to reject the usual perfectionist conception of maturity. (ix)

There is nothing final about maturity in the sense intended here. Another, and the first, meaning of the word "maturate" listed by Webster is "to suppurate—to discharge pus." To ooze white corpuscles as a defense against invading internal organisms may be a useful metaphor for much one does throughout life. The ghosts of significant others may affect us like viruses or germs. White corpuscles are necessary defenses against them.

Other aspects of "maturity" as discussed by Boelen give further insight into this project. Boelen likens "personal maturity" with artistic creativity, philosophical reflection, and authentic love. Each of these qualities is characterized by ecstasy, enthusiasm, inspiration, and gratuitousness. According to their Greek and Latin roots, these expressions connote being outside oneself, being in a supreme being, to be breathed into and to be given to freely. In each case the quality is something given to us. We can be open to it as a gift. It is not something we can will or manipulate. Each of these qualities contains "something of wonder" about it. It is "wonderful" because it cannot be predicted, controlled, or constructed. It is not a problem to be solved. In a mature state of being, one is in dialogue with the child in oneself, and with one's internalized parents. The study facilitated this dialogue for each of the women who participated. It would be ironic if I had not also reflected on this dialogue of my own as part of understanding what the study was and meant.

Having gleaned away the biases of developmental theory, its remaining golden threads can be woven into the tapestry of a hermeneutic phenomenology which allows for the patterns of the women's lives from childhood to appear. In the context of oppressive economic, social, and environmental conditions, burdened by the ghosts of their immature parents and childhood adversities, most of the parents of the women in the study exhibited various kinds of "immaturity." These immature parent–child relationships coupled with continual socially situated pressures and adversities result in what I have called "ghosts." Mature parent–child relationships led, on the other hand, to the internalization of "spirits." These ghosts and spirits, in turn, effected the adults' lives, including the way the women acted as parents to their children.

A Grounded Theory of Mature Parenting

The theory of mature and immature parent–child relationships was not formulated until after the results from the study were completed. It provides the basis for an overall understanding of what the women experienced. The theory of mature and immature parent–child relationships is grounded in the written narratives and verbal discourses of the fifty-three women who participated in this research. Characteristics of child-rearing based on immature and mature relationships are presented.

The major point of this book is the elucidation of what it means to be mature, and the implications of this for understanding and improving our relationships with others, particularly in our roles as parents and children. First, it was necessary to formulate and distill the narratives which the women wrote, describing various kinds of childhood adversities and how they were overcome. Having completed this, a pattern of mature and immature relationships which the persons in the study experienced became clear. The theory is explained in Chapter 4 because it is the link between the quantitative and qualitative aspects of the research. The characteristics of mature parenting will be briefly sketched here. It is intended to be an ideal. The possibilities of realizing it will be discussed later.

The mature parent will possess certain qualities. The first of these is the ability to provide a secure, unruptured bond with the infant and later the child. Second, the mature parent adequately recognizes and mirrors the full range of the child's expressive emotions. This parent is empathic toward the child. He or she does not abandon the child or project his or her feelings and attributes upon the child. He or she does not expect the child to take care of him or her or to parent younger siblings in his or her place. The mature parent communicates to the child his sense of uniqueness, worthiness, and competency. The child is expected to become mature in his or her own unique way.

The mature parent does not squelch and destroy open communication with the child through arbitrary displays of parental power. Rather, the parent will communicate his or her feelings and expectations directly, presenting no contradictory or double messages. The parent ideal does not blame, placate, distract, or objectivize in his or her communications with the child. The messages from parent to child are congruent and clear. The mature parent does not have a divided self as does the abusive parent. Since the mature parent fully understands and dialogues with the immature side of him- or herself, he or she does not make the child into a victim of abuse, ridicule, or neglect—a scapegoat. The child does not need to split off an aggressive side but can be an integrated self. Incongruencies of life and life's adversities are handled by the mature parent in the comic rather than the tragic spirit.

Having appropriate self-control and developed skills of artistry and love, the mature parent can foster these qualities in the child. Mature parents are in the habit of defending themselves from life's adversities through humor, altruism, anticipation, creative sublimation, or suppression (as when they temporarily set aside anger until it can be handled constructively). They do not deny, delude, distort or repress reality, nor do they act out either violently or passive aggressively. The mature parent values the precious time spent with offspring.

Accepting the inevitability of death, time is experienced as meaningful by the mature parent. He or she does not subject the child to a stressful experience of measured time, but a joyfully shared temporal flow, marked by shared festivities of a memorable nature. Morally, the mature parent does not act primarily out of personal survival concerns or out of the need to be socially acceptable. Rather, the mature parent nurtures him- or herself and the child within the context of a network of supportive others in a caring community.

Organization of the Book

Hermeneutics involves the movement back and forth between the texts or actions as texts and the understandings of the interpreter. As a result, it is often referred to as a "circle" or "spiral" that one follows to deeper levels of meaning.

Chapter 2 describes the research design, techniques, and group processes used in the study. The theories of George Herbert Mead, (1934, 1938, 1959) Alfred Schutz, (1970, 1973) and Jurgen Habermas, (1973, 1979) which served as a basis for the research, are first briefly discussed. The kinds of narratives written by the women are described and examples are presented. The way the documents were coded is discussed and the group processes are evaluated. The women's self-assessments of the effects of being involved in the research are summarized.

Chapter 3 presents a description and summary of some of the quantitative analyses resulting from coding, computerizing, and statistically analyzing the data. Included in the analysis is the extent to which the women accepted or rejected the attributions of those close to them from childhood onward. These results support the overall premises of the study that others close to one in childhood have a profound effect on who one becomes as an adult. The results of the phenomenological time-memory study, comparing the way time was experienced by the women as children and adults are also presented. These findings confirm Schutz theories (1973:114b) about the temporal nature of experience. They indicate that childhood memories of time center on major disruptive changes, such as a geographical move or the death of a parent.

These efforts at quantification and systemization of the findings did not capture the essential qualities of the experiences described and discussed by the women. If I had stopped here, I would have ignored deeper meanings of the research results in terms of the actual life experiences of the participants. Those readers interested in sociological theory and research methodologies and how they were used in the study, should pay special attention to Chapter 2. Chapter 3 summarizes the findings from the quantitative and systematic analyses in regard to relationships to significant others, and the experience of time. Chapter 4 describes the effect of childhood on women's lives in relationship to the theory of immature and mature parent child relationships. The theory was not developed until after the case constructs (presented in chapters 5 through 9) were written. As the conceptual anchor of the rest of the book, it is presented first.

The case constructions represent types of experiences reported by participants. Each chapter presents two or three case constructs centering on kinds of childhood experiences including the following: physical and psychological abuse, death of a parent, incest, poverty and neglect, and "mature" caring. Identifying information has been changed to protect anonymity. Events and sequences have been abstracted and/or altered so that each example incorporates reports of other women with similar experiences. While there are extensive quotes from partici- pants' diaries and autobiographies, these were selected to illustrate typi- cal patterns found among women with these kinds of experiences. The case constructs were selected and written to exemplify the range of types of childhood adversities reported on by the entire group of women.

The narratives written by the women varied greatly in depth and in- tensity because they were not all ready or willing to equally reveal them- selves. I did not fill in the blanks and gaps in the narratives, since to do so would have been more fictional than true to their original forms.

My interpretations of each case construction are not based on any one case or even the one quoted. Thus, while the actual writers of the quotes may recognize them, they may not recognize themselves in the sur- rounding narratives and interpretive material, which is based on their's and several other similar cases. Where she could be located (for many had long departed to other states or countries), each woman whose quo- tations were used extensively was contacted prior to publication and has given her permission for the use of her documents in that specific con- text. This does not necessarily mean that she concurred with my inter- pretations.

The lives of each woman has changed since the time of the study, and certainly their interpretations of the same events will also be different in retrospect. Therefore, they were given the opportunity of writing an addendum to the original quotations. The quotations in the case studies are for the most part direct quotes from the women's written docu- ments. However, identifying information has been changed or deleted, and grammatical and spelling errors have been corrected. Because of these and the above-mentioned alterations, the women's lives as pre- sented are called "case constructions" rather than case studies, indicat- ing that the facts and interpretations represent summary constructs of the researcher and not necessarily the experiences of any actual woman in the study.

Case constructions of three women who were physically abused as children are presented in Chapter 5. I have called them "Rebecca," "Gloria," and "Greta." Chapter 6 contains the accounts of "Delores" and "Beverly," who represent typical experiences of those from incestu- ous families. The poverty and neglect which marked the childhoods of "Barbara" and "Michelle" are described in chapter 7. Chapter 8 contains studies of "Shelly" and "Laura" who as children lost a parent through death. Chapter 9 exemplifies the stories of two women who experienced "mature" parenting as defined in Chapter 4. "Pam" is currently coping with a divorce and "Glenda" with a custody suit. This chapter causes us to reflect on problems in the social context of parent–child relationships. Religious, political, and other cultural institutions impact on the family and affect one's becoming mature. This directs the hermeneutical spiral back around toward better theoretical understanding of the context of becoming mature.

Chapter 10 summarizes the quantitative and qualitative results of the study. The elements of the theory of mature and immature parenting practices are used as a basis for comparing the case constructs. Social and cultural forces that mitigate against or facilitate mature parent–child relationship are analyzed.

When parents must work and function in situations of low resources, it is less likely that they will be able to act "maturely." Job insecurity, massification, depersonalization, destruction of the ecological environment, power-distorted political and religious communication, distorted and untruthful communication on the part of commercial institutions, rigid and tyrannical work organizations, stressful time schedules, repressive and rigid religious institutions, all contribute to a context making mature parent–child relationships difficult to maintain. This constitutes our fourth and final hermeneutic turn in this book. It looks toward what Paul Ricoeur called "the world reached for by the text."

Entering the Hermeneutic Circle: A Note to Readers

As a reader you are asked to enter into dialogue with me, the writer, and with the ideas of the theorists that guided me. Most importantly, you are entering into dialogue with the fifty-three persons who participated in the study, and with the ghosts and spirits that they came to recognize. As you do so you will compare yourself with them, and share their pains and their triumphs. You will be reminded of your own ghosts. Thus the reading of this book, if entered into with the hermeneutic spirit, will change you. It will present a model for self-reflection and possibly suggest ways you may redirect your life.

Although some readers of this manuscript have said that it paints a rather bleak picture of men—this is *not* its aim. Female "ghosts" and women who participated in the study also behave immaturely at times. The persons who participated in the study were self-selected. They were women who had some issues they wanted to discuss. I make no claims that they "represent" all women. What a hermeneutic approach tries to do is to meaningfully interpret experience. A phenomenology attempts to find what is essential in their experiences. In this way each reader can judge for him- or herself the extent to which he or she shares some of these life events. The reader is asked to join the writer in delving into these lifeworlds.

Although this study of becoming mature was based on the experiences of women, I did not emphasize this in the title of the book or in the theoretical analysis. One reason for this is that much of the work in developmental theory has been based on single-sexed studies, for the most part, based on male samples. Kohlberg's theory of moral judgment was based initially on a study of men. Vaillant's (1977) work on defense mechanisms in adaptation through life was based on an all-male group. Yet neither of them presented their work as a theory of "male"development. Gilligan's (1982) critique of Kohlberg was based on a study of women's moral judgment. Yet no one has applied her methods of looking at moral judgment in real life situations among men. Men, too, may experience ethical dilemmas in terms of "survival, goodness or care" (Gilligan's stages of moral development in women). This study is about women's becoming mature, but like the work of Kohlberg, Vaillant, and Gilligan, it is also about human beings of the other sex.

Men also suffer from immature parenting practices and low resource contexts. They too are physically, psychologically, and sexually abused, are neglected, and lose parents through death. Some men are fortunate enough to have had mature parents. I have worked with men clinically who were beaten and raped by their fathers as small children, verbally abused and molested by their mothers and mothers' boyfriends, and sexually abused by uncles, brothers, and cousins. Some of these men became perpetrators of abuse with their daughters and sons. Men too must deal with the ghosts of their childhood.

This is not to say that boys and men do not experience childhood differently from women. The impact of negative attitudes toward women and sexist institutions bears more heavily against girls and women than boys and men. Also, girls are apparently more likely to be sexually abused than boys. Boys may be more likely to question or reject the attributions and expectations of significant others. They may be less likely to experience reversal parenting, because it is more typical to place girls in caretaker roles. Both boys and girls are equally likely not to receive adequate mirroring. The mirroring they do receive is distorted in different directions for males and females, however. Anger is more heavily repressed in girls, and sadness in boys. Boys, in order to identify with the male sex, are forced through sanctions and ridicule to break their primary bond with their mothers at the oedipal stage (see Chodorow, 1978:115). This may mean that to have a ruptured, or at least somewhat torn, primary bond is endemic to being a male. Each of these questions remains to be explored in studies that compare becoming mature in males and females.

This study is about human beings becoming mature. These human beings were women. Some aspects of what they experienced are shared by all of us, some by none of us, some perhaps, only by women. Since its focus is on women, this research properly may be seen as a contribution to "women studies." There is a kind of subtle sexism involved in that once a work is labeled "women's studies" it is thought not to be generally applicable to human life experience.

The illumination of any lifeworld has something to say about human experience. What I discovered in analyzing these lifeworlds is that the way to human maturity may be arduous, but it is fitting that we undertake the journey. As Hegel emphasized, historically, the knowledge we have accumulated about human development and human communities has moved us in the direction of greater self-awareness.

On Reading and Emotions: A Letter to Readers

The object of writing a book is to share thoughts with readers. I would like to be there with each of you as you read. I would like to speak with each of you during and after your reading. Since in most cases this will not be possible, I would like to address you more directly. If I were to write you a letter, this is what I would say:

Dear Reader:

I would like to feel I am sharing the experience of reading this book with you. This cannot be a mutual experience if you attempt to shield yourself from whatever emotions you feel in reading about the lives of the persons involved in the research. Please do not shut down your impulses to cry or laugh or become enraged as you read this book. Become a mature parent to yourself in reading this book and let yourself "adequately mirror" your feelings and thoughts. It would be wonderful if you would care to share some of them with me, and thus let the hermeneutic spiral continue to expand. Please write to me and let me know of the ghosts and spirits of childhood you may have uncovered while reading this book.

Yours sincerely,

Valerie Malhotra Bentz

Group Communication and
Narratives in Research _____ 2

Introduction

This chapter is about the way this research was conducted as a critically reflective process. The theories of Mead, Schutz, and Habermas are first briefly described as they inspired the research design and group interaction. The group processes are analyzed in relation to Habermas' theory of communicative competency. The narratives which the women wrote are described with examples given. The women's assessments of the effects of writing each kind of narrative on their lives is also presented.

Ethical considerations were foremost in the research design. From an existentialist point of view, it is important that the act of carrying out the research with others have some intrinsic value. If research as an act is simply a means to an end it becomes a waste of the life and time of those involved. Even if due to some event or stroke of fate the results of research could never be written or published, the research process itself should be of some immediate benefit for the women. The research must certainly not harm the participants, who must be freely and voluntarily involved. Research designs should be flexible enough to allow participants to effect the procedures. In this way, the knowledge that can be learned from participants will not be blocked. The researcher must keep in tune with him- or herself and with the participants so that the process will not be alienating but will yield insights and inspire positive change.

Ghost Finding

The self-concept, the way time is experienced or "spent" and the way one communicates are essential aspects of understanding persons. Therefore, three major social psychological theorists provided the initial theoretical basis for this study. George Herbert Mead, the Chicago school pragmatic philosopher, developed the most recognized theory of self in sociology and was a founder of the school of "symbolic interaction" (1934). Mead also wrote landmark works on the experience of time (1938, 1959). Basing his sociology of the lifeworld on Max Weber's *verstehen sociology* and Husserl's phenomenology of consciousness, Alfred Schutz (1970: 60f, 1982) provided a framework for the analysis of temporality as experienced. Of the theorists who focus on communication, Jurgen Habermas is outstanding because of the way he analyzes communication distorted by power relationships. By combining several different theories in the same research, each with a pertinent methodology and relevant techniques of data collection, a strategy of "multiple triangulation" was employed (Denzin, 1978). Such a research design promises to reveal something of the complexity of what is being studied, including the possibility of contradictory findings (see Malhotra, 1979b).

The research process was a way through which the women discovered the ghosts within themselves. George Herbert Mead's social psychology stresses the way self is built upon communication with significant others. The voices of important early caretakers are parts of our initial way of thinking about who we are. When these others were immature, or inadequately nurturing to us as children, they will remain within us as ghosts. These ghosts haunt us as we unconsciously speak to ourselves the way they would have. Their voices drive us to become workaholics, alcoholics, codependent or whatever may have been important ways that they learned to cope with stresses. These ghosts continually remind us of our failures, ugliness, clumsiness, stupidity, or inadequacy. As developed selves, we in turn become ghosts to our children and those around us who exhibit many of the same human foibles. Thus we become driven contributors to distrust, alienation, and war.

To Mead, the self has three parts, the "I," the "me" and reflectivity. The "me" of each person's self is made up of their impressions of what these significant others think of them and what they expect of them. The "I" is the self as actor, that influences these others. Mediating between the "I" and the "me" is the reflective intelligence, where in internal conversation with oneself one decides the meaning and value of the attributions and expectations of others (see Malhotra, 1977). One can find ghosts and exorcize them, or change them into "spirits."

Time was crucial for the women, for each of them had multiple obligations as students, mothers, wives, and employees. Schutz investigated the difference between "duree" or the experience of inner time, and the external socially imposed measurement of time (1970: 60f; 1982; 1983). By verbally reconstructing their pasts, the women endowed it with meanings pertinent to their present circumstances. This is accomplished by applying words and their inherent standards, i.e., categories, concepts, and values to experiences (Schutz, 1970:62).

Through the sharing of experiences in direct and indirect social relationships, meaning is created. Each person's biography also effects how she interprets events. Language models each person's temporal experience (Schutz and Luckmann, 1973:247) around events and purposes of cultural value in the lifeworld. Each individual's life plan is constrained by the limits of "world time" and one's "life plans" that must be contained therein (Schutz and Luckmann, 1973:92). Plans are ultimately ended in death, an unavoidable boundary for one's life. In terms of daily plans, time is limited by immediate necessities or "imposed relevances". Things must be done on a "first things first" basis (Ibid). Typifications which exist in the cultural environment already present a coherent and meaningful image of the world.

As insightful as Mead and Schutz are about the constitution of the self and of meaningful experience, neither of them deals adequately with the effects of domination and power on these processes. Since these women had been impacted upon by male-dominated institutions and sexism, it is important that a theoretical perspective sensitive to such issues inform the study. Jurgen Habermas' theory of communicative competency (1979), of power-distorted communication, of technical-instrumental action vs. symbolic interaction (1970), and of the colonization of the lifeworld (See Rasmussen, 1982: pp. 15–16) fits the situation aptly. Habermas (1973) draws a parallel between psychoanalytic psychotherapy as a means of liberation from distorted internal communication, and liberation from social oppression through the uncovering of ideologies. To achieve understanding through dialogue with others in relation to one's past is liberating.

Habermas lends critical (political) connotations to the Husserlian–Schutzian concept of "Lebensvelt" (lifeworld). To the extent that communicative relationships are distorted by the force of governmental and commercial institutions, these relationships are "colonized." This colonization tends to transform education into the training of technical experts. Family life becomes an efficient consumption apparatus. Marital and parental communication mutates into hassles over power and resources (see Malhotra and Deneen, 1983). The life cycle itself has been codified into a series of tasks watched over by "experts" (Karp and Yoels, 1982).

What Habermas calls "fragmentation of everyday life" is also part of this colonization. Diverse and competing commercial, governmental, and ideology-producing institutions (churches, schools, voluntary and professional associations) demand more of a person as student and as wife–mother–homemaker. The "colonization of the Lebensvelt" (life-world) is accomplished as meaningful discussion is replaced by bureau-cratic processing (1970). Rational-instrumental action efficiently and sin-gle-mindedly is oriented toward the realization of a predetermined end. It is the hallmark of the technocratic world view which makes all objects, animals, and persons into means. Symbolic interaction, on the other hand, is the process of communication involving face-to-face relation-ships in which meanings, minds, and selves are created, maintained, and transformed. In the tradition of Marx, Weber, and Toennies, Haber-mas points out how the rational-technical process of modern civilization proceeds at great cost both to the natural and the human world.

Alleviating Power Dynamics in the Research

Habermas (1979) clarifies the social situations where undistorted com-munication can occur. In such symbolic interaction, freely established goals and objectives can be realized. Ideally speech acts of discourse must be "institutionally unbounded" if they are oriented toward disclo-sure of valid understandings. They must occur outside of normal orga-nizational structures which can exercise sanctions against unpopular or critical ideas. Only in such situations, can the norms of the ideal speech situation operate. These norms are: "truthfulness," "truth," "normative comprehensibility," and "understandability." "Truthfulness" means that the speaker, within the limits of self-awareness, is attempting to be truthful. The "truth" criteria means that what is present does coincide with verifiable knowledge about the actual world. "Comprehensibility" (normative appropriateness) means that the speech act makes sense to others given the situation (cultural world), and understandability means that the speaker has the linguistic skills necessary to "make sense." Habermas contends that societal breakdown would occur if we did not normally assume these four norms of communicative competency to be operative, even though for the most part they are not.

Typically, those low in power, such as the mentally ill, criminals, the elderly, children, minorities, and animals, are the "subjects" of social research. The structure of the research reinforces such alienated rela-tionships between researcher and those "subjected" to research tech-niques. The researcher, as the one in power, can benefit from the rela-tionship with little or no benefit to the "subjects" who may in fact be "victims." Most often, the low power of the subjects of research is mag-nified because they do not have the opportunity of communicating with each other. Therefore the normal processes where situations are as-sessed and evaluated in symbolic interaction are usually not available to research subjects.

It would have been ironic to have designed a study of persons likely to have experienced the effects of sexism in a form and style which paralleled and reinforced power distorted communication. To study developing and changing selves as temporal, communicating selves, the form and format of the research must be dialectical and reflective. The methodology for this research attempted to avoid a false division between researcher and "subject" and between theory, research, and practice (Malhotra, 1984a, 1986b; Nebraska Feminist Collective, 1987).

Steps were taken in the structuring of this project to eliminate or alleviate the effects of power in the relationship between researcher and the persons volunteering as "subjects." From the beginning of the project on, the providers of narratives and documents (the 53 women) were called "participants" rather than "subjects." This symbolized a shift away from the asymmetrical researcher/subject tradition. In addition, participants were involved in open, small group discussions through which they had an impact on the research techniques. These groups also functioned as support/growth groups designed to have a beneficial effect on the members (Malhotra, 1987b).

Participants had the option of choosing not to provide any aspect of the data. This option was utilized. One woman did not produce the audiotape of a dinner time conversation at home due to a custody battle with her former husband over her teenaged daughter. This daughter refused to be taped. If participants chose to provide data, they were under no pressure to disclose information. It is evident in the narrative texts provided by participants that the depth of their involvement varied. Some diaries are soliloquies about deeply personal and important conflicts. Although one woman said little in the group discussion, she used her diary to explore her feelings about her disintegrating marriage. Some diaries were written at a superficial level, demonstrating that pressures upon participants in regard to level of disclosure (or alienation) were minimal.

The fifty three persons who participated in the research were divided into five small groups which met for $2\frac{1}{2}$ hours a week for 15 weeks. These groups provided the vehicle for the research and therapeutic process. Confidentiality was a working agreement in the groups. Anonymity of the documents was guaranteed by a signed agreement with the researcher. All of the documents were kept by number only, not name. The discussions were about everyday life situations, but took place outside of their usual contexts and of all immediate consequences. Every attempt was made to facilitate trust and inhibit fear in the groups.

The women encouraged each other to reflect on their experiences and to offer interpretations. As such they engaged in hermeneutics. The groups provided a vehicle for a critical eye to be cast upon the effects of childhood experiences and cultural institutions and values upon the women's lives. The truth content of the claims made by the participants was also checked from one document to the next, or between statements made in the group and disclosures in the diaries and other documents. Marilyn French's *The Women's Room* (1974) was discussed at initial group meetings. This is a novel about women's confrontations with male domination in their personal lives, and particularly, in work and education. The participants could openly discuss their feelings about issues without having to talk directly and immediately about themselves.

Blockages to critical reflection were evident. For example, participants who reported experiences very much like the victimized characters in the novel were often condemnatory of the novel. This condemnation took several forms. One participant commented on the accuracy of the novel's descriptions of the experiences of women and gave examples from her own life of similar experiences. She did not like the novel, however, because she found it "depressing" to think about these things. Several others displayed a hostile attitude about the novel and were silent as to whether or not they had comparable experiences. Their autobiographies and diaries indicated, however, that they did have similar experiences. One woman wrote that she "struggled" through most of it and then had to "quit" because she was dealing with similar problems in her own life. Another wrote that it made her depressed; she could not discuss it in the group; "I never wanted no (*sic*) one to know that much about this part of my life."

The distinction between researcher and participant was further alleviated by an open invitation for all of the women to be involved in the study to any extent they wished, including analyzing data and writing up results. This came to actualization in the form of several women writing and presenting professional papers about aspects of the research. An additional effort was made to offer each aspect of the research for group discussion. In this way, the women participated in criticizing the research design itself. The style and format for the time schedules, for example, was changed as a result of such a discussion.

Analysis of Group Experience[1]

The groups were structured to maximize the ability of the members to communicate freely and openly and to engage in a dialogue with the

[1]An earlier version of this section of the book was published as, "Habermas' sociological theory and clinical practice with small groups." *Clinical Sociology Review* 5, 1987, 181–192.

other members (see Malhotra, 1987c). This allowed them to understand the structures within themselves and in the organizations and institutions with which they live. In many cases, they came to realize that these organizations—school, church, employment—both assisted and hampered their self-realization. Habermas views discourse leading to such realization as "emancipatory." The groups were intended to alleviate the effects of institutional patterns and to foster what Habermas called "competent communication" free from power distortions.

This section describes the group process based on direct observations. Following this, quantitative attempts to measure "communicative competency" are presented. These include an assessment of the "truth" content, "truthfulness," "understandability," and "comprehensibility" of each group member by the group leaders based on the videotapes of the groups early and late in the process. Assessments were also made of the communicative competency of the women in interaction with their families at home, based on the transcripts of audiotapes. Finally, assessments were made of the nature of the group process on the tapes by independent teams of observers.

Much like the hermeneutics of reading a text or a psychoanalytic dialogue, the small groups provided the occasion for a critical eye to be cast upon childhood and cultural influences upon the self. The *"comprehensibility"* aspect of the group communication was consistently high. Disclosure of intimacies was common. The verbally fluent members were patient toward those whose expressive capabilities were poor. For example, one of the women was from Ghana and had difficulty with English. Her family life was considerably different from those of the other participants. However, the others continued to gently question her until they had a picture of her experience.

"Understandability," or communication within appropriate norms, seemed to come easily within these groups. This was due partly to the fact that group norms were openly discussed and established at the initial session and reaffirmed as necessary throughout. It was agreed that both open self-disclosure and the decision not to self-disclose were acceptable. No instance of an individual or collective attempt to demand self-disclosure was observed.

The *"truth"* content was high in the groups because the intent of the discussions was continued self-understanding. The expression of deviant viewpoints took place consistently and was encouraged. There was continued support and acceptance at the personal level of those who disagreed. For example, a supporter of patriarchy continually went out for pizza and beer after group sessions with several others who were highly critical of her position. Yet she was accepted as "one of us." A wide range of political responses to related issues continued to be expressed throughout the group process.

An additional example of a challenge in discourse to the truth content of a fellow participant's assertions centered on the issue of "unconditional positive regard." A participant asserted that the emphasis on equal power within the male–female relationship would not work in her case. By applying Carl Rogers' (1961, 282) therapeutic attitude, she tolerated her husband's abusiveness as well as his economic and emotional dependency. Under the supposition that her consistent high regard would transform him, this student of counseling continued to hope for an improved relationship with him, despite his cold indifference to her two daughters from a previous marriage and his disparaging remarks about her judgment. His nickname for her was "Butt-breath." The group continued to challenge her interpretation of her situation.

"Truthfulness" (sincerity) tended to be high. There were few or no sanctions for a particular belief. One example was observed where the truthfulness of a participant was questioned by several others in the group. This woman boasted consistently about her highly successful business career and equalitarian marriage. Some group members doubted how ideal her marriage really was. She brought her husband to a group session to demonstrate directly to the group that she was telling the truth about their relationship. The husband affirmed that they shared in all household tasks and domestic decisions.

Assessment of Communicative Competency in the Groups

Using Habermas' criteria, the two research assistants who were leaders of the support groups participating in the study and I made judgments about each participant's communicative competency. The judgments were based both on overall observations and on viewings of the videotaped sessions. The same judges also assessed communicative competency for each member in their interaction with family or friends. These assessments were based on the audiotape recordings and transcripts of a dinner time conversation. (See Appendix I, Figures A2 and A3.) A factor analysis of the results of these judgments revealed the emergence of four consistent factors. (See Appendix IV, Tables A15 through A18.)

Factor One is called "Coherency of Communicative Competency." This factor indicated that participants tended to display consistently competent communication as judged by the raters throughout the 15-week period. The factor also included the components of being supportive and stimulating.

Factor Two indicated that support and hostility were inversely related throughout the group process. Factor Three showed a relationship between communicative competency in the home with aspects of communicative competency in the groups. For the most part, communicative competency in the groups was higher than in the home, thus indicating that we were successful in creating a group environment for therapeutic, competent communication. Further analysis of the data showed that there was less domination in the groups than in the home settings.

Comprehensibility, understandability, and truthfulness were rated higher in the videotaped groups than in the transcripts of conversations at home. Comprehensibility was rated as consistently higher in the groups. Understandability was also higher in the group than in the home and increased during the study. Truthfulness was rated as higher in the group setting than in the home with a slight decrease over the course of a semester. Objective truth content was rated as slightly higher in the home setting. Overall, the women shared and communicated on a more competent level in the groups than in the home examples. The home conversations seemed to be distorted by power and strategic forms of communication. Evidently, the attempt to alleviate these distortions in the group were successful. (See Appendix IV, Tables A19 through A23.)

Analysis of the Videotapes

Coming to an agreed upon coding system for the videotapes was itself a process of group analysis and negotiation. The six graduate student volunteers who worked on this part of the study and I established a coding system. Body language was determined to be open or closed. "Open" body language was indicated by unfolded or outstretched arms and legs and extended bodily posture. "Closed" body language included folded arms and legs and abdominal area bent inward. Speech patterns were judged hesitant or confident. "Hesitant" speech patterns were those where words were disjointed or cut off with little or no eye contact or indication of emphasis. Whether or not the women initiated topics, and offered support or disagreement to the points made by others were also coded for each tape.

Three pairs of research assistants and I systematically viewed the videotapes of the group discussions. Each coding decision was made by the pair watching and reviewing the tapes together. The two all-male pairs experienced little difficulty in agreeing upon the way most items should be coded. The male/female team had frequent debates about a coding decision. They always resolved them, however, without having to ask a third opinion. These pairs of volunteers did not complete the coding of all of the tapes. Two research assistants working as a team, attempted to code the remainder. They frequently could not agree about how a particular speech pattern should be coded. Subsequently, the remainder were coded by two other assistants.

Coding reduces the complex to the simple. Two or more coders attempting to analyze an involved group discussion will often disagree. Coding was itself a learning experience in group process. Attempting to clarify and systematize judgments also either confirmed or disconfirmed prior interpretations. Such quantitative supports for arguments are convincing to many who have come to believe in the power of "science" and who find numerical arguments appealing.

Often, such behind-the-scenes difficulties with quantification are glossed over when results are reported in neat tables. Quantification makes order out of chaos. This order is socially constructed and therefore reflects the ways of perceiving and thinking of those who do the ordering. With this in mind, let us review these quantitative findings.

Overall, more confident then hesitant speech patterns were exhibited. The amount of confident speech patterns was higher on the second taping. Only three persons on the first taping and two on the second exhibited hesitant speech patterns. Greater role crystallization in the second taping was indicated by the fact that fewer persons exhibited a greater number of confident speech patterns on the second taping.[2] Two persons exhibited hesitant speech patterns one time at each taping. This indicates greater role crystallization with an increase in the overall amount of confidence expressed by the time of the second session. The lack of comfort symptomized by hesitant speech patterns was minimal throughout.

Increased role crystallization was also shown by the fact that fewer persons exhibited open body language more often on the second taping then the first. No closed body language was observed on the second tape. This indicates less resistance among group members as time progressed.[3]

[2]In the first taping nine persons exhibited a total of twenty-four confident speech patterns. The range for number of times each person spoke confidently was from one to five. Hesitant speech patterns were exhibited by three persons only one time each. During the second taping seven persons exhibited confident speech patterns a total of thirty-nine times with a range of between one and eleven times each.
[3]During the first taping nine persons exhibited "open" body language with a spread of from one to five times per person for a total of twenty-five times. Seven of the persons exhibiting open body language were over age 25, thus

On the first taping only one person (who was over age 25) originated a topic. In the second taping this increased to three persons. Overall this indicates that members continued looking to group leaders for initiation of topics, with a slight increase over time of member-initiated topics. The taped sessions were atypical in this respect from the other group sessions. Normally, more persons originated topics and emotional outbursts and expressions were more frequent. The women may have been intimidated by being taped.

The first taping found nine persons exhibiting supporting comments a total of seventeen times. In the second taping four persons made a total of twenty-eight supporting comments. This indicates that certain persons (one in each of the four groups taped) took on a rather crystallized role as supporter.

These attempts to systematize observations about "communicative competency" (Habermas) supported the success of establishing group communication patterns which alleviated power distortions and allowed for interaction which assisted the women in self-understandings, and which empowered them to make desired changes in their lives.

Narratives as Data

Dorothy Smith (1987) points out that women carry out many necessary but culturally invisible functions. Therefore an understanding of the becoming mature of women must be contextually situated. As Smith affirms, the social phenomenology of Alfred Schutz is particularly adept at delineating the way persons are temporally and socially situated in their lifeworlds.

Narratives are always stories about changes that occur in time. Each of the documents gathered as part of this study made a different kind of time or a different time frame relevant for the writer. The phenomenological time studies attempted to get at the experience of time directly. However, each of the other narratives accomplished the same end indirectly. The autobiographies made relationships with significant others from childhood to the present thematic in the recounting of experience. The time schedules revealed how clock time was "spent" for a week.

---

indicating a slight tendency for more openness or calmness among the older participants. On the first taping, closed body language was exhibited by two persons, both over age 25. On the second taping, seven persons exhibited "open" body language with a spread of from one to eleven times each and a total of thirty-nine times. No one exhibited closed body language on the second taping.

The diaries provided reflective analysis of the meaning of activities and events throughout the day. Each of these narratives were already reflective exercises infusing experience with language and meaning. Each was guided by an intentionality. As Wagner points out: "Phenomenally, there is no 'memory image' outside of intentionality" (Wagner, 1983:78).

Schutz expressed this view repeatedly in his later phenomenological works: "My memory does not mechanically register the experiences of my inner duration; it affects them in a different form: it integrates them" (1982:45).

In each instance, others, perspectives, and values of the lifeworld, and one's own biographically related situation determined the experience as recounted in the narratives. Schutz discussed in detail how language is an element "already on hand" in earliest "we" relationships. This language already contains within it a view of the natural and social world, and thus becomes a "model" for everyone's subjective experiential structure (Schutz, 1976: 29–30, 58f).

Schutz (1970) emphasized that all experiences were grounded in the body, which in its actions and movements makes inner experiences compatible with the social world. In the act of reflection, immediate experience is pushed into the background. What is gained is the endowment of meaning upon an action in the past. This is accomplished by applying words and their inherent standards, i.e., categories, concepts, and values to experiences (p. 62).

Schutz overlooked the way words simultaneously ascribe meaning in immediate experience. Once language is learned, while awake or dreaming, words accompany experience, denoting meaning along with the flow of somatic sensations and bodily movements. Reflection is not the point at which meaning is ascribed. Rather it is a new act of interpretation of an experience that may already be meaningful prior to reflection. The relevance of immediate context and interest is crucial to the nature of this interpretation. The writing of narratives about one's life is such a reflection. Writing changes experience by endowing it with meanings that are pertinent to the current life situation of the writer. A meaning structure was already imposed on the documents by the intentions of the researcher and the face-to-face interaction among researcher and the participants. The time-memory narratives were discussed in the groups before they were written.

Group discussions served as a spur to memories, especially of the more distant past, like early childhood. Some of the participants had difficulty remembering when they were in first grade until after these informal discussions. The interaction in these groups was much like Schutz' description (1976) of making music together (p. 59f). Observations of these discussions made it clear that the verbal, gestural, and emotional reactions of the one stimulated contrary, supportive, or amplifying comments in the other.

These aspects of experience which the groups focused upon influenced each woman's memories as reflected in the narratives. Likewise, the research context framed the memories and the narratives. Memories and narratives were already endowed with a special, superimposed significance, for the women knew the questions were of importance to a funded research project and to the researcher. The "stocks of knowledge," shared evaluations, and typifications brought to the event by each participant about such activities already colored their context. (That the women knew that the documents were kept only by code number not by name may have mitigated this effect to some extent.)

The women were asked to evaluate how writing the narratives and discussing them in the groups effected their understandings and actions. They were asked to state whether their understandings of themselves or others had changed as a result of involvement in that project. In addition, the women were asked to what extent participation in the research had changed the way they acted in relation to others. Following a description of each type of narrative, the results of the evaluation will be briefly summarized. Although the effects of writing each narrative were analyzed separately, it is important to remember that none of the techniques were carried out alone or in isolation. Each was embedded in the ongoing group process and was carried out amidst group discussion of that technique. Therefore it cannot really be determined whether the effect reported was due to technique alone or to the discussions or to both.

Sensory/Memory Bracketing Narratives

In attempting to capture experience of time, the women were asked to remember one day in their lives from the time they woke up in the morning until retiring. To facilitate memory of actual experience as embodied, a technique of sensory bracketing was used. The participants were asked to remember what they said, smelled, tasted, heard, and touched throughout the day. The resulting narratives made the difficulties of capturing such a sequence apparent. What frequently resulted were not descriptions of the flow of sensations, but lists of fragmentally remembered feelings and events, or interpretations of sensory memories deemed relevant. However, this artificial separation of sensations helped them focus on specific events of some emotional relevance. Indeed, writing the accounts seemed to elicit memories of significant expe-

riences. The women remembered a day in first grade, as a way of elicit-
ing emotional meanings from childhood. They also wrote about a day
in their lives at the present time.

The women similarly reflected on longer term temporal experiences
in the present and as remembered in first grade. They recounted events
that stood out as important for that entire year as a child and as an adult.
They described their thoughts about the past and about the future at
these two points in their lives. Finally, they reflected on their views
about death in the past and at the present time.

One respondent, writing of the sounds remembered throughout the
passage of one day when in first grade, is typical in the way her descriptions are infused with meanings, cultural typifications, and feelings:

> When I was in first grade my mother used to come into my room and wake
> me up. I remember the sound of her voice. I would lie in bed a few minutes
> and she'd go back to the kitchen. I remember hearing the pots and pans
> rattling and the water running in the bathroom where my father was shav-
> ing. At school I remember singing songs and saying the alphabet out loud.
> The nuns wore big, long rosaries on their habits and I remember them rat-
> tling as they walked down the halls. At noon I remember hearing the bells
> of the church ring for the Angelas, a noon day prayer. The bells always had
> such a sacred sound. I remember the sounds of laughing and yelling on the
> playground at recess. At home in the evenings I remember listening to the
> radio. I loved the mystery show called "The Shadow." It had creepy sounds
> in it that made me get goose pimples all over. It scared me but I liked it
> anyway. At night I remember hearing the hum of the attic fan, and the
> chirping of the crickets outside my window.

The next narrative almost succeeds in giving the impression of recounting a day's experiences through memory of sounds:

> The perking of the coffee pot and the splashing of the shower extend the
> early morning solitude. The silence ends abruptly as my older son turns his
> radio full volume to a rock station, and my youngest son yells at me to go
> away when I try to get him up. Sounds of scurrying around through break-
> fast and dressing occupy the next hour. Accusations, arguments, and dis-
> cussions are heard between the children. Polite but strained conversation
> is the ride to work with my husband. The rest of the day is filled with
> work sounds, friendly chats, serious talk, telephones, and typewriters. The
> evening is kitchen meal sounds, the television and a radio in someone's
> room, discussions of the day's events with the children, arguments with
> the children and among themselves. At last, the semi-solitude of my room
> for an hour or two of study with interruptions from the children for ques-
> tions or an extension of an earlier conversation.

Yet even in this narrative, it is clear that purposes, and culturally
determined necessities fuse the memories of sounds. The narrative is

not a description of the sounds as they were heard, but rather a recounting in abstract fashion of those sounds which stand out as meaningful in the course of the day's activities and relationships.

One narrative consisted simply of lists of remembered objects seen throughout a day:

Bathroom facilities
Image in mirror
Traffic
Office building and environment
People working and moving about
Clients paper work
School: professors and students
Books, newspapers

This list reflects this woman's day of necessary activities as a professional and a graduate student.

The following narrative describes the passage of one day of time through memories of sights. This narrative makes clear the way relevant things seen can serve as markers or familiar guideposts that may serve as anchors of one's day. Especially illuminating in this regard is her description of visual markers while driving and how these have come to mean a definite clock time:

I wake up and see the big mobile over my bed. It used to be very artistically arranged, but the wind/kids have permanently arranged it so it looks like junk hanging from the ceiling. I hit the floor which is bright purple and shows every little piece of lint. I am standing in front of a ten foot floor-to-ceiling mirror. Sometimes it is nauseating to have to look at my body first thing in the A.M. The den is in it's usual mess. I shake my head in amazement at how dirty a carpet can possibly get. There are books of all shapes and sizes everywhere. I need a bookcase so desperately. I think the room would improve 100% if the books were picked up. I paw through the laundry room to see what there is to wear. There's always a big pile to do even when I feel like there couldn't possibly be any more anywhere. I don't know how I'd act if my house wasn't terminally cluttered. There's an endless string of cars on the highway on my way to school. I pass some familiar landmarks that draw me closer and closer to town. The lake means 9:05 A.M., the Fishin' Hole means 9:10, etc. Every landmark has a time attached to it because I know what time I have to be at certain points in order to be in class on time. TV is on, as usual. Some of the shows interest me now and then. Most do not. *All in the Family* is the last show I normally watch before I go to sleep.

It was evident in the group discussions that emotionally significant contents were emerging from the exercise of recalling events of a day in terms of sensory memories at the present time and as remembered from childhood. The majority of the persons involved in the study (87%, N = 46) reported changes in their lives as a result of doing and discussing the phenomenological time studies. They reported such effects as greater acceptance of others, greater sensory awareness, and realization of the bases of their morals and values in their past. They also reported the following changes; different reactions from others, a tendency to look more at the present rather than toward the future, making more of their own decisions, gaining greater acceptance of their own pasts, changing their perceptions of things and events, and entering psychotherapy.[4]

Autobiographies

The women wrote autobiographies in which they recounted their experiences from childhood to the present in relation to George Herbert Mead's theory of the self. They were asked to specify who their most important others were throughout their lives, and to recount their memories of what these others expected of them and what qualities they attributed to them. They were asked to state their reactions to these perceived attributions and expectations from significant others. The women also wrote about their conceptions of society in general and specific institutions as they were growing up and their evaluations of them.

What the autobiographies amounted to was a reflection on the situations as biographically determined (Schutz, 1973: 76–77). All of the geographical, cultural, and social conditions and systems of relevances and typifications were involved in their producing narratives which allowed them to "make sense" out of their lives in this framework. As Lakoff and Johnson (1980:173) demonstrate, the narrative form of the autobiography assumes that one will make a coherent story out of one's experience, highlighting those which "fit" the story line.

The following segments of an autobiography are illustrative of this infusion of time, memory, and meaning with relationships with others in the context of culturally based values, typifications, and relevances:

> I was born in 1938 in Texas. My father was in the army and my mother was a homemaker. World War II began during my preschool years and being a military family this had an influence on my life. The main thing I remember about this time is the different houses we lived in. My father was stationed near the Texas/Mexico border when and where I was born. Then he was sent to officers' school. When the war started he was stationed in California.

---

[4]Four percent (N = 2) reported no effect from having completed the phenomenological time studies.

> We followed him to these places, which resulted in living in quite a few different homes . . . My parents were divorced when I was 5 years old and this ended my strong military connection. My father made a career of the army and between wars (WWII and the Korean War), he was stationed in Europe quite a bit, so I did not get to see him very often. However I have had a strong feeling for the military and one of my big regrets in life is that I did not join some branch of the service when I was young. My mother and I moved back to Texas and lived with my maternal grandparents for the next 8 years. Of all the people who had some influence on my life, my maternal grandparents and especially my grandmother have been the strongest influence. She and I were alone all day while my mother and grandfather were at work. Her love for animals, flowers and books have all rubbed off on me . . . Life was very quiet on the farm, my nearest friend lived about 1 mile away. Most of my playing was done alone until I was 11 years old and got a bicycle. I always loved dolls and played with them often . . .

The autobiography goes on to describe various radio programs she listened to and the characters she admired. She later describes the positive influence of her grandfather and the negative effect of her stepfather after her mother remarried.

A second example of an autobiography makes it apparent how another respondent's existence at a particular historical point influenced her:

> This autobiography cannot be complete without knowing the time period of birth, September 26, 1938, and the influence in force because of the social and political air. Of course, 1938 was before World War II—but a time of brewing in Europe. It was a time of growing and rebuilding after the stock market crash of the late 1920s and early 1930s. The average families were struggling to make ends meet. Even the wealthy were hurt.

These autobiographical narratives make it clear that others are the key to one's central experiences. Feelings, values, and self-concepts all center on the interplay with others and were perceived as having positive, negative, or mixed effects on the self. Such autobiographical narratives place one in time in relation to family, culture, and perceptions of one's achievements and valued accomplishments. The narratives reflect what Schutz (1982) refers to as the constraints of "world time":

> Our I-experience is banished into time and space; it is tied to consociates through language and emotions; it is accustomed to thinking, that is to spatialize streaming changes of quality and to form them into concepts. (p. 32)

Systematic reflection on childhood was a new experience for all participants. The discussions surrounding this process were frequently highly emotional. Several women discussed early experiences involving severe physical and verbal abusiveness on the part of parents or spouses. They received understanding and support from the group.

Most of the participants (88%, $N = 47$) reported that writing the autobiography had changed their lives. They reported such effects as more awareness of the following: the effects of others on them, the causes of their own behavior, their own past, their own limitations, their role in making life choices, and the effect they had on others. Some reported having greater acceptance of their own lives and greater acceptance of others. One said her childhood goals were reinforced through participation.

The women reported the following changes in their behavior: greater strictness with children, less tolerance of others' lack of responsibility, developing the motivation to begin a new project, greater self-confidence, improved relationships with significant others, and entering psychotherapy.[5]

Diaries

The respondents were asked to keep daily diaries throughout the 15 weeks of the study. These diaries illustrate the way: "the fixed course of world time conditions subjective actions; it forces the principle of 'first things first' on daily plans" (Schutz and Luckmann, 1973:92).

The respondents were not given any directives about what to write about in the diaries except "whatever is of concern to you at this time." However open ended this was, the "diary" already has the cultural connotation of the secret, the personal, and the reflective. Diaries are often sold with a lock and key attached, reinforcing this personal, secretive aspect. However, these "diaries" were known from the start to be documents which would be read (albeit anonymously) by the researcher and perhaps others. This brings with it the possibility that what is written in the diary may have been oriented to a potentially broad eventual audience. At times in discussions, the term "journal" was interchanged with "diary" to encourage those who may not have been oriented toward personal disclosure, but more toward an "objective" descriptive recounting of the days' events.

The diaries ranged from personal and analytically reflective to more "objective," curt, and superficial. The majority of the respondents wrote personally disclosing diaries. One respondent's diary served as a way

---

[5]Nine percent ($N = 5$) reported no effect from having written and discussed the autobiography; 3% ($N = 1$) did not respond.

of reflecting on a failing marriage and impending divorce. The evening after her husband returned from the hospital after a hernia operation she said:

> . . . he left the house about 8:00 and didn't return until midnight. I'm watching everything he does as if it has nothing to do with me at all. . . . It's as though I'm watching my marriage slip out of my hands, and I can only move in slow motion. . . . Saturday night, and I'm spending it as I want, studying. My husband went out with his friends. He said he might not be home tonight. . . .
>
> [My husband] said he didn't believe there was any hope for us at all, that I made him feel inadequate in every way. He said it might be irresponsible of him, but he just didn't want to deal with the kids and their problems or the grind of putting me through school. . . . To add insult to injury he confirmed that he is involved with a girl from his office—she's only one year older than our daughter!

This diary continues throughout the 15-week period where the respondent seeks the help of a counselor and works out a divorce agreement with her husband.

A second participant reflected in her diary about a book we were reading and discussing as a group. The book was *Neurosis and Human Growth* by Karen Horney (1950):

> Last night I had a terrific insight when reading the Horney book. I re-read the part about ambition. As I read this I realized something about some of us so-called over achievers but I'm going to save it for my book—the one my idealized self thinks I'm going to write someday. I don't think I care so much for power over others but I surely do want recognition . . . I am going to read more in the Horney book today—it is a good day for it—pouring down rain and very gloomy. Actually, in spite of finding myself on every page, I like the book—well like is not the right word. I think I appreciate reading a book that helps me gain understanding of myself and others even if the insights occasionally make me want to hide under the covers.

One of the participants, a student from Iran, took the idea of writing a diary so literally that she turned in a traditional diary with a lock and key. In this diary she reflects on her feelings about being in a foreign country, and feelings of missing her family, about cultural differences, and political problems. She also commented on having written the autobiography:

> Doing the autobiography and having to think back brought up so many memories, old, dear memories that I cherish some, and like to forget some other. . . . There is a new girl from home in school. She reminds me of myself when I came here 3 years ago. She is so trustful in everybody. She

looks at the bright side of everything. I think that she has not known people as they really are. She is the same age when I came here, 18. We heard our grandfathers death news from a distant relative. It made all of us more mad than sad. They never tell us anything, no bad news because we are all students here and we should not be disturbed with bad news. It makes me think who else is dead and we don't know. I had a nightmare last night. I was talking to grandpa. He was wrapped in a white shroud, and he looked so pale. He was telling me how much he wanted his grandchildren to be with him at that time, but we preferred being away and studying. I told him how sorry I was, but he didn't hear me. . . .

In their diaries, respondents expressed feelings and evaluations about their daily experiences. These evaluations were directly related to how they perceived their relationships with others according to cultural standards of what these relationships should be like. The daily diaries kept by the women were doubly reflective, for they wrote about their experiences in the research, as well as other aspects of their lives at home and as students. In one of the journals the participant indicated that after a group session her husband had asked her what they had talked about. After she told him it was about the double burden of career and home life, her husband voluntarily cooked lunch and dinner for the first time in their 5-year marriage!

The majority of the women (83%, $N = 43$) reported a change in understanding and/or behavior as a result of keeping the daily journal. Most realized that their problems were not unique but experienced by others. In Mills' (1959) sense they were able to convert "troubles into issues." For example, one woman realized that she became too upset about some things. Some learned about the causes of their behavior.

Changes in interaction with families which resulted from the exercise included the following: becoming more distant from husband, starting to yell at husband, a change in sex life, becoming more assertive, and putting less pressure on husband and children. Other changes reported included: becoming a new "self," becoming more patient, learning to say "no," making better use of time, improving personality traits, and learning to set priorities.[6]

For some participants, it was difficult to say whether they should be counted with a change in understanding or a change in behavior. For them, the act of writing the journal was in itself a behavior with certain direct effects including: the release of hostility, the experience of pain in writing, and feeling better while writing. The journals' value was described by one participant, who was also a research assistant, as "thera-

[6]Eighteen percent ($N = 10$) reported no effects.

peutic." Katherina Anna (the name she wishes to be called in this book) indicated that the journals showed how the various aspects of the research on the self, temporality and communicative competency, were integrated. She described the therapeutic advantages of the journals for the women including the following; monitoring one's own behavior and environmental influences, exploring the possibilities and limitations of one's own life space, working out role conflicts, providing support for self-nurturing, being able to see oneself more positively, and clarifying goals. Commenting on this aspect of the journals, Katherina Anna said:

> In suggesting the use of a journal for therapeutic as well as research purposes, we do not in any way encourage it as an end in itself, or as a substitute for action. However, it can serve as a kind of blueprint in which to chart new and desirable courses of action.

Time Schedules as Narratives

The way the women kept their "time schedules" makes it clear that when one is asked how one "spends time" one emphasizes work and purposive activity. Little of the women's thoughts or feelings or bodily states were expressed in these calendars. It is interesting to note that in spite of extremely busy schedules as students, employees, wives, and mothers, they projected the sense that they had not really done anything or accomplished anything. One of the participants in fact presented a paper on the effect of keeping the time schedules which she titled "So Busy Doing Nothing." A typical time schedule for a graduate student who was also a mother and employed as a counselor in a junior college reads as follows:

6:45 Arose and had prayer
7:00 Washed up
7:15 Dressed daughter for school
7:40 Prepared breakfast and lunch for daughter
8:05 Saw daughter off to school
8:10 Made bed
8:15 Had bath and dressed self
9:00 Made phone call
9:20 Cleaned up kitchen and dining areas
9:45 Left for work
11:00 Arrived in class and administered examination
11:55 Left class
12:00 Had conference with student
1:00 Worked on report for meeting
2:00 Attended meeting

5:00 Drove to the university
10:00 Arrived home, checked on daughter
10:30 Changed clothes, had a snack
11:00 Studied and read
12:30 Sleep

For the second and third weeks of keeping clock time schedules, participants decided (based on a suggestion coming from one of them in group discussion) to add a column to these documents where they would comment on these daily activities. This was motivated by a discussion of the first time schedule, where a discussion centered on the fact that it was enlightening to see what they did "on paper" but what this felt like or meant to them needed to be included. Indeed these simple descriptive tabulations of actions appeared to them to distort their experience. What was missing was the story behind them, or the narrative, which would make sense out of the events by connecting them with prior events or with feelings and evaluations. These commentaries were often simple adjectives such as "felt tired", "aggravating" or "what a relief!". Some of them were true narratives in that they related the actions to other persons or events such as: "my mother always makes me wait like that" "my husband does not appreciate all of this effort on behalf of the children which I put out!" "no matter how much laundry I do there is always a pile remaining to be done. This is the story of my life." "I am tired of entertaining and felt guilty for not getting my studies done."

The limitations of what-must-come-first in daily life of the world within actual reach are evident in these schedules. Likewise is the phenomenon of "waiting" as one's own calendar does not mesh with others' or as biological calendars conflict with social calendars or prescribed events: "Waiting is the expression for a system of relevances imposed upon us" (Schutz, 1970: 182).

Most of the participants reported that having kept and discussed the time schedules had changed their understandings and/or behaviors (74%, N = 39). They reported greater awareness of the following; their use of time, their subservience to the demands of others, their own selfishness with time, their frustrations and feelings surrounding time use. They also reported increased appreciation for how much they do. Many of them adjusted their use of time to better reflect their values and goals. Family patterns of responsibility were changed in some cases. Decisions were made to be more lax about housework or to obtain more help from family members.[7]

[7]Twenty-one percent (N = 11) reported no effect of the time schedules.

A participant who gave a presentation on the effect of keeping and discussing the time schedules called her talk "Making Nothing a Reality." She spoke with other participants about the effects of keeping the time schedules. They reported realizing how much they did even though they would respond "nothing" if asked what they did on a given day. This was especially true of married students and student mothers. The time schedules kept the week prior to entering school showed the women assisting children and spouses in preparing for school and work activities, with no time to prepare themselves and no one assisting them in their preparations.

Discussions, Tapings, and Coding

To determine the power distortions in communication both in the groups and at home, audio and videotape recordings were made. Each group was videotaped twice—early and late in the process. Each woman audiotaped a dinner time conversation in her home. They transcribed and analyzed the segments of these conversations which they thought important. These tapes became living narratives for interpretation along with the written narratives.

The women analyzed their tape-recorded conversations with family members (or close friends if they lived alone). They transcribed these conversations and looked at such factors as who talked the most, who interrupted, and who governed choice of topics.[8]

The largest category (30%, $N = 16$) reported having changed their behavior as well as understandings as a result of doing the taping and analysis. Some of the behavioral changes indicated were the following: showing more respect and appreciation for family members, turning off the television more frequently, becoming either more or less assertive in conversation, becoming more humorous and less critical, becoming less defensive in interaction with a domineering husband, and becoming more fair with children.

Thirty percent ($N = 16$) reported changed understandings only. Increased awareness of the following were reported; multiple interpretations of situations, poor usage of language, greater appreciation for the influence of self on others, and the need to become more self-confident.[9]

[8]Cicourel (1973) and Speier (1973) discuss some of these techniques; Malhotra and Deneen (1982) further developed the techniques.

[9]Twenty-six percent ($N = 14$) of the participants did not complete the conversational analysis because of fears on their part or on the part of family members. Indeed, the conversational analysis was the most intrusive of the techniques used. Twelve percent ($N = 6$) reported no effect from having completed the conversational analysis.

Continuing with the critically reflective process involved meeting with research assistants who also read the documents, and reviewed the video- and audio tape recordings. Coding categories for the documents emerged from the group discussions. Thus these categories may be seen as "significant symbols" in the Meadian sense of a socially negotiated meaning. These categories were then "tested" by actually trying to code several documents and using them before they were finalized. Following this the documents were coded and computerized.

Summary

This chapter has described the research process as a hermeneutics of written and spoken texts. The guiding theories for the study of Mead, Schutz, and Habermas were briefly summarized. The kinds of narratives written by the women were then reviewed in relation to Schutz' theories of time and memory in narratives. The study of the group processes based on the videotapes indicated increased communicative competency and group cohesiveness over time in the five small groups.

This research was designed to increase the self-reflective awareness of the participants as they wrote self-descriptive and analytical narratives. The small discussion groups were structured to facilitate communication freed from power or distortions based on strategic interests. In this way, the relatively open communication in the groups stimulated the private recollective and reflective activities of the women. Overall the women reported positive effects of being involved in the research.[10]

Catching the "Bug" of "Quantophrenia" and "Abstracted Empiricism"

Sorokin (1956), the astute and caustic sociologist, said modern American sociology suffers from the disease of "quantophrenia." This is a delusional illness whereby the sociologist comes to believe that if she can put something into numbers and add them up and put them into tables, she is a real, hard core "scientist" and her results will thereby be more valid and respectable. In an attempt to alleviate the stress of looking

---

[10]Summarizing the reported effects of participation in all aspects of the research showed the following: over all techniques 34% of the women changed both behaviors and understandings, 45% changed understandings but not necessarily behaviors, and 12% reported no change from participation. Nine percent did not complete the evaluation. (See Appendix III, Table A14.)

directly at and coping with the worlds opened up by the project and the meanings in the narratives, I succumbed to a hypochondriacal attack of this bug.

C. Wright Mills (1959) rediagnosed this disease "abstracted empiricism." The abstracted empiricist tries so hard to make her findings "real" and concrete that she objectifies her created abstractions. This reification—objectification process is stage two of the disease. It occurs when the results of a self-induced illness become real in themselves. This is the hang-over suffered after overindulgence in quantophrenia.[11]

For a while I became obsessed with producing more and more computer printouts of tables and charts. I accumulated hundreds of such tables. All of this kept me safe from comprehending the depth and scope of the effects of childhood adversities experienced by the women on their adult lives. My own "ghosts" did not want me to recognize this.

I look back on all of this intellectualization as an attempt on my part to defend myself against the implications of the profound meaning of the results. As I was in supervision in my private practice in psychotherapy with Robert Langs, M.D., I became aware of the tremendous lengths to which therapists and patients will go to avoid dealing with the most profoundly meaningful issues which come up in therapy. These include death and painful childhood experiences. Indeed, Langs' work is testimony to the way therapists hide the truths about them-

---

[11]This "defense mechanism" was promoted and enforced by the institutional arrangements under which the research was conducted. Having tried and failed to obtain support for qualitative research on this topic, I reframed the research proposal in the language of positivism and added the quantitative component. Subsequently I did obtain funds. I have seen this socially induced tendency to quantophrenia effect the research efforts of numerous graduate students. Typically, the student will start our with a project idea which has deep personal meaning for him, such as how to deal with a dying parent. By the time the research design gets through the committee and university research structures, he will be measuring something on a scale of one to five and lose touch with the significance of his original interest.

This is not to say that all those social scientists who count are "sick." If you quantify something that requires it, and is not inherently obfuscated by it, this is an important undertaking. (Don't mistake the symptoms for the disease.) Quantitative sociology is a necessary effort to understand large-scale segments of social reality. For example, we do need to know how many people are likely to get heart disease so we can prepare adequate prevention and treatment programs. Even on a smaller scale, the systematic coding and analyses of the narratives from this study was of value, demonstrating the nature and extent of the effects of others on the maturing self, the management of time, and the experience of temporality.

selves through their work with patients (Langs, 1982). I then started to wonder: Had I been doing the same thing with this research? My reexamination of my own research processes led me to realize that I too was attempting to escape from realizations about childhood adversities, death, and painful aspects of my intimate relationships.

This research process has been a long existential struggle for me in carrying it out in such a way as to illustrate the striving for maturity of the fifty-three women who participated. When I finally paid my debt to the objectivist in me and overcame the "quantitative defense mechanism," I came back to the cases, the real life experiences of the women who participated in the study as they told them directly and through their narratives.

After reviewing the theories and methodologies upon which this research was based and the related theories of human development, I felt that the bedrock of the women's experiences was not yet fathomed. Theories are conceptual enterprises. They are tools for abstracting aspects of life which are of relevance for onlookers and interpreters. Theories and methods are double-edged swords which both cut through weeds and cut away beautiful wild flowers. Thus theories and research methods both facilitate and mitigate against understanding. As rational enterprises, they screen out emotional qualities. As categories, they operate against recognition of unique human experiences. Narratives are attempts to capture these uniquenesses. Phenomenological description moves from these rich descriptions to essential shared meanings of these experiences.

It was not until I visited Fan Benno, a well-known psychic, that I realized that I had not yet written the book which was most important. With no prior knowledge of my work, Fan told me that I had two books to write and that one of them was about the lives of women. Following Fan's insight and the dictum of phenomenologist Edmund Husserl, I went back to the things themselves and read once again the more than 4000 pages of narratives written by the women. This led me to realize the inadequacy and incompleteness of the prior analyses I had made of the data and also of the inadequacies of existing theories to explain these experiences.

Following the data gathering stage of the study, the long process of interpretation of the documents began. In spite of the coding and counting of the results, data analysis was a hermeneutical, critical, and ongoing task, involving myself and numerous research assistants and volunteers. Some of the results of this process are described in Chapter 3.

Self, Time, and Temporal Experience 3

Introduction

This chapter summarizes the major findings which resulted from systematizing and quantifying the information provided by the women in relation to the theories and concepts of Mead, Schutz, and Habermas. This effort centered on the themes of self, time, and temporality. The data which was analyzed included the autobiographies, time schedules, and phenomenological time studies. While the phenomenological time/memory studies were not actually coded and computerized, the results as reported in this chapter were obtained by systematically grouping the open-ended responses. Typical ways the women experienced temporality as children and adults were established.

Each narrative related a slightly different temporal focus. The autobiographies, inspired by George Herbert Mead's concept of significant others as the grounds for the self, covered the time of childhood until the present seen in relation to others. The diaries spoke of personally determined relevances for each particular day. Participants' time schedules, while not strictly narrative in style, told stories of how time was accounted for during a week with a focus on time as something to be "spent" in purposive activities measured by the clock.

Finding "Ghosts" and "Spirits" by Writing Autobiographies

The act of writing the autobiographies was a way in which the women discovered the existence of "ghosts" and "spirits" in their lives. The women were asked to specify who their significant others were at the following stages: preschool, ages 6–12, ages 13–18, ages 19–25, and age 26 and older. For each significant other, they were asked to state what they thought this significant other thought about them (attributions) and what they expected of them (expectations). They were then

asked to analyze how they evaluated these attributions and expectations—did they agree with them or not? On what basis did they evaluate
them? The women also evaluated each significant other by specifying
what kind of impact the significant other had on them and whether they
thought well of the person or not.

The autobiographies also included analyses of the nature and effect
of organizations and institutions on them at each of the above stages in
their lives. This was an attempt to ascertain the effect of what Mead
called "the generalized other" on the women. Outside of these guidelines, the autobiographies were to be completely open ended. (See Appendix I, Fig. A1.)

As with each aspect of the research process, discussions in the groups
centered on issues related to the writing of the narratives. The women
discussed the effects of parents, grandparents, siblings, friends, and
others on their lives and in the process clarified and worked through
their feelings about them. These discussions also helped some of the
women remember aspects of their childhood which they had forgotten.
The discussions freed some of them to evaluate things which they had
completely repressed. These discussions no doubt "biased" the documents. However the "bias" was in the direction of greater depth of understanding and thus contributed to rather than detracted from the
overall aims of the research. The group process also made possible the
related goal of empowering the participants.

Writing and discussing autobiographies was a way of reflecting upon
the effects of those whose voices later became the "ghosts" and "spirits"
of the women's everyday lives as adults. For the most part, they had not
previously been consciously aware of the extent to which the attitudes,
values, and ways of acting toward them of these significant others had
effected their ways of becoming mature.

Evaluation of Significant Others

Overall the women evaluated their significant others in a positive
manner.[1] This finding held true for those who mentioned many signifi-

---

[1] The coders agreed that only the first three significant others mentioned for
each age group would be coded according to their relationship to the participant
and according to sex, due to the cumbersome nature of coding all of those mentioned. Of course, sometimes the women wrote on less important significant
others prior to mentioning a most important one, thus leaving the most crucial
ones out of the quantitative analysis. The attributions of significant others were
coded as to whether they were "self-oriented," "other-oriented," "negative per-

cant others and for those who just mentioned a few. Overall, 58% of the evaluations of significant others were positive, 39% were mixed, and 2% were negative. (See Appendix III, Tables A7 through A9.)

The sex of the significant other seemed to have some effect on the evaluation at preschool age, teenage, and age 25 +. At preschool age, 74% of male significant others as compared with 64% of female significant others are evaluated positively. At teenage years, only 43% of male significant others are positively evaluated as compared with 56% of female significant others. For those age 26 +, both male and female significant others are more positively evaluated (female 71% and male 77%) with males gaining the lead. At ages 6–12, both males and females are evaluated positively to about the same extent (43% female and 41% male) and at young adulthood this percentage is increased for both males and females (female 55% and male 55%). On the average, significant others are evaluated most positively at age 26 and older (71% positive), the lowest overall evaluations occurring at ages 6 to 12 (42%). The autobiographies suggest that female significant others may have tended to be evaluated less positively at preschool age because the fathers had little contact with many preschool daughters and when fathers did relate to them it tended to be in more playful situations. As one participant put it:

> My mother was once again in the background loving and, unfortunately, playing the heavy at times. She had to discipline me, so I really liked her the least of the two, but I knew I loved her. I more-or-less observed my mother. I don't remember feeling very attached to her at that time. She expected me to grow day by day and all of us in the family did my daddy's biddings. That was our life—to do what he wanted.

For the teenage years, evaluation of boyfriends tended to bring down the overall evaluation of males. Overall boyfriends tended to be evaluated lower than fathers. Young adulthood brings the second lowest

---

sonality traits," "developed appreciation" or "other." Expectations of significant others were coded into the following categories; family activities—positive, family activities—negative, school or work—positive, school or work—negative, future activities—family, future activities—school or work, positive personality traits and negative personality traits. Each attribution and expectation was also coded as to whether or not the women accepted or rejected it. The coders also recorded their judgments about whether the women evaluated each significant other in a positive, mixed, or negative manner.

overall evaluations of significant others. This seemed related to the stresses of establishing economic independence and becoming new wives and mothers. One young woman, a student from Nigeria, was faced with crises in all these areas simultaneously:

> During my nineteenth to twenty-fifty years, my husband and my Chemistry teacher . . . were the significant figures in my life. It was a time of hardship for me. My marriage was in the process of breaking off, I lost my pregnancy due to poverty, and at the same time took a very tough teacher in my Chemistry class, a required course for my major. In my marriage, I considered myself as too young to be married, and also as foreigner I could not get a good paying job to help straighten my life out. With all these pressures on me, I could not agree with my husband and everything was going upside down for me.

The evaluation of significant others was analyzed according to who the significant others were. Those least frequently evaluated positively were boyfriends, other friends, and God. The women frequently had bitter feelings toward their boyfriends, who they felt had misused their affection. Those most negatively evaluated were brothers, other friends, female children, and God. It is of interest that female, not male, children were evaluated negatively by their mothers. Those who mentioned "God" as a significant other expressed strong feelings about God, whether positive or negative. In cases where the feelings were negative, God was a source for their condemnation of themselves or others.

The general tendency toward positive evaluations of significant others in the autobiographies are in part due to the coding system and in part due to the tendency of the women to gloss their experiences by mentioning first or most often those persons who had a positive effect on them. An example of excluding a negative significant other is as follows: One women, a 38-year-old recently divorced mother of three, does not mention her former husband. She comments only on supportive women friends before and after the divorce. An example of positively evaluating a significant other who had a negative effect on the women is the case of a woman who wrote about her father's attempts at incest with her when she was 7 years old, his overly punitive actions, and his actual incest with her sisters. When the mother discovered what was going on, she divorced the participant's father. Speaking of her parents at that time, during her fifteenth year, she wrote: "I realized I loved them both but something was wrong with my father and it was best for us to separate and find ourselves again and maybe he could too."

The extent to which the women accepted or rejected the attributions and expectations placed upon them by significant others was also coded and analyzed. Overwhelmingly, the women accepted the attributions, which they perceived others placed on them. At no age group did more than 5% of them reject any attribution of a significant other. This was true of both positive and negative attributions. The data thus support Mead's contention that the self is constructed by looking at oneself from the viewpoint of significant others. (See Appendix 3, Tables A1 through A13.)

Reflectivity, in Mead's sense, is the ability to critically evaluate the influences of significant others and social institutions upon oneself. It is the ability to accept or reject them, and change one's life accordingly. Reflectivity is stimulated by the necessity of working through contradictory attributions or expectations presented by one or more significant other. For example, one woman mentioned being scolded and hit a lot by her mother as a preschooler. Her mother viewed her as essentially "bad," "uncreative," and "unimaginative." By contrast, her grandmother viewed her as "good," "kind," and "intelligent." At the time of writing her autobiography she was still working through these contradictory aspects of her self. Her significant others at work and school were like the grandmother, thinking her good and intelligent. At home, her series of inadequate and exploitative boyfriends and spouses demeaned her.

As with attributions, expectations of significant others were similarly accepted by the women. Over all age groups, 74% of the expectations of significant others were accepted by the women. The highest level of acceptance occurred at preschool age (85% acceptance). The lowest level of acceptance of expectations occurred at young adulthood (56%), perhaps indicating the need for establishing independence at that age, perhaps also indicating the new situation of the women, many of whom were currently at that age and entering the university.

The nature of the expectations reported varied with age group. For preschool age, positive personality traits were the most reported expectation. For ages 6–12, the expectations centered on daily life at school and at home. Teenagers experience more expectations in regard to the future. For young adulthood and older age groups expectations turn back toward the present life with family and toward career and school activity.

The autobiographies overwhelmingly supported Mead's contention that the self is constructed by looking at oneself from the viewpoint of significant others. Both positive and negative attributions and expectations, from both positively and negatively evaluated significant others, were for the most part accepted as valid by the women. This finding overall supports the notion that others in early life and throughout life have a profound effect on the self. Furthermore, it makes little difference whether others are perceived as good or bad, positive or negative, or whether they think of one in a positive or negative matter. Regardless, their attributions and expectations will become part of the building blocks of the self. The positive attributions and expectations become the "spirits" and the negative ones the "ghosts" which continually hinder or inspire one's daily life.

Since others effect one in this way, the development of the capacity to critically evaluate these effects is of the utmost importance in human becoming. The way the ability to cope with and critically reflect upon the influences on oneself develops and is exercised was not captured by the coding and analysis.

Some understanding of the initial development of critical reflection in the participants could be gleaned from the autobiographies. Frequently, the women would mention contradictory attributions and expectations between varying significant others. For example, perhaps they had a mother who attributed negative qualities to them but a grandmother who was more accepting. One woman never thought about her intelligence or lack of it until she had a teacher in the fifth grade who thought she was extremely bright. Prior to this time she thought she was stupid, because this was the attribution about her that was commonly shared and projected by her parents and teachers in grades one through four!

A similar conflict was experienced by another participant between her mother's attributions and her father's. Her father ascribed her qualities as "stupidity," "clumsiness," and "lack of determination." On the other hand, her mother thought she was pretty, clever, and capable." She explained how she was able to accept both parents' attributions by ascribing her mother's to her relationships with those close to her and her father's to the outside world:

> In reflecting upon the combined impact of these attributions and expectations, I see the beginning of a kind of a contradictory self-concept, which has followed me throughout my life thus far. There was a very strong maternal acceptance of me, and this greatly added to my self-esteem and confidence in relation to others. I have somewhat internalized this in relationships to loved ones and friends and consider myself a worthy person in this respect. On the other hand, the critical evaluations of my father, marks what has been the beginning of a very strong sense of inadequacy and incompetence which has prevailed throughout my life in relation to the larger world.

While conflicting attributions and expectations between various significant others (and at times coming from the same one) instigated some critical reflection on the part of the women, this did not mean that they would not accept all of them. What happened in such instances was that an emotionally divided self (see Denzin, 1984) was formed.

Lifestyles and Time Schedules

Keeping Time

The women were asked to record everything they did for each of 4 entire weeks. The first time schedule was done retrospectively about a typical week prior to their taking a job and/or entering college. The second and subsequent time schedules were done at monthly intervals thereafter. Because the participants suggested and agreed upon it, the second, third and fourth time schedules included comments and evaluations of the activities mentioned.

The time schedules vary greatly in detail and precision. The decision was made initially to sacrifice the neatness and convenience of predetermined and prescaled measures. The categories as coded are to be viewed not as "measurements" in fact, but rather as patterns which emerge as objects in a social process of reading the documents. Like all social realities, the frequencies and means in the tables which follow represent negotiated realities resulting from a process of social interaction. Here the relevant interactors were the researcher and research assistants, the students who made up the coding system, the primary coder, and the participants.

Coding as Hermeneutics

The coding and analysis of the time schedules was itself a complex, messy, social process. It would indeed be misleading to report the results of research designed as a reflective, symbolic interaction process and make it appear as if the results were not negotiated social realities. The "facts" as presented are in their present form only as a result of a web of communications between the many persons involved in producing and processing the data. Constraints of time, limited resources, and the pressing immediate problems and needs of the students involved as participants and researchers continually impinged on what was initially thought to be an "ideal" research design.

The time schedules were read by a group of research assistants, and a system of coding categories was established. The final coding categories were by no means seen as "definite" or even "final" by those involved, but merely as workable. The documents were then coded by an assistant. When a second assistant began to help with the coding, she discovered discrepancies in the way the two coded the data. The problem seemed to lie in cultural differences, since the initial coder's primary language was Chinese. These discrepancies were analyzed and the data were then recorded.

The data were summarized by computing weekly totals for each type of activity for each participant for each of the 4 weeks. An intuitive reading of the documents showed differences between age groups and marital status groups in the way they spent time. Consequently, the data were analyzed by age, marital, and parental status.

The Rapid Pace of Life: Losing Sleep

The single category with the largest average number of hours of time spent per week was "sleeping" (mean of 34 hours). The daily average of hours of sleep was consequently less than five. The other activities were ranked in order from larger average amounts of time spent to smaller amounts. These activities ranked as follows (from larger to smaller amounts of time spent): leisure, work, education, bathing, dressing and eating, shopping, driving, medical/dental appointments, household duties, and religious activities. The greatest single difference in time spent between married as compared with single or divorced women was in time spent working. Single or divorced women worked an average of 13 hours a week more than married women. Single or divorced women spent 5 more hours a week at leisure activities, while married women spent nearly an equivalent amount of time in leisure activities with children.

Childless women spent 8 more hours per week at leisure activities than do women with children. Women with children spent more time than childless women at household chores (3 hours) and at shopping and driving (4). Women with children cut back 10 hours a week of leisure time with children after beginning school or work. They cut back 2 hours bathing, dressing, and eating with children, and 5 hours a week shopping, driving, etc. with or for children. Thus hours spent with children were cut back by 17 per week on average. At the same time, they reported an increase in time spent in educational activities of 10 hours.

The biggest difference between older and younger women students in terms of time expenditure is in the area of work and education. Younger women spent 12 more hours per week than older women (age

25 and older) at work. Younger women also spent 9 more hours/week on the average in educational activities than did older women. Those age 24 and under spent about 3 hours/week *more* than older women at leisure. In all the other areas analyzed, older women spent more time on the average than did younger women.

Those age 25+, married with no children, slept on the average 61 hours per week, followed by those single or divorced age 25+ who slept on the average 50 hours a week. Those age 25+ and married with children slept 34 hours and those 25+ and single or divorced with children slept 31 hours. Those who slept the least were those 24 or younger who were married but with no children (28 hours/week). It appears that having either children or a husband lessens the chances of getting a good nights sleep!

Single/divorced women with children under the age of 24 spent four times as much time in educational activities (20 hours per week) on the average, as those 25+ and single/divorced with children. The single mother age 25 or older spent 10 hours a week at leisure activities as compared with 20 hours a week for those age 24 and under.

This quantitative analysis of the data tells us little about the pace of life for these women. Only reading the time schedules as whole entities in relation to other documents gives one any sense of the flow of daily activities. For example, "Betty" is a single woman, age 27, without children and never married. She is a library science major from a small town and of Jehovah's Witness background. Her typical schedule contrasts with the highly demanding schedules of single parents who attend school and work. One of her four weeks she became a live-in baby-sitter for a friend's two small children. During this week Betty's day began at 5:30 A.M. since she needed to be at work at 8:00 A.M. and had to feed and dress the two children and take them to the day care center. After work and before her evening class (between 5 and 5:30 P.M.) she had to pick them up at the day care center and take them to another baby-sitter. After class she picked up the children and ran errands such as grocery shopping. At 9:00 P.M. she put the children to bed. She then studied until she fell asleep at about 11:00 P.M. Her commentary on the number and kinds of activities she engaged in during this week is twice as dense as her normal, childless weeks.

Responsibility for others, such as children, who may be slow, recalcitrant, or demanding and unskilled at basic self-maintainence tasks can be anxiety and tension producing on a minute to minute basis. For example, "Carol" remarks one weekday morning at 6:30 A.M.: "Alan is refusing to get up! Looks like I'll be late for work!" One day when waking up at 5:20 A.M. she comments: "I know these few minutes of quiet and privacy will be my last until approximately 9:00 P.M. tonight. I relish each moment."

"June," a 33-year-old high-level civil servant and doctoral student begins her day at 5:30 A.M. and does small household chores, drinks coffee, and dresses. She leaves the house at 7:00 A.M. to drive fifteen miles to work. One or two days a week she works until 9 P.M. since she conducts evening group therapy sessions. Two afternoons a week she drives to school for the afternoon and evening classes. Arriving home typically between 9 and 10 P.M. she eats supper, reads mail and the newspaper. From 10 to 11:30 or 12 she studies or prepares for the next day's work.

The most hectic schedules were those of the single mothers, most of whom were also working and attending school. "Nancy" is an example. She has been divorced for 2 years and is the mother of a 12-year-old girl and a 6-year-old boy. she works 30 or more hours a week as a real estate agent, attends school part time (6 hours a semester), and must commute in different directions for both work and school. Nancy's schedule is a whirlwind of car pooling, taking her children to after school activities and doctor's appointments, shopping, doing yard work, housework, and mending, studying, etc. She is constantly worried about unpaid bills. At one point in her schedule, her son gets ill and her whole schedule collapses.

These brief examples illustrate the limited interpretability of the quantitative analyses of the time schedules, which in themselves leave no picture of the actual flow of time through a day or week. [See Malhotra (1984a) for a more detailed analysis of time schedule data.]

Time, Temporality, and Becoming: Narrative Explorations[2]

Time/Memory "Phenomenological" Narratives

These narratives were written in an open-ended manner in response to the general questions (see above). A double-leveled reflection was involved in the descriptions of participants' memories of their thoughts about the past in childhood. For the purposes of this study, the narratives were read with an intention of constructing a range of types of

[2]An abbreviated version of this section of the chapter is published as "Time and memory: A social psychological etude inspired by Alfred Schutz." chapter in Lester Embree, ed., *Worldly Phenomenology: The Continuing Influence of Alfred Schutz on North American Social Science*, pp. 101–123. Washington, D.C.: University Press of America, 1988.

responses to each question. The analysis focused on the selection of characteristic responses.

The Past in Childhood and as Adults. Consistently the women said that they thought less frequently or not at all about the past as *children* as compared with as adults. Many said that when they were in first grade the past did not exist. One said: "The past was for me, the present." Or, the past was described as being earlier in the day, a few hours ago, or a week ago at most. Only in cases where they had experienced a geographical move to a new home prior to the first grade did the participants have any more extensive thoughts of the past:

> I thought a lot about the past when I was in first grade because we had just moved and my old friends were back in the other town. I thought about the security and contentment before that time and wondered why we had to move.
>
> . . . that we lived in Iowa in a big white house with stairs and I had a friend named Ruby who I found out was a "nigger" when we moved to Texas.
>
> I thought about my grandmother in Oklahoma and friends I had made there.

As *adults*, the participants were divided in terms of how frequently they thought about the past. Some thought of it often, others rarely or not at all. The way the participants thought about the past at the present time was according to feeling, mood or purpose. The feelings were frequently related to remembrances of their relationships with others (Schutz' "Thou-related I"). These included the following:

> (*Happy Feelings*) What I recall most about the past was love, carefreeness, and relationships with family which were close and comfortable.
>
> [*Painful Feelings* (this was by far the most frequent expression about the past.)] I recall how hard it was for me to express my feelings to my father . . . reflections of the past include agony, pain, hurt, frustrations, resentments and a million questions that I am unable to find answers to.
>
> I reflect on how miserable my teen years were. . . .
>
> I have very strong and hurtful feelings about the past.
>
> My impressions of the past was hard times, all having to share, having to give up our paychecks to our father to help make ends meet, never getting what we wanted.
>
> When I think of the past I get a troubled feeling in my stomach.
>
> (*Nostalgic Longing for Past*) I think about the days before I married, my own apartment, of solitude instead of tension and severe strain.
>
> How I regretted being married.
>
> How I missed my friends.
>
> The 'good old days' of senior year in high school.

(Purposeful Repression of Unhappy Feelings) I try not to think of the past often because it is so painful.

I usually think about the good things in the past and censor as many negative events as possible.

(Purposeful View of Past as Basis for Development) I try to use all of my experiences, good and bad, to mold my character.

I remember my past in order to avoid mistakes I have made.

I view the past as a series of people, places and events that have helped to mold and shape the individual I am today.

Impressions of the Future. For the most part, memories of thoughts about the future in *childhood* were very immediate:

The future for me was the next day.

I had no thoughts of the future nor worries.

The memories they did have of the future as children centered on phantasies of being grown up:

I always.played being a schoolteacher.

I fantasized about jobs, doctor, teacher, artist, airline steward, rancher.

I always planned to get married and be somebody.

As in the case of the past, experiences of the future in childhood were in terms of a difference. To have a future when you are a child means to be able to imagine not being a child.

As *adults,* perceptions of the future centered on goals, plans and the completion of projects such as school, getting married, getting a job, having more money, marrying a rich man, their husband earning more, or being a mother. Such plans and projections were accompanied by feelings of doubt, anticipation, or fear:

I see the future now more in the context of limitations and frustrations.

My impression of the future is a dark place and I have to make a choice.

Maybe marriage won't be as bad as I've made myself think and maybe motherhood won't be the burden I've told myself it will be.

The Present as the Child's World and the Birth of Ghosts and Spirits. Of particular significance for childhood experience of temporality is the pervasity of the present. Children live intensively in the existential "here and now." Only geographical moves or other profound changes give children any sense of the past. Likewise, the future is immediate for children. It is the next hour, or approaching supper time. Only as they imagine no longer being who they are, no longer being children, do they conceive of a long-term future. This realization has profound implications for understanding the impact of "ghosts" and "spirits" from childhood. Since the present is so intense, the child is profoundly effected by others. The world of the child *is* the immediate presence of others. As adults, these others are the ghosts and spirits which frame everything that we were before. This is why as adults our sense of the past is highly emotionally charged. It evokes feelings of joy or sorrow about the entire world that we were. The child's conception of the world as immediately present others is reinforced by the bracketing studies that follow.

Sensory/Memory Bracketing: Sounds. When asked to bracket all *childhood* memories except for sounds throughout a day, most of the participants remembered the voices of others, especially family members. Speech of significant others was the omnipresent auditory memory.

For *adults* the world of sound is different for one living in a family as compared with a single person living alone. Those who were currently single focused more on objects such as the sound of running water in the shower, doors slamming, and traffic noises. Even for these women, radio and television fused the home environment with human speech. For those living with husbands and/or children the sounds of their voices predominated the descriptions.

Nearly all of the participants mentioned also such sounds as the noise of the car running, car radios, chatter in the hallways at the university, chalk on the blackboard, the falling of a coke in the machine, and teachers' voices.

Even nonverbal sounds were related to the human world of meaningful sounds. For example, one woman mentioned the sound of a dog barking and was angry with her neighbor for not taking care of it. Even the sound of an animal was perceived in terms of cultural norms involving the concept of a good neighbor and laws about rights and obligations of animal ownership and control. She also mentioned classical music as a familiar sound which colored her mood and which she mentally associated with friends in the fashion of Wagnerian "leitmotives."

Sensory/Memory Bracketing: Sight. Visual memories of *childhood*, like those of sounds, were mostly associated with persons:

> I see my sister and hope that she will leave me alone today.
>
> How pretty the teachers were.
>
> Seeing my mother and kissing her goodbye.
>
> I see my teacher. She was short and stout and braided her hair and wrapped it around her head.

Other *childhood* remembered images were those of culturally significant objects and things in nature:

> The flag as we said the pledge of allegiance.
> The school bus coming.
>
> Large green Catelpa tree leaves, white flowers, profusions of red blooms, running water in the creek.

One person reported not a memory but a memory of having had a fantasy as a child:

> I would fantasize images . . . the teacher has one of the children bent over a desk and is spanking him with a ping-pong paddle.
> I would imagine my mother waiting for me near a fire plug and my dog waiting for me at home.

As *adults* at the present time, visual memories tended to be more environment- then person-centered. For example, subjects mentioned aspects of their natural surroundings such as:

> The sun high up in the sky.
> Wild flowers in green grass.
> . . . raccoons playing in the trees outside my bathroom windows. I could see their babies getting fatter.
> A frozen forest that looks like a palace.

Or they described their home environment:

> The wallpaper in our tiny living room, it was new, but a hideous pattern.
> I wake up in an apartment with white walls. They are too sterile. It is sparsely furnished.

Those who were married and/or had children also described the sights of persons:

> Our daughter playing the piano. She nods her head and grimaces at each mistake.
> My husband's eyes, that unusual shade of hazel that seem to reflect whatever color he is wearing.
> My husband asleep on the couch by the television.
> My dearest friend, a comfort to know he is here.

Sensory/Memory Bracketing: Smell. Childhood memories of smell centered on food, which varied due to the cultural background of the children. For example, a Mexican-American woman recalled the contrast between the smells of corn tortillas and beans in the mornings at home and the "strange" smells of casseroles and green beans at the school cafeteria. She associated these smells with feeling happy at home and tense and anxious at school and with the sounds of the Spanish language at home and unfamiliar English at school. (The children were forbidden to speak Spanish at school.)

Food smells associated with *childhood* memories included:

> milk boiling over and burning on the stove
> boiled eggs being peeled, soup in the lunch room
> vanilla in ice cream bars
> the smell of popcorn means nighttime T.V.

Other smells of *childhood* remembered were associated with familiar persons and activities:

> my father's shaving lotion in the mornings
> the smell of Crest toothpaste which I used all my life at home
> deodorant and soap
> the smell of daddy's pipe chokes me up

Smells associated with school and other children were also mentioned:

> chalk, trash cans, restrooms, dusty hallways, paste in large jars
> kids who smell like sour milk
> the heater on the school bus, new books
> hot bodies after lunch when we all had to put our heads down on our desks

As *adults*, the memories of smells mentioned most were of food smells:

> coffee perking, bacon and eggs frying, McDonald's down the road at lunch

Or, the smells of bathing in the morning:

> the minty fresh smell of toothpaste, cosmetics and perfumes in the morning

Smells associated with school or work were also mentioned:

Xerox machines, floor wax, stale odors from the restrooms
Honeysuckle on the walkway

The sense of smell produced a consistent description between childhood and adulthood. Food was the primary remembered smell, followed by the scents of daily activities associated with familiar persons, followed by the scents in nature and in objects.

Sensory/Memory Bracketing: Touch. Memories of touch in *childhood* were mainly about that of family members as they came in contact throughout the day:

parents gently shaking me awake
the feel of my father's face after he shaved
my mother patting me on the back to wake me up
grandma's hugs
dog's cold nose against my face
dad's whiskers when he kisses me good night
I remember rolling my grandmother's sagging skin between my fingers

Tactile memories of family members also including frequent references to unpleasant forms of touch:

my mother would discipline me in public by pinching me under the arms
I remember being spanked with a hair brush which really hurt
I don't remember my daddy ever touching me, the only thing which touched me with love was my dog, or so I thought then
I remember very well the touch associated with frequent spankings.
Teacher raps me on my knuckles with a ruler

Other childhood memories of touch centered on familiar objects:

chenille cloth of my bedspread
chalk on my hands that made me feel like I needed to wash them
the tickle of June bugs in my hand
crayons, paint and clay
stiffness of the dresses mother starched

Memories of the sense of touch throughout a day for the participants as *adults* were similar to those remembered from childhood. Like in childhood, the primary tactile memory was of being touched by other persons or pets:

> scratchy kisses from my bearded husband
>
> baby moving around in my stomach
>
> my girls' kisses and hugs
>
> holding a patient's hand for reassurance, hugging them when they were discharged to go home
>
> cuddling and petting my dog
>
> the fat body of my cousin's baby who will be in my arms for the next four hours
>
> my cat sleeping on my legs at night

Memories of the touch of significant others were often revealing about the nature of those relationships:

> being hugged by anyone except my mother
>
> my husband washing my back, holding hands and good sex
>
> the constant demand for sex or being hit
>
> although we can't tell each other how we feel verbally, we hold and hug each other

The next most frequent tactile memories were of familiar objects and their temperatures:

> warm water of the shower
>
> cold steering wheel in the car
>
> the softness of the new carpet in the living room
>
> touching the dusty, cold floor with my feet
>
> cool sheets against my naked body
>
> the hard chairs at school feel like concrete

The World as Bodies with Others. The sensory memory exercises illustrate the pervasive way the world is a world of bodies with others. By far most of the sensory memories involved the sights, words, smells, and touch of significant others. Sensory memories of others were always of others and thereby endowed with meaning. Others were loved, appreciated, dreaded, hated, in moods of joy, anxiety, disgust or pleasure. Frequently bodily needs and awarenesses were mentioned, especially when it came to smells and food. The sensory recognition of objects used in everyday life, and memories of the natural surroundings were similarly important.

The Experience of the Passage of Time Throughout a Year. The cultural shaping of the experience of time over a longer period, a year, was clearly evident in that most of these memories centered on shared holidays or special events with family members. This was true of *childhood* memories of all participants:

> Christmas when I would get to see my grandparents
> joining the church picnics in the park with my family
> birthday parties for me and my brothers.

Other *childhood* events in the passage of time throughout a year which were remembered centered on school events and activities with friends:

> being mascot for the school basketball team
> being dressed as a head of lettuce in a Peter Rabbit play
> Thanksgiving festival at school

Memories of the passage of time throughout a year as *adults* similarly centered on family holidays such as Christmas, birthdays, weddings, and deaths. Those who were not married differed in that they emphasized culturally prescribed events such as Christmas and birthdays less. Instead they remembered parties and other activities with friends:

> going to see a punk rock band
> having diaquiri and margarita parties with my boyfriend, his friends and their dates
> pledging Algaians
> ballet exam
> my dog being stolen

Time as Moving Slowly or Quickly Childhood. memories of the speed of the passage of time were associated primarily with whether the events were pleasant or unpleasant. For some, time at school passed slowly, for some rapidly, depending on whether they experienced school as unpleasant or pleasant. Similarly those who had happy family lives experienced time at home as moving fast and those with less pleasant family memories experienced it as moving slowly. This is, as Wagner pointed out (1983), a commonly recognized experience, which was substantiated by this data.

Who one was with had a significant impact on the perception of time moving rapidly or slowing. Time was perceived overall as passing rapidly when one was enjoying oneself and slowly when one was not.

For most of the *adult* women, and all of the women under age 25, time passed slowly when they were with their family of origin (parents and siblings) as compared with when with their own immediate family (husbands and children) or friends:

> time I spend with my family is rather boring, all we do is watch T.V. When I'm out shopping or with my friends time passes fast
>
> time passes slowly when I'm alone with either of my parents
>
> I know how fast time goes when I'm with my family because tensions tend to increase the more time is spent among ourselves

Several respondents, all of them over age 25, expressed experiencing the passage of time with their extended families as being precious and passing too quickly.

The Experience of Time in Relation to Thoughts About Death. Thoughts about death as children and at the present time were clearly illustrative of Schutz' profound statements in regard to awareness of death as only possible intersubjectively, through communications from others about death and through syllogistic reasoning about one's likeness to other mortals (Schutz and Luckmann, 1973: 46). Most of the participants said that as *children* they did not think about death or if they did they did not comprehend it:

> death was not a reality to me
>
> I didn't think about death because I felt it only came to older people.
>
> I thought only my parents could die a long time from now
>
> I didn't realize what it meant to be dead until my uncle was killed in a car wreck and was not at my grandmother's any more when we came to visit

A few remembered thoughts of death as children centering on images of a life after death:

> I fantasized being in heaven with God and all the angels and being free to do whatever I wanted to do
>
> I did not really die; I just left my body
>
> I remember seeing myself in a coffin with a long white gown on and looking like an angel with wings

Currently, as an *adult*, many of the respondents did not think about death. If they thought about it at all it was the death of someone else. Thus the temporal limits of one's own life did not seem to have an effect on the way these persons experienced the passage of time.

I think about others' deaths but ignore my own.
Death is maybe my pet's death or my mother's
Death is a long ways off.
I do not think about my own death.

Those who did think about it expressed feelings of fear and pain:

I don't want to die yet, I haven't accomplished anything yet. This makes death scarey.

I fear that death will catch me off guard. I do not like anything I cannot control.

The older I get the more I am afraid about being in a fatal car accident or getting cancer.

A few respondents expressed their feelings about death in relation to an afterlife:

You leave your body as a spirit. It will be fun to be in heaven.
I believe death is a freeing of the spirit.

Some respondents reflections on death became an impetus to the way they lived in the present:

The inevitability of death has made me more closely examine what I am doing with my life. My greatest concern is that I have enough time to do the many things I still want to do.

A Heideggerian interpretation of this last statement would be that this person had approached authenticity through such an acceptance of death. Schutz had a similar view (Helmut Wagner, written commun., 6 Sept. 1986).

The Time/Memory Narratives and Schutz' Phenomenology

Language pulls away from *duree* (immediate temporal experience). It mitigates against direct experience, makes reality play upon itself, and transforms biological life into cultural existence. For a being who knows language there is no *duree*, except perhaps in glimpses during transcendental meditation. Experience of time is always experience of something in time—it is not ever pure. A simple description of swimming in a cold lake is an example:

I am swimming in a very cold lake in Mid-July. I feel surges of energy coming from my body. My heart is pounding and my breath is rapid. I feel the
rhythm in my legs and arms as I kick and pull, kick and pull. The water is
somewhat rough, and gets a lot rougher as motor boats occasionally pass.
The smell of seaweed, pines and cedars in the air is overcome by the smell
of gasoline. I occasionally gulp down some water, and get some in my nose
and ears. My legs are tickled by seaweed from time to time. This startles
me because I think it may be a fish, or worse. While swimming, I see the
shoreline and my sister lumbering through the water holding on to her
inner tube. My brother-in-law and his dog sit on the pier. I worry about
getting "itch." I think of my mother who had a lake cottage but never
swam.

Unlike narrative structures common in everyday life, this narrative
specifically attempts to focus on a bodily activity. Nevertheless, as the
narrative moves on, cultural and social meanings start to emerge. Implied in the words "speed boat" and "gasoline" is the whole technological culture. Once "the swimmer's sister and brother-in-law, his dog, and
her deceased mother" are brought in, the whole network of this particular biographical situation in the world comes into play.

To attempt to write a narrative about the experience of time one must
already move that experience from immediate flow based on soma and
feeling into a purely cognitive conceptual realm. While immediate experience is based on body and is influenced by ego, narratives are based
on ego and are only effected by body if a special focus requires it. Narratives tend toward repression of awareness of bodily experiences.

Normally, the swimming narrative alone would have begun with a
sentence like "I went swimming at Clear Lake with my sister and brother-in-law". When asked by a passing acquaintance, "how was your
swim?" the relevant information, if it is a lake, is "the water was cold."
This involves bodily awareness, but only at a general level. Water tem-
perature is thought relevant in this community where the water is often
too cold for many potential swimmers.

According to Schutz, summaries and quotations from narratives
such as those in this research are illustrative of a conceptual process
which removes them a step away from the experience itself into the life
form of conceptual thought. It is like trying to capture a piece of air
while one breathes it in and out. You can hold your breath, but while
you do so you do not capture the experience of breathing. Context and
the whole system of cultural and personal relevances influence the
structure of narratives. As I tried to capture the experience of swimming
by simply describing how my body felt I could not do so without remembering the mood and feeling of a particular time.

Sensory memories were most often associated by the respondents with moods, feelings, purposes, and meanings. The sensory-memory bracketing exercises (sensory experiences throughout a day from morning to night recounting one sense at a time) resulted not in narratives descriptive of the flow of time for a day, but rather in conceptualized fragments of sensory memories. Some of the narratives give an impression of movement throughout a day, but they are like snapshots, abstracting from the flow of experience.

Memories of sounds were pervasively of speech and hence thou-related. This was true of memories of childhood and of adult experience. Adults living alone experienced a significantly less thou-related auditory world then they did as children. Memories of visual images as a child were primarily of other persons. As adults, most visual images recounted were of objects in the home, work, school, or natural environment.

For both childhood and adult memories, food was the central smell remembered. This was followed by familiar smells of others. Tactile memories were primarily of the *touch of others*. Those memories were immediately associated with pleasant or unpleasant feelings.

The more enjoyable the activity, the more time was perceived as having passed rapidly. The more an activity was perceived as painful, tedious, or boring, the more slowly was time perceived to have passed during that activity. This illustrates the way one cannot describe simple bodily experiences without getting into biographical particulars.

The experiences of past and future hinge on being able to conceive or imagine being in a different place or situation. Memories of a past in childhood were most clear only to those who had already experienced a geographical move. Memories of the future as children were structured by the respondents around conceived differences between their current states of being and images of being an adult. *Children live intensely in the present.*

Memories of the *past* were primarily *other-oriented*. They were colored by feeling and purpose. Happy, painful, or nostalgic memories of the past were evaluated this way based on a conception of one's relationship with others. [This supports the validity of Denzin's sociological conception of emotions (1984).] The past was also purposefully structured by some to repress painful memories or to use the past as a springboard for development.

As for the past, a conception of *difference* was the key to the construction of the future. As long as things remain the same, there is no future only the continuation of the present. These differences were in terms of obtaining a job, having more money, graduating, having certain material possessions, etc. Feelings of doubt, hope, anticipation, and fear accompanied such constructions.

Memories of the passage of time throughout a year centered on family and culturally prescribed holidays. This was less true for the single, where events were social gatherings with friends.

The autobiographies illustrate the way in which "world time" and "cultural time" are articulated through relationships with others. One's unique biographical situation occurs in relation to world historical events mediated through we-relationships. Feelings about one's life relate to how one evaluates these relationships against typical expectations of them. The autobiographies speak of the "world which was in reach" (Schutz, 1975: 186). The biographical situation, based on the categories of meaning which exist in the lifeworld provides the basis for "life plans." These, in turn, effect relevances, choices, and meanings in the course of a day (Schutz, 1975: 122–123).

Time schedules contain mostly actions geared toward meeting necessary goals and tasks of work, school, and family life. They tell of "interests and projects which determine the course of a day's activities" (Schutz, 1975: 122–123).

Most of the respondents said that they had no concept of death as children. This supports Schutz' notion that awareness of death occurs only in an intersubjective context. How death is experienced is structured in the lifeworld of shared meanings and typifications. Adult thoughts of death tended to be repressed. Most respondents said they thought little about death except that it would happen a long time from now or happened to other and much older people. Others mentioned religious doctrines about life after death. For a few respondents, knowledge of death led to an authentic valuing of the present experience.

This exploration into the experience of time as remembered and described was inspired initially by Alfred Schutz' distinction between *duree* or inner time and outer time. In the course of the investigation it became clear that the Bergsonian-inspired notion of inner time could not be captured in narratives. The narratives did make it clear, however, how central many of Schutz' other concepts were to an adequate understanding of experience. His emphasis on bodily/somatic experience as a basic feeling link to the social world was supported by the sensory/memory bracketing studies. Schutz' analysis of the subject as at the same time ego-centered and Thou-related became apparent in the narratives. Each of them told a story filled with meanings, purposes, feelings, and values. The way meaning is constructed linguistically in retrospect was illustrated in the narratives. However, language already infuses experience at the initial happening. Later these meanings may be reinterpreted. The importance of the question of relevance to memory and meaning was illustrated throughout the documents. Since the analysis was a collective one—that is, the narratives were analyzed into categories instead of interpreted in relation to the overall experiences of each woman—little can be said about any one woman's temporal experience, except to relate it back to her life in case study fashion.

Summary: Back to the Things Themselves

The hermeneutic process of understanding the women's experiences as adults as related to sedimentations from their childhoods began with an initial reading of all the documents which they provided. This was followed by an attempt to code and quantify the documents, including entering the resulting data on the computer and analyzing the results. Many research assistants and volunteers were involved in trying to find common themes in the documents and on the videotapes which could be coded. The decisions about coding emerged from a process of interaction in which meanings were negotiated. The quantitative and systematic analyses of the documents and videotapes resulted in support for the theories of Mead, Schutz, and Habermas. The study also illustrated the way being involved in the research process had effected the becoming mature of the women. The study itself was a reflective process which resulted in behavioral changes and changes in self-understandings.

Having completed the quantitative and systematic analysis, I remained unsatisfied. I did not feel that these results alone justified the effort put into the study and the process by these women. The meaning of their written and spoken texts had not been fully elucidated. Therefore, I bracketed these results as advocated by Husserl (1970), who emphasizes the importance of setting aside the scientifically based knowledge and assumptions about the world being studied in order to return to "the things themselves." In this case, when I bracketed the "scientific" results reported above, I was left with an uncomfortable feeling. I had read the documents with a scientific mindset—namely, to glean out the most systematic data I could which would relate to the theories. This is a different attitude than I took when rereading the documents to simply understand the full meaning of them.

When I took the next step suggested by Husserl, that is bracketing one's assumptions from everyday life, these emotions intensified. In everyday life we cover up painful experiences, especially those which are private, and possibly induce shame. For example, we tend to "deny death" (Becker, 1973; Langs, 1986; Heidegger, 1962) in this everyday, inauthentic realm. When I allowed myself to be more fully open to the women's experiences, I hit rock bottom in the recognition that I was one of them. I too had hidden from the ghosts of my childhood and had to recognize and exorcize them or change them into spirits before I could write any further. The next step in the hermeneutic circle entailed re-reading the documents "without memory, anticipation or desire" (Langs, 1982). In this case the repressed memories of my own childhood pains had been brought to the surface and no longer blocked my under-standing of the texts. I therefore no longer desired to obscure or cover up these meanings in a deluge of numerical and "factual" information.

I realized that the theoretical boundaries of Schutz, Mead, and Haber-mas, as indepth and broad as they were, did not in any sense cover many of the important aspects of the processes of becoming mature re-ported on by these women. I realized I would have to broaden the theo-retical scope of the work in order for the theory to accommodate the data. This process is a step beyond what is called "grounded theory" (Glaser and Strauss, 1967). The theory *was* grounded in the data. How-ever, an explanation and elucidation of the data required relating it in-tertextually to other theories. In this way I was able to make greater sense out of the patterns of pain, adversity, joy and fullness of life ex-pressed by the women. The result from this third turn through the her-meneutic spiral of this work is a theory of "mature and immature par-ent/child relationships." I will present this theory in Chapter 4, before I present the case constructs, even though it did not emerge until after the constructs were formulated. By doing this, the reader will be better able to relate the constructs to the resulting theory and to integrate them as he or she reads.

Mature and Immature Parent Practices _____ 4

From Narratives To Theory

This chapter presents a theory of human ethical and emotional maturation. The theory was formulated hermeneutically, going back and forth between the documents, the group discussions, and the existing theoretical literature. Only those theorists and ideas that are congruent with the data from the study are included. Therefore, the resulting theory is both grounded and hermeneutical in that it stems from the data but also pulls in existing theoretical texts that are consistent with the results. The process involved first gaining grounded insight into special experiences of the women through direct, informal interaction with them. The most promising social psychological theories, namely those of Mead, Schutz, and Habermas, were consulted initially and used as a framework for designing the research process. As the research continued through the initial stages of data analysis, additional theoretical texts were consulted as they helped to explain the emerging understandings. This technique seemed to be more appropriate to theory development than to generate "new" concepts from the data which may have already existed in theoretical writings. In this way the most pertinent concepts of the best theories which explained the data were arrived at. Theoretical writings were used intertextually with the documents in that they helped me read the documents more fully and deeply.

This chapter reviews aspects of existing theories which emerged as congruent with the data from the study and which helped in the interpretation of the data. The result is a theory of two kinds of parent–child relationship: mature and immature in regard to emotional and ethical nurturing. In Chapters 5 through 9 the theory is applied to the analysis of eleven case constructs that exemplify typical patterns of parent child relationships as described by participants in the study.

Ghosts and Spirits of Childhood

Freud's discovery of the importance of childhood experiences for later development continues to be supported by evidence and experience. In the process of this research, 53 women were asked to write autobiographies and diaries. Unexpectedly, nearly two-thirds of them had suffered adversities such as abuse, death of a parent, poverty or neglect as children. This high number may have been due to self-selection, for those interested in participating in the research may have been those troubled and seeking an opportunity to work through problems. On the other hand, recent studies of child abuse, sexual abuse, and neglect indicate that the number of females having had such misfortunes is astoundingly high. In addition, investigations from the history of childhood indicate that this may not represent an increase in incidence. Rather, the work of sociologists, psychologists, and child development researchers during the past 50 years has increased the sensitivity of parents toward children and their ability to empathize with them.

Having completed the quantitative data analysis, I felt that the results were incomplete. They provided insights into the importance of others to the self in the process of becoming and of the way time is experienced with and through relationships (see chapter 3). These results did not capture the essential aspects of what the women spoke and wrote about. Bracketing these results I realized I was avoiding the issue of childhood pain and the tremendous effect it can have on later life. Childhood experiences live in and through the bodies of adults. They are presented in words and phrases which echo the voices of significant others, past and present.

Many of the participants in this study attained outstanding successes despite childhood difficulties. Yet each woman, in her own way, exemplified the way such experiences do have lifelong effects. While little can be concluded about childhood in general from 53 examples, it is important that what is suggested by the pattern be fully clarified. The categories of childhood experience discussed are the following: physical and psychological abuse; death of a parent; incest, poverty and neglect; and happy childhood.

Rebecca had to care for an emotionally withdrawn and weak mother and suffered severe beatings and psychological abuse from her stepfather. She was determined to succeed in spite of all obstacles. She is critical of all those who have not succeeded, referring to them as lazy and unworthy. Rebecca avoided serious relationships with men until her late twenties, when she married a much older man. She had no children of her own.

The subtle ways in which being abused as a child results in a tendency to abuse one's own children is illustrated in Gloria's case. The poignancy of Gloria's example is that her abuse of her stepson almost catches her by surprise, for it is mixed with dedication and concern for his well being. The psychological and physical abuse Gloria suffered led her to have low self-esteem. She indeed believed at a basic emotional level that her mother's attributions of her as stupid and uncreative were true. This influenced her choice of mates. Gloria consistently chose inferior, and emotionally and physically ill partners.

Greta also had difficulties in experiencing positive relationships with both men and women. Up until the present time, Greta and her daughter suffered the consequences of the sometimes violent relationship that Greta had with her mother.

Both Shelly and Karen, who as children lost a mother and a father, took on the characteristics and responsibilities of the deceased parent. Shelly became the mother in the family, assuming all household duties in zealously caring for her father and four brothers. Although she frequently reflects on the injustices she and other women were experiencing, she has assumed a perfectionist attitude, cooking, shopping and cleaning for her husband and adult son. Even when her husband offered to hire someone to help her with the housework, she refused. Now a full-time student, she suffers migraine headaches and back problems, and still receives no help from either her husband or her son in performing household duties.

In addition to taking on her mother's role, Shelly followed her mother's advice to become an elementary school teacher. It was not until in her fifties that she realized in a dream that she had no desire to be a teacher. At that point she enthusiastically went back to school, finally pursuing her interest in nutrition.

Prior to her father's death Karen was "daddy's girl." At the time of his death, Karen took on aspects of his role. She was the only one not to become hysterical, taking control, and making the necessary phone calls. As with Shelly, she took over her deceased parent's role and obeyed his injunctions. He had told her of the limited avenues open to women, and that her primary role was that of being wife and mother. Only after marrying and bearing two children, did Karen continue her education and pursue her own career. Like her father, Karen developed a weight problem. Like him, she is concerned with obtaining the outward appearance of status in terms of clothing, home, and life style.

Janet and Delores came from families where their fathers had incestuous relationships with their sisters and were sexually abusive to them as well. Both are successful in academic and professional endeavors, but have had difficulty in their relationships with men. The ghost of Janet's father has made her afraid to have children for fear she may physically abuse them. She harbors continued resentment toward the men she works with and seeks only women for intimate companionship. Delores is married and a mother. Her diary reflects her continued struggle to remain in a relationship in which she feels oppressed.

Barbara, who had adequate material support had negative, distant, and rejecting parents. As in the case of Gloria, Barbara developed a negative self-image, which directed her attraction to narcissistic and cold men. Now divorced, she feels lonely and unattractive, and is at times overwhelmed with dealing with her teenaged children's problems. Still, Barbara is engaged in numerous worthwhile charitable causes, indicating maturity in sublimation along the lines of altruism (see Vaillant, 1977). Her camping trips with her children and memberships in environmentalist organizations reflects her sense of values and commitment.

Michelle suffered from extreme poverty as a coal miner's daughter. Her alcoholic father was self-serving, expected care and concern from Michelle. Through strength and determination, Michelle obtained two degrees and was currently working toward her doctorate. A faculty member at a private college, she wrote of a close companionate marriage to a man with whom she raised two daughters. The other women in Michelle's group questioned her idealized self-portrayal.

The two studies of Pam and Rhonda illustrate the life-coping skills of women who did not experience particular childhood misfortunes. Both grew up in warm, loving, intact homes where they experienced nurturing, respect, emotional closeness and, encouragement. Their parents demonstrated maturity in their relationships with their children. They came from traditional families. In a male-dominated society, traditional families foster sexism which had a negative impact on both Pam and Rhonda. The sexism in their schools and churches also inhibited their ability to freely and fully develop intellectually. Pam, more so than Rhonda, experienced some degree of reversal parenting, for her young mother projected independence upon her from her infancy, expecting her to be both her sister and to also help care for the younger siblings. Pam's premarital pregnancy and early marriage resulted in her leaving town in shame with her young husband. The marriage ended in divorce after 20 years, as Pam's husband entered his delayed adolescence at the same time as their three children.

Pam and Rhonda exhibited maturity in their relationships with their adolescent children and admirably handled the adverse experiences of divorce and a custody suit. This was reflected in the mood and tone of their narratives. Their sense of puzzlement was directed more externally, to the understanding of others and events and the analysis of ways of coping. They wrote more about their happy moments amidst hassles, and delighted in small pleasures of shared activities with their own children.

The women in this study who were victims of abuse, neglect or incest inevitably were raised by parents who were "immature" or maturational "children" in regards to their own emotional and ethical development. The women who suffered the effects of misfortunes, such as poverty or death of a parent, were also deprived of adequate care. The social context did not provide adequate resources for parents to function at a "mature" adaptational level, especially in times of crisis. Even in those cases where the parents exhibited mature caring for their children both emotionally and ethically, the children suffered indirectly from the effects of inadequate social supports. Specifically, they bore the burdens of sexist economic and educational institutions and of repressive religious institutions.

Emotional and Ethical Becoming

There are eleven aspects to mature parent–child relationships: a continual primary bond; an authentic temporal experience; empathy; adequate mirroring; positive and clear attributions and expectations; competent communication; congruent communication; comedy as a dramatic model; caring as a basis for moral judgment; mature defense mechanisms; and self-control, artistry, and love. The fulfillment of these aspects of mature parenting facilitates the process of becoming mature in the child. The opposite facilitates the development of immaturity as characterized by the emotionally divided self. Table 4.1 summarizes each of these aspects of the parent–child relationship, indicating the source of the concept. Following this, each concept is briefly explicated. Special attention is given to the primary bond, for it is the basis for all the other elements of the theory.

Existential Phenomenology and the Primary Parent–Infant Bond

The establishment of an unfractured, sustaining bond to a primary caretaker is an essential first step in becoming mature. The insights of existential phenomenology, especially those of Martin Heidegger (1962) and Jose Huertas-Jorda, (1979) are essential in appreciating the nature of this bond. A complete existential phenomenology of infancy cannot be developed in the context of this work. However, aspects of Heideg-

Table 4.1. Immature and Mature Parent–Child Relationships

Relationship elements	Immature	Mature

Primary bond
  Heidegger, Huertas-Jorda,
  Schutz
	Fractured	Continual and
		  stimulating

Time/temporality *Heidegger, Schutz*	Unauthentic/stressful	Authentic, meaningful

Parents' relationship to child
  deMaus
	Projective, reversal
	  double image
		Empathic

Mirroring
  Miller
	Narcissistic pride
	  vicious cycle of
	  contempt
		Adequate

Attributions and
  expectations of
  significant
  others
  Mead
	Negative or confused	Positive, clear

Communicative environment *Habermas*	Power-saturated	Competent

Parent–child communication
  Satir
	Blaming, placating,
	  irrelevant,
	  objectivistic,
		Congruent

Model of dramatic action *Duncan*	Tragic, scapegoating	Comic
Moral self *Gilligan*	Survival, goodness	Caring

Defense mechanisms
  of significant others and
  society
  Vaillant
	Psychotic,
	  immature,
	  neurotic
		Mature

Ethical self
  Weinstein
	Resentment and
	  self-indulgence
		Self-control, artistry,
		  and love

Emotions and self *Denzin*	Divided	Integrated

ger's and Huertas-Jorda's work provides important insights into coming into being of the child, especially as this may be affected by adversities.

There is no more dramatic instance of being "thrown-into-the-world" than birth. Already in the uterus, the nascent Dasein[1] exists as other, as

---

[1]Heidegger's term for the human being is *Dasein* which means at the same time "being there, at and with." For more complete explanation of the richness of Heidegger's concept see Malhotra (1987b).

liquids, flows, warmth, chemical tensions and relaxations, movements, and sound. From such beginnings, it is "being-in":

> When Dasein knows an object it does not get out of its inner sphere to gain knowledge of it. Dasein is already outside always alongside the entities it encounters. (Heidegger, 1962:89)

As babblings become responsive to the other, first words are used searchingly, poetically. Out of these, initial meaning patterns emerge, based on repetitions and variations, each one a wonder of identity, resting on objects handled, caressed, eaten, needed, and loved. Growing into a larger world, the infant is always other/self. Other is recognized as an object prior to the recognition of oneself. What is for the infant *is* other. The primary other leaves, and so the infant cries for the loss of its parts. When Mother returns, the infant relaxes. The word "Mama" once spoken becomes a call, an appeal to that part of self-world to bring comfort. Each departure of "mama" signals "death" or "lack." This ebb and flow of desire and fulfillment is the emergent Dasein's temporality.

Caring falters in the face of heartbreak. Departures, pain, hunger, tell of the Nothingness against which being thrives. With adversities, the infant cries. Yet it hurls itself forward and becomes enraged. In all of this, the infant exists within essential ontological structures pointed out by Heidegger, but without awareness. Prior to speech, the infant does not "find itself" *(Befinden Sie Sich?)* therefore cannot yet be Dasein. It does not attach a mood but exists already as enraged, joyful, or content. The infant simply is becoming, but is not yet Dasein. With the word "no" the infant can negate the world—and only through the possibility of its negation does the world exist for Dasein, which chooses its mode of being.

With this entry of language and self-consciousness, the obstinacy of the world multiplies along with its possibilities. Until the inevitability of death is realized, authentic Dasein cannot exist. Fear and anxiety have already been experienced, death as departure and loss and nothingness as nonfulfillment. Each experience of loss calls the Dasein to authentic self-awareness.

Huertas-Jorda has provided a basis for making sense of the depth of the relationship with primary others in earliest self-beginnings. Huertas-Jorda's phenomenology of "living presence" describes the structure of primal perceptual ties to mother (the first other). Basing his descriptions of the essential structures of pre-egoic consciousness on Husserlian phenomenology, Huertas-Jorda writes of the "primal perceptual upsurge." The infant's consciousness consists of a sequence of sensory experiences. The experience involves "stasis" and "flux." Aspects of a feeling are sustained from initial awareness and other aspects change. The infant senses that more may still be coming into the field. As stasis, awareness of the possibility of more, of change, presents itself as a *lack*. As flux, experience presents itself as powerless to hold on to what was:

> The imperviousness of the primal perceptual upsurge to it (unsatisfied hunger V_B) is then the originary experience of *negativity* at its simplest and ontologically most fundamental, namely, the horizonal experience of fragility, superfluity, threat, absurdity, of being *"de trop"*, of being a powerless witness to a wanton presencing which allows no temporal thickness (no control) whatever. (Huertas-Jorda, 1979:92)

An essential aspect of earliest pre-egoic existence is intersubjectivity. Initially, the other is experienced as motion—not originated in one's own body (Huertas-Jorda, 1979:146). Since the ego is not yet aware, there is no self, and the other is apperceived in the horizon of awareness:

> The apperception of the *not-self* is as *an echo with a void*, a facade in the perceptual continuum between stasis and flux. (Huertas-Jorda, 1979:147)

The pre-egoic basis for the apprehension of the other is incongruent. The motion of the other is not perceived as matching one's prereflexive self-awareness. A key moment in developing self-awareness occurs when "other" as one's mirror image is perceived as self. Prior to this recognition, which Lacan (1977) has placed between 6 and 18 months for most infants, a reflection of oneself in the mirror is perceived as other. Only when one perceives one's own moving body to coincide with the moving body in the mirror does one identify the image as one's own. This "mirror stage" is to Lacan, and to Huertas-Jorda, the beginnings both of self as image, and of self as alien. There is thus a split, a dividedness, at the very root of the self, from its initial self-apprehension. If this split is reinforced later (which must happen in abuse or incest), the self becomes a "divided self" (Denzin, 1984).

An infant who, in this pre-egoic state, is already abused by the motions of the other would have a primal experience of the "other-as-pain." The neglected infant would feel the *absence* of needed warmth, motion, and touch as lack, as hunger. In either case, the pain inflicted by other or circumstances through and with other may even be prior to earliest other-recognition. It is still fused with the initial sensory awareness of the world ("the primal perceptual upsurge"). Thus in the case of the abused infant, pain is perceived in the earliest, pre-egoic state as part of self, in that the cleavage of experience exists prior to any sense of self.[2] This split allows for a being whose very presencing is bifurcated—one part of which is pain. Part of existence is existence as pain or the inflicting of pain by the motion of the barely apperceived other.

Even in the case of the nonabusive, loving mother or other primary caretaker, other will at times be perceived in this pre-egoic state as correlative with absence of met needs. Since the perfect caretaker also will not always be able to be available, lack and pain and hence the basis for an alienating split in the self exists in every infant. A parent who does not adequately mirror the child's expressions will intensify this split, building misperception and denial into the pre-goic consciousness of the infant.

Likenesses between one's primal perceptual upsurge and that of the perceived "other" allow other to attain the status of "alter ego." For if the other is too different in level of complexity of patterns of motion and rhythms from one's own primal perceptual upsurge, the other may be not perceived at all (as in calls of animals too high pitched for the human ear, or which move too fast to be accommodated by the eye). There must be sufficient congruency of the motion, touch, rhythms, and sounds of the other and that of the pre-ogoic infant in order for an other to be perceived as alter ego. Once so perceived, the other is significant in the Meadian sense—is internalized as an aspect of the nascent self. In the case of abuse, the self becomes divided, one part abusive to itself and others. In the case of the death of the other, the intensity of alter ego's life in the child's ego may become overwhelming.

Once an other is internalized as alter ego at both the pre- and post-egoic stage, the other's way of organizing its presence with other, its typical sequence of actions, and its own sedimentations, becomes a basic core for the presencing of the nascent self. This is what Huertas-Jorda calls the "resonating pedal point" of the self. Internal and external presencing of these primary pedal points produced initially by significant others must be present for the self throughout its existence.

[2]The implications of this ethic of care for infants who are born with painful afflictions are profound. Similarly, the implications for the infant whose natural mother is lost to it after birth by death or adoption, for the already recognized motions, rhythms, and sounds of mother experienced as a fetus would be lost to it as an infant. In many cases, the bodily chemicals and rhythms of the adoptive parent are more beneficial in nature than those of the natural mother. The effects of such a positive rupturing of the primal bond have also been too little studied.

Whether kindly, abusive, dead, neglectful, cruel, incestuous, violent, or loving, the pedal point of these others is essential for the self:

> A new and complicating factor is introduced in the field of presence of the perceiving awareness: the other's own "index of refraction," namely, its own manner of organizing transpresence, its own primal layer of sedimentations together with its own sequence of lived experiences, the "pedal point" of its own resonating presence. (Huertas-Jourda, 1979:151)

An example of the nature of the "pedal point" of other as alter ego within the self was given by Huertas-Jourda. While riding on a crowded bus in Toronto he observed a small girl, perhaps 20 to 24 months old sitting quietly next to her mother. The little girl sat with her head down, in a rather dejected manner. She was skinny and pale, and coughed from time to time. Her clothing was soiled and too large for her. The child was extraordinarily quiet and well behaved throughout the bus ride. Indeed, she said nothing the whole time, her hands on her lap. The mother, who was heavily made up and looked to be between 15 and 18 years old, stood up suddenly and pulled the cord for her stop. She bumped abruptly against the little girl. Then, as the bus came to a halt, she reached out with her left arm, and grasping the child around her waist picked her up like a sack of potatoes, leaving the child's head to hang down in front and her feet behind in a most undignified position. She also slipped a shopping bag on her left wrist, directly in front of the girl's face. The mother, jerking and handling her roughly, said in a loud, abrasive tone of voice, full of conviction and sincerity: "You are such a burden, a little brat."

The beginnings of the child's alter ego and her nascent self existed as a burden, as a sack of heavy, unwanted potatoes, a source of pain. The "pedal point" of her young being was as an unwanted task. To exist as herself she *must* treat herself as a burden and/or have others who treat her as a burden. Or, in later life, as a mother, her child in turn is her heavy load.

Significant others are not experienced as merely communicative voices (as Meadian social psychology implies). Rather, they are experienced in a totally embodied manner, as described in Heideggerian and Huertas-Jordian terms. Phenomenological descriptions are necessary to deepen understanding of the major importance of primary others in becoming. This is necessary for a view of human beings as embodied, and as existing in moods and emotions.

One's fundamental being-in-the-world is already from the outset "being-with-others" (Heidegger, Schutz). Because one's existence as self (conscious self) is based on a continued "pedal point" to these others, it is likely that one will maintain emotional ties—symbolic and at the prereflective level—to primary alter egos (significant others). Shifts in cathexis, from parental love objects to friends and lovers, are likely to be to those who furnish patterns of stasis and flux, of time and motion, of verbal and nonverbal relating as did original others. For these are *the* patterns in relations to which the self has been constituted. For the little girl on the bus, to exist at all is to exist as a heavy weight. The child who is beaten, exists as one who must be beaten to exist. She is likely to love one who will beat her like her parents did.

Other Aspects of Mature Parenting

Schutz stressed the temporal coordination between persons in a "we-relationship." Each person in a face-to-face interaction is aware that the other has a life and a consciousness similar to her own. No pretense of actual knowledge of the other or the other's internal experiences is necessary for a we-relationship to exist. Through sharing time and space together, Dasein becomes aware that the body of the other is a field upon which his inner consciousness plays. I can observe the other as I cannot observe myself—from the outside. In the we-relationship, one can observe the other in ways one can never observe oneself. To the child in its early we-relationships, the other is more real than the self. Because the ego forms as it practices the patterns of motion and emotion of alter ego, the self will be divided, unless alter ego was an adequate and supportive mirror of the child's own emotions (A. Miller, 1984).

In constrast to such an empathic temporal relationship, there is a stressful experience of time, where goals and objectives are externally imposed and time is quantified by the clock. Such an experience of time would be deemed "inauthentic" by Heidegger, or part of the world of "external time" by Schutz. The mature parent allows for the child to experience time authentically as opposed to mechanistically in a stressful and measured manner.

Imagine baby Delores' infant experience in the crowded Los Angeles Mexican–American ghetto. This youngest of five had a mother who, of necessity, had to leave her in the care of older siblings and others while she worked. The stresses of her mother's life did not allow for a continual primary bonding or for authentic temporal experience. Incest occurred in the family; even the baby sister used Delores to meet her needs. The child experienced hunger and a lack of constant and warm contact with her mother which consequently fostered her need to with-

draw into a perfect, fantasy world. Of all the women, Delores expressed
the most profound fear of death in her childhood memories. Her surroundings annihilated her even as an infant. In a rat-infested apartment
(such as the one Delores lived in), some infants are literally eaten alive.

Mature parent–child relationships are characterized by what psy-
chohistorican Lloyd deMause calls "the helping mode." The premise
that childhood is a treacherous process for many is congruent with de-
Mause's (1974) reading of the history of childhood. Drawing upon diaries, letters, sermons, and other documents, deMause concludes that in
the history of Western society, most children were what we would today consider abused. deMause contends that child rearing went
through the following stages in Western history: infanticidal, abandonment, ambivalent, intrusive, socialization, and helping. The helping
mode is just beginning to emerge, with the socialization mode the most
prevalent among educated persons. According to deMause (1974), the
helping mode occurs where:

> . . . both parents are the child's servants, and strive to interpret the child's
> conflicts, provide stimulation and objects for its growing emotional needs,
> tolerate its regression, and in general produce a strong, independent, gen-
> tle, sincere and happy individual. (p. 54)

These modes are not entered into by all persons in society at each
historical period. Even at the present time, some child-rearing practices
are still perpetuating patterns of infanticide, abandonment, ambivalence, and intrusive modes. The most widely accepted and generally
advocated child-rearing mode of today is "socialization" with a few parents and educators venturing into the "helping" mode.

The helping parent is empathic in his or her way of relating to the
child. deMause characterizes parent–child relationships in four ways:
projective, reversal, double-image, and empathic. The farther back in
Western history one goes, the more likely one finds projective, reversal,
or double-image parenting. In *projective parenting*, the child is a waste
basket for parents' imaginings, and is often seen as the embodiment of
evil or demonic forces. In *reversal parenting*, the child is seen as a pro-
vider of love and companionship and as caretaker of the parent. *Double-
image parenting* involves both projection and reversal. The child is simultaneously the parent's emotional waste basket and is expected to provide love and care for the parent. Projection has been used by parents
throughout history to justify beating, torturing, and even killing their
children. Parents who act in the reversal manner frequently exploit their
children emotionally and sexually. Reversal also feeds into projective

child rearing when the infant does not provide the mother (or other primary caretaker) with the love she feels is her due. The mother's rage may result in her battering the child. When Gloria's great need for love and recognition was not met by her stepson, she lashed out at him physically (see Chapter 5).

What is of particular significance about deMause's historical interpretation is that it makes the large numbers of women in the study who had experienced childhood adversity comprehensible. It makes it all the more important that theories of the development of self include the effects of adversity.

Mature parents provide adequate "mirroring" of the full range of their infants' feeling. It is appropriate for infants to be narcissistic and to have their caretakers cater to their needs. Based on her study of the effects of inadequate mirroring on her patients, psychoanalyst Alice Miller (1984) found that many of her gifted and successful clients were "prisoners of childhood." The process involves a narcissistic parent, whose ego is overinvested in her child's living up to an ideal. As a result, she does not mirror, reflect back, and show understanding of the child's natural emotions. Rather, she ignores those emotions that are out of her range of acceptability. For example, exuberant joy, or, on the other hand, sheer rage may be unacceptable to her. She will therefore not mirror these when they naturally occur in her child or she may punish them.

Only in empathic parenting is adequate "mirroring" possible. Good parental mirroring means that the child's own emotions and responses are understood clearly as the child's expressions and responded to appropriately as such. For example, Pam was able to correctly assess her 15-year-old daughter's need for structure. In spite of lack of support from her immature husband, she was able to stand firmly. She communicated congruently with her daughter, and took the necessary steps to enforce the limits she made on her behavior. Were she in a reversal mode, she would not have been capable of this because she would not have been able to bear the emotional strain of his angry responses to her disciplinary measures.

The narcissistic parent produces a narcissistic child who becomes caught up in alternative modes of grandiosity and depressions and the "vicious cycle of contempt." In "narcissistic disturbance" the ego is identified as "I exist as success." The individual therefore must succeed in order to exist as the best, the most healthy, strong, loved and admired. When normal adversities, such as illness or financial set backs occur, a feeling of overwhelming annihilation occurs, forcing one into a mode of despair. The self of the narcissist is split three ways. Not only between grandiosity and depression as alternating modes of the false self, but also between the false self and the real child who was never allowed to exist.[3]

The patterns of communication between parent and child are crucial aspects of becoming mature. George Herbert Mead's profound insights into the development of each unique self through relationships with significant others perhaps goes the farthest in explaining the uniqueness and yet the social conformity of children. A basic premise of this theory is a Meadian one: the self or identity of the person is formulated during interaction with significant others and influenced by social conditions. The participants in the study were most decidedly effected in their identity formation by parents, stepparents, grandparents, siblings, friends, teachers, and respected members of their churches. These individuals projected directly or indirectly attributions about the kind of person each girl was, and the kind of woman she was to become. Expectations of acceptable and unacceptable behavior were similarly communicated. The quantitative analysis found that significant others' attributions tended to be accepted by the women.

For each woman, the attributions and expectations of primary others became the mainstay of her identity. Gloria, who as a child was frequently hit by her mother and told that she was worthless and uncreative, became involved with men who confirmed both her worthlessness and her superiority. Helen, another woman in the study, was constantly criticized by her parents. Her mother frequently commented about how large she was for her age. She was made to feel like she had to take care of everyone else's needs. After divorcing a husband who severely beat her and her children she remarried. This man was a mentally ill veteran. While he did not beat her, he was critical of her figure, called her derogatory names, and ignored her daughters from the previous marriage. Rhonda, on the other hand, perceived herself as able and happy, just as she had heard she was from her positive and giving parents as a little girl.

The mature parent will provide an atmosphere for communication free from power distortions. (See Chapter 2 on Habermas' theory of communicative competency and power in relationships.) "Competent" communication, to Habermas, is consistent with what Satir (1983) calls "congruent."

---

[3]Miller, not phenomenologically grounding her work, is unduly harsh with the primary caretakers, making them appear culpable when they may simply not move and act in ways that they had not experienced. Nevertheless, she does provide valuable insights into the dynamics of parent–child relationships.

Satir speaks of the "great international cultural conspiracy"[4] whereby persons do not allow their thoughts to be congruent with their inner feelings or tell the other what they really feel and think. Families as subsystems within cultural systems unconsciously reinforce and punish certain kinds of communication (Satir, 1983). Such "lies" or failures to be truthful are felt necessary for family stability. The cover up of incest in families is a startling example.

One example of nondisclosed incest was related by a counselor at a shelter for battered women (Juniper, pers. commun., 1986). A 13-year-old girl had just returned home, having been sexually molested by her young uncle while out playing. When she came in the house the girl, "Jana," was crying and bleeding and her clothing was torn. She looked at her mother and said "Amelio" in dismay and outrage. The mother immediately hit her and said "what have you been doing." At that moment it became clear to Jana that the whole event was her fault and that she was terribly guilty. The abuse by the uncle continued for 4 years, always under threat that her mother would be told. Since the tension between her parents was great, Jana feared that additional problems would cause the family to break up. It was only when her younger sister was molested by the same man that Jana sought help. It turned out that her mother had been molested by a close relative and had been punished for it, as if she were the guilty party. This case illustrates also that power and fear are often at the root of incongruent communication.

For Satir, communicating "congruently" means that one expresses one's true feelings, thoughts, and desires to the other. Such communication requires self-understanding and empathy for the other. One cannot communicate one's feelings if one has not learned to recognize them. If a child was raised by unempathic parents who did not adequately mirror the child's feelings and emotions, the child never recognizes them as valid. As a result, many persons are angry but unaware of it. Similarly, others do not recognize their feelings of joy or exuberance because they were not allowed in their childhood home environments. Direct expression of feelings is not necessarily "congruent communication." A mother screaming with rage at a 12-year-old daughter who stayed out all night is not clearly denoting what behaviors on the part of the daughter upset her, and why and what she wants the child to do about it. Rather, screaming simply projects blame.

There are four varieties of "incongruent" communication: blaming,

[4]As stated by Virginia Satir at a conference on conjoint family therapy, Dallas, Texas, June, 1985.

placating, irrelevant, and objectivistic. Persons tend to habitually communicate in one of these four modes. The *blamer* is the person who projects the responsibility for his bad feelings on others. The *placater* is one
who typically accepts responsibility and tries to make amends. *Irrelevant*
communicators change the subject or use other distractive measures to
dissociate themselves from what is occurring. *Objectivists* intellectualize
everything, appealing to reason. Satir shows how, with the help of a
therapist, families can understand and change these patterns. This implies, however, that the person or persons in power in the family are
willing to be involved in family therapy and have the resources to pay
for it. Or, it is assummed that some external source of power (such as
a child's protective services agency) requires such participation.

Mature parents will provide a comic, rather than tragic form of dramatic interaction in the home environment. For Hugh D. Duncan, the
self is constructed according to *how* communication occurs between self
and others—that is its *forms*. Two levels of Duncan's analysis are important here: communication as comic or tragic and his typology of audiences.

Using a dramatistic model of human action, Duncan hypothesizes
that communicative action may take comic or tragic forms. In the tragic
model, often reinforced by religious mythology, social order is disrupted by disobedience or failure to live up to accepted principles. In
real societies and social relationships, such failure is inevitable because
some of the rules may contradict each other, or situations may change,
presenting unpredictable challenges. Failure to live up to the rules of
social order leads to chaos or disorder. Order is restored by torturing or
punishing the guilty, or by finding a scapegoat. The inflicting of pain,
death, or torture on the scapegoat appeases the gods or restores social
order (Duncan, 1962).

A scapegoat may be internal, as when we do not fulfill the demands
of alter ego or significant other and punish ourselves. We feel guilt and
alleviate it by killing the internally guilty self. Or we may abuse or hurt
an external other, projecting the guilt outward. As de Mause has demonstrated, children have consistently functioned as objects of projection
and as scapegoats.

The way internal scapegoating occurs is clarified through Duncan's
typology of audiences. Communication to oneself is "soliloquy," or the
"I" talking to its "me." It is in this linguistic form that one may resolve
and negotiate between the demands of various others and of social institutions. There are actually multiple "me's" and "I"s within the self. A
very effective way of punishing oneself is to select an abusive significant

other. The abused child is often made to feel guilty and indeed responsible for the abusive acts. An aspect of a child's "me" is "me-as guilty," and unworthy of better treatment.

Mature parents make decisions based on principles of care, rather than on concerns for personal survival or of social acceptance (goodness). Gilligan characterized the stages of moral development in women as moving from *survival*, through *goodness*, to *care*. Gilligan interviewed women who were considering having abortions to study their levels of ethical decision making. In morality of survival, the woman makes the decision she feels she has to make in order to survive, whether this means to have an abortion or not. At this survival "stage" the woman feels little or no support from anyone. At the stage of "goodness" the woman feels the need for approval from those who support her. She sacrifices her own interest in order to be considered "good." Realizing that in self-sacrifice she ends up not being able to really take care of others either, she may move to the stage of "caring" where her needs and those of others are balanced.

What is most important in Gilligan's "stages" for the understanding of the experiences of the women in this study is the way she ties the stages in with the social context. "Survival" ethics are used when the woman feels absolutely no support from others. Survivalist ethics occur where the woman feels she must decide as she does to ensure her own emotional, physical, and/or economic survival. Such is the likely ethical level of the abused child, who must bear the abuses, and yet function as demanded in the family environment upon which she depends. Such too is the ethics of the incest victim who is threatened should she tell (Juniper, 1986).

At Gilligan's next level of moral development, the incest victim accepts the abuse out of a sense of "goodness." She is sacrificing her interests to make her father or stepfather happy and to keep the family together. Goodness implies some connection, for at least the woman is receiving some rewards for pleasing those close to her. With adequate internal and external strength, she will decide to care for herself as well as others, and that to harm herself to meet other's needs is not an inherent good. In so doing, she must overcome the split in herself and the pull of primal pedal points. "Caring" implies that she is secure enough in the family and social network to be related to others in a reciprocal manner.

What is not at all demonstrated by Gilligan is whether these are truly stages. Some of her examples seem to be at the "goodness" stage and may have always been there. The key to which "level" the woman is on must lie in her network of social relationships and the social context for them, rather then in a mysterious internal process of "development."

The kinds of defense mechanisms used by the mature parent will be "neurotic" to "mature," following Vaillant's analysis, rather than "immature" or "psychotic." The person using mature mechanisms of defense according to Vaillant will also be acting in a more ethical manner than those who use neurotic or immature defenses. While we reject the strictly "developmental" aspects of Vaillant's theories, the concepts that persons vary as to the kinds of defenses they typically use, and that these relate to their levels of ethical behavior in relation to others is most pertinent to this study. For it is clear that "psychotic" defenses, such as denial, projection, and distortion of reality are most harmful to others and to oneself. Similarly, Vaillant's "immature" defenses of fantasy, projection, passive aggression, hypochondria, and acting out are harmful.

The person who regularly employs immature defenses cannot be an adequate nurturer or cultivator of either one's self or of others. Even those using primarily "neurotic" defenses will not allow for the full emotional and ethical maturation of their children. Intellectualization, repression, displacement, reaction formation, and dissociation all deny emotional realities and the issues that are of imperative ethical relevance. Only those parents who regularly use "mature" defenses will be able to foster their children's affective and ethical development. These are: sublimation, which recognizes emotions but expresses them only in creative harmless ways; suppression, which manages negative emotions away from possible harm to self or others; anticipation, which furthers continual motivation for artistry and love amidst unavoidable adversities such as loss, illness, and death; altruism, which is the very essence of ethical behavior; and humor, which takes pain and turns it into communal joy.

The mature parent practices the ethical principles of self-control, artistry, and love, respectively (Weinstein, 1985). As Weinstein states, one cannot practice artistry in any task, not just the fine arts) without self-control, nor can one love another except as one is self-accomplished. The kind of love advocated by Weinstein is one that cultivates the artistry of the other, and does not seek to control others. He notes, in addition, that ability to rise above resentment and self-indulgence may be self-cultivated, through such endeavors as meditation, self-analysis, and dream analysis. Weinstein's ethical person has a cultivated overego, which guides and directs the various role-specific egos. The overego is not Freud's superego, for the overego allows for failure without undue guilt and accepts foibles and obstacles in a comic-ironic mode. Two main temptations exist—the appeal to ecstasy and self-indulgence, on the one hand, and resentment in the face of life's inevitable adversities, such as illness and death, on the other.

The Emotionally Divided Self

When a child does not receive mature parenting, the child will develop a "divided self." In the language of quantitative social science, the eleven elements of the theory of mature parenting are "independent" variables; an emotionally divided self in the child is the "dependent" variable. Denzin's social theory of emotions shows how self-feelings constitute emotionality. For our theory of child becoming in inadequate or damaging contexts, Denzin's discussion of the emotionally divided self is most pertinent. The child who is abused, neglected, or not given adequate mirroring is likely to have crystallized her identity development around a falsified self. When the false self loses its social supports a feeling of overwhelming emptiness or hollowness is experienced. In a state of depression, this is also what occurs. Sometimes alcohol or drugs will be used to escape the falsified self, or to ease the pain of emptiness or depression. However, this makes it all the more likely that rage in the form of self-condemnation and/or violence toward others will occur. Since the damaged self is likely to be involved in close relationships with others who perpetuate this self-condemnation, she experiences divided feelings about these others as well:

> First, they are near to the subject, as intimate, warm points of reference, even sources of stability, yet also distant, as vague, unnamed "others." Second, they are threats because they are so near. Third, the other's perceived "normality" or stability is threatening. Fourth, the other is a source of resentment, anger, and guilt. Feelings from the past are directed to the other. An aversion to the other is felt and sensed, yet the subject cannot be free of him. She feels a debt of emotions toward him. If he dies before the debt is repaid, resentment is added to guilt as a feeling that binds her to him. Fifth, feelings are "emptied out" on or at the other, often through violence, withdrawals of affection, or inward obsessive dwellings on the other's emotions and expectations for the person. (Denzin, 1984:207)

The others overwhelm the self and the self that complies with the wishes of the other is perceived as a false, or inauthentic self:

> Outwardly she complies with the wishes of others. Inwardly she rebels. Outwardly the behavior of her false self appears normal. Yet this is a facade.

She perceives herself as living a lie. Inwardly she feels intense anxiety, hatred, fear. (Denzin, 1984:208)

A part of this divided self will consist of the child's originary motions and emotions. The other side will embody the patterns of feeling and acting recognized, reinforced, and required by alter ego. If alter ego was an abuser, this part of the self will be self-abusive and/or abusive to others. Since she knows what the pain of abuse is like, she does not want to inflict such pain—but, on the other hand, not to do so requires that she recognize, then kill, and mourn for the dead abusive part of herself. She must first acknowledge and mourn for the childhood she never had, for the originary aspect of her divided self.

The case of death of a parent traumatically forces the nascent self to become the lost alter ego. Freud was phenomenologically accurate when he said in *The Ego and the Id* that when one looses a love object, one increases the power of his own ego. "Loose a loved one today and internalize him or her as alter ego tomorrow" may have been his bumper sticker. Freud pointed out that one adopts the characteristics of lost love objects. He did not demonstrate phenomenologically how and why this must occur, as did Huertas-Jorda.

Karen and Shelly (see beginning of chapter), illustrate Freud's point well. Only after dealing with the effect of their parent's deaths on their adult lives did they break the patterns. Karen lost weight, developed a career in higher education, and renegotiated an egalitarian relationship with her husband. Shelly, now in her 50's, rejected the "shoulds" she had internalized from her deceased mother and cultivated a new career.

The incest victim's primary alter ego was also her lover—but a lover who abused power, exploited her, inflicted pain, and caused her to feel shameful and guilty in relation to the larger culture (or to what Huertas-Jorda would call the "proto-symbolic"). One is made into a wife-lover when one is daughter. Alter ego, usually feared and respected and sometimes also loved, is one who threatens, uses, exacts payments, makes unnatural demands, does not truly *care* for you, is not your protector, and yet is jealous of you.

The incest victim and aspects of the significant other—perpetrator—take root in the identity of the child as aspects of the child's divided self. This part of the incest victim's ego exacts payments from her, does not care for her, seeks uncaring partners, or seeks partners over whom she can exercise pleasurable powers. Delores had great difficulty with her marriage and in coping with the demands of her relationship with her infant daughter. Janet, also an incest victim, directed the rage she felt for her father toward her dog. She was afraid to marry for fear she would abuse her children in some way. Through psychotherapy she confronted and exorcized the ghost of this part of her divided self.

Due to the structures of a divided self, incest victims may abuse power in relationships, or, they may tolerate and subtly encourage their boyfriends or spouses to exploit their daughters. They may then see their daughters as seductive and guilty. To brutalize a child is to simultaneously create a brutal aspect to that child's self. In Schutz' (1970) terms, the we-relationship between parent and abused child becomes the me–I-relationship as the child internalizes a "me" that abuses its own "I." This "I" is likely to abuse others, especially in the parallel situation of parent–child. This fact will be resisted, for to come to grips societally with this reality is to face head-on the terror of living in a culture with millions of persons who have brutal internal selves.

Mature and Immature Parent–Child Relationships

The theoretical concepts when placed together provide a diagnostic tool for the analysis of parent–child relationships. The extent to which parenting practices are adequate for the maturation of the child can thereby be ascertained. Parents' actions vis-à-vis their children are assessable in relation to these criteria. Two types of parent–child relationships or family climates are delineated. These are called "mature" or "immature" families as parents either function in an adult (mature) or a childlike (immature) manner. They may also be called "low-resource" and "high-resource" families, with resources defined as emotional, empathic, communicative, and care-giving. In the parent–child relationships studied, most were "immature" or "low-resource" families. Even these families were not loveless, but their love and concerns were expressed as burdens.

Descriptions of parenting practices written and discussed by most of the women in the study indicated that their parents were themselves immature, and thus looked to their children to supply them with unmet developmental needs. Becoming "mature" requires a social context, familial life, and relationship with ones' parents with particular qualities.

Mature parent–child relationships have recognizable characteristics. There exists a strong primary bond, which is both stable and stimulating. The primal patterns of movement, rhythm, and tone are continuous and provide variations from soothing calm to safe excitement. There will be no violent emotional or physical interactions between parent and child. The full emotional range of the infant/child's expressions are adequately mirrored by parents who do not narcissistically project contempt or pride. The parents are empathic to the child, avoiding projection, reversal, and double-image constitutions. Mature parents avoid blaming, placating, irrelevant, and objectivistic communicative patterns between themselves and their children. Instead they clearly communicate feelings, thoughts, expectations, and hopes to their child. The communicative atmosphere is a competent one, exhibiting truth, truthfulness, understandability, and comprehensibility. It is not distorted or synthetic ("pseudo") due to power distortions. Parents regularly use mature to neurotic defenses (sublimation, altruism). They do not act out or use denial, hypochondria, or passive aggressive strategies with their children.

The dramatic environment in the home is comic in form. That is, all are participants with unique but acceptable foibles. Roles in the family are not crystallized along hero-scapegoat lines. Through gentle and unpossessive love, the self-control, and then the artistry of the child and all other family members is fostered. Because of this atmosphere of mutual support, the level of ethical action displayed by family members tends toward caring, as members nurture themselves and other members. Time is experienced in a free authentic manner, as family celebrations, and meaningful rituals and events mark the importance of their shared lives; they experience together the full gambit of emotional life, from joy to mourning. Parents who provide such a family environment with their children are "mature" in this particular emotional and ethical sense, and will facilitate their children's becoming "mature." Their relationship to their children is not emotionally divided, and they avoid encouraging a "divided self" in the child.

Immature parents, as 'child-adults" (Postman, 1982) provide fractured bonds with their infants and children, interrupted by violent emotional and physical outbursts (acting out). Unable to be empathic (since they did not receive empathy), they expect their infants and children to meet their needs, holding them in contempt when they do not do so. They consequently inflict, and project their violent and negative emotions on their children and each other. In response, their children become emotionally divided selves, feeling both love and hate toward their parents. The child represses unacceptable or fearful emotions, and a psuedo-self emerges. This is because parents do not reflect back or mirror the child's constitutions and responses but instead project their own emotions and needs onto the child. The narcissistic pride of parents encourages this development of an equally narcissistic pseudo-self in the child. When these grandiose expectations fail, depression follows, as all are locked into the vicious cycle of contempt.

Communicative patterns of blaming, placating, irrelevant or intellectualistic avoidance abound, crystallizing into role patterns for each family member. As a result, negative or confused messages of attributions and expectations are made. The "me" of the child's developing self thus tends to be negative or divided. Parents and children release their frustrations and tensions through acting out (physical or emotional violence, alcohol and drugs, sexual deviances, physical ailments or accidents). Strategic, or pseudo communication abounds, as each member struggles for his or her share of the limited emotional resources and rewards available in this resource-draining situation.

The dramatic action between parent and child takes a heavy, tragic tone. There is a victim or victims in the family constellation, who provides constant places to "dump" unwanted emotional projections and garbage. A feeling of bitterness and resentment is experienced by all who feel shortchanged and unappreciated. In these kinds of everyday life situations, the level of moral judgment exhibited by family members is survival (where no family resources are available to help the members) to "goodness," where the person sacrifices herself to garner an ounce of appreciation. All feel like victims of Shylock, who demands one "pound of flesh" and then another. Time is experienced by members in an unauthentic manner as constant pressure and stress. Little opportunity for experiencing time as authentic flow is allowed.

What we know philosophically, ethically, and scientifically is good and essential for human becoming is difficult to achieve. This is because many parents and adults did not have the interactional and contextual supports to become socially mature, nurturing parents, significant others, and associates, nor did they learn to adequately self-nurture. Along family lines, generations of adult "boys" marry adult "girls" and, therefore, are unlikely to be able to be empathic, adequate mirrors, congruent, authentic, caring, integrated, and competent communicators who use mature defense mechanisms such as sublimation and altruism. Such a situation becomes self-perpetuating over generations. Given environmental stresses, such as unemployment or unresponsive work environments, many persons will tend to act out against themselves (as in eating, drinking or drug disorders) or against others (as in violent abuse or the infliction of negative emotional climates). Parents who have not been adequately nurtured and who have inadequate social networks will tend to be reversal or double-image parents who will need and expect their children to love them and take care of them.

In this study, the majority of families functioned in the immature mode. In each of the case studies, the result for the child and later for the grown woman was devastating. In some cases, physical and/or emotional abuse of the child occurred. In others, incest (acting out) or neglect (passive aggression) were experienced. In some examples (Shelly and Karen), the lack of adequate caring resulted not from immature parents but from the loss of a parent through death. Poverty or illness are such factors which make becoming mature more difficult.

Mature parents are the greatest asset a child can have. "Pam" and "Rhonda" had parents who exhibited most of the qualities of maturity in their relationships with their children. They were also the happiest and most mature parents as adults. This was true in spite of the fact that they both went through difficult times. Pam had to deal with premarital pregnancy, poverty, and later divorce. Rhonda also went through divorce and a custody battle. That they had more childhood spirits then ghosts was a major reason they did so well with these crises.

The next five chapters of this book present in-depth analyses in the form of eleven "case constructs." Each chapter represents a different kind of childhood adversity experienced by women in the study. The theory of immature and mature parent–child relationships is applied to the way the parents of these women seemed to relate to them when they were children.

The Childhoods of Rebecca, Gloria, and Greta—Ghosts of Battering Parents _____ 5

Introduction

Frequently women in the study spoke of forms of physical abuse they experienced as children. Physical abuse leaves scars and traces. Gloria, now a stepmother and Greta, a mother, abuse their children. Rebecca, the most severely abused as a child, had no children, except for stepchildren who were already grown when she entered their family. However, the ghosts of her abusive stepfather and mother haunted her as she held in contempt others who did not meet up to her high standards, including her husband.

In each case the parents lacked the maturity to adequately nurture and care for their daughters. The first, "Rebecca," 43, has succeeded remarkably in her career. The ghosts of Rebecca's childhood still speak to and through her. In the group discussions, she was consistently severely critical of those who had not attained her level of achievement, and expressed the strong conviction that those less fortunate are most likely simply lazy and lacking in motivation. She dominated the group discussions with descriptions both of the severe abuses she suffered as a child and of her pride in her successful career and marriage. She exhibited what Miller (1984) refers to as "narcissistic pride" and "the cycle of contempt" for any who do not meet her standards.

Gloria, 29, has continued a pattern of entering into relationships with dependent, inadequate men. While she has done well academically and professionally, she is transmitting her ghosts to her stepson, whom she abuses. Greta, 27, and the youngest of the three, is still embedded in the abusive cycle. Her mother, who takes care of Greta's preschool daughter, still hits Greta. Now Greta hits her back. Greta's daughter shows every sign of being severely abused herself.

Rebecca—The Ghosts of a Violent, Immature Stepfather and a Passive, Negative Mother

Rebecca Sealey, is a successful hospital administrator in a large city. She is also a spokesperson for a national organization of hospital administrators and teaches part time at a prestigious private college. She is slim and attractive, with her long, dark hair usually drawn up and back. Her well-articulated facial bones make her photogenic. One often sees her at grand openings of new community hospitals and ribbon-cutting ceremonies, in newspaper photographs.

While maintaining her private, modern designed condominium in the city near the hospital, she commutes on weekends to a 300-acre lake estate. Her husband is a youthful, widowed businessman in his late sixties. Rebecca had admired him for years prior to their marriage. In fact, as a teenager, she served as live-in housekeeper in his home, which was, at that time, also a haven for Rebecca from the beatings she had been receiving from her stepfather and the verbal abuse of her mother. As she writes in her autobiography:

> I have very few, if any, happy memories of my childhood. I remember it being one of struggle and poverty. It was not the poverty that hurt,—but the lack of love and feeling of being OK concerning my parents. This truly left its mark on me for many years. I look back now and understand that they were the product of their own times and programming by their parents. . . .
>
> I know very little about my father except what others have told me. He was married three times. I have a half-sister ten years older than I by his first marriage. My mother was his second marriage. We (Rebecca and the older half-sister) are friendly now. I have a sister two years younger than I. I also have a half-sister approximately twenty years old as a result of his third marriage. He was a victim of a very bad background and as a result never used his brilliance and potential for good. With my parents' divorce when I was three years old, I was alienated from the presence and love of my father. I am told I was his favorite and as a result the child most hurt by not being with him. I resented my mother for not letting me make the decision on my own as to whether he was good or bad. I sought him out when I was twenty-four years old. I felt guilty because I knew my mother would not approve. He frightened me. I never saw him again or talked to him again. I read about his death in the newspaper and attended his funeral. I felt cheated and I could not tell anyone how I had longed for him all my life. . . . I just hope if he knew what I was doing while growing up, he was proud of me.

Rebecca also had a "very confused" relationship with her mother. Until Rebecca was 40, she saw her mother as the root of all of her emotional problems. Rebecca never called her mother "mother." Rebecca's early childhood relationship with her mother was fragmentary. Her mother frequently had to leave her in the care of others as she moved from job to job. In fact, Rebecca functioned from the age of three as a mother to her mother and to her sister, taking on the role of primary nurturer and comforter in the family. Rebecca as a child/mother to her mother was involved in "reversal" child rearing, where the child is expected to provide the love and care needed by the parent (deMause, 1974). Yet, as Rebecca said, "No matter what I did to please her, it was not enough. My feelings ran from hate, pity, disgust, guilt, resentment and a great amount of confusion."

Following the break-up of her first marriage, Rebecca's mother remarried, this time to a man who beat her mother, and, when he was still angry, beat Rebecca "without mercy." Rebecca felt that her mother favored her younger sister. The voices of the ghost of her mother from her childhood contain phrases like; "you are a bad girl," "you are like your father," "you can not expect to ever be anything," "dress right or men will lust after you" "men are no good—a woman is just their slopjar." She also remembers her mother's good qualities. Her mother was educated at a private school and at a young age taught her social graces, cooking, sewing, and all other household duties:

> My pre-school years were mostly spent from housekeeper to boarding house because my mother had to work to support us. Usually there were other children belonging to the housekeeper or the person we were boarded with. There was always friction. Sure enough, guess who got blamed (by mother) for everything! Teachers, whose names I cannot remember, became mother figures to me. I would only feel good and then have to go to another school, leaving a trusted person behind. I remember my mother coming to visit us when she could. I remember the longing for her and watched her as she walked out of sight. I would gather my little strength and tell myself I had to be a big girl. To this day, when things go wrong and I don't feel the support I need from a loved one, I gather my spirit and tell myself, "I will show you—I can do it by myself."

Rebecca shows a remarkable determination to cope. Her internalized image of herself is strong enough to "stand alone." At the same time such forced independence, where a basis of love and support do not exist, fosters the vicious cycle of contempt and resentment. Today Rebecca deeply resents those who she perceives as lazy, such as women collecting welfare. She strongly believes that everyone should be able and willing to make his or her own way because she did.

> My life from age 6 to 12 was one of utter turmoil. In 1945 my mother remarried. The man she wed was supposed to be a substitute for my father. She

did a worse job in marrying him than if she had stayed with my father. This man was uneducated, cruel, a wife and child abuser, insecure, overbearing and liked to have a conflict going all the time. He had had three marriages before and was certainly not ready for a five and seven year old.

My first introduction to this man was when my mother brought him to the house where my sister and I were boarded. He took my sister on his lap and gave her some gum. When I came to his side, hoping for some gum, too, he pushed me away. I never forgot that. Was it me? Why could not just one someone love me? They married and the family moved to a ranch in Nevada. There we went to school with Latin American children, some of whom were to become life-long friends. I had the responsibility of keeping the house, working in the fields, and all the things described before. This was my introduction to my stepfather, who was to play the most depressing role in my life of anyone. He would get mad at my mother, beat me and dare me to cry. If I cried, he would beat me more. I hated my mother for letting him beat me. I was expected to always bring honor to the family, in person, in grades, in behavior, and in deeds. I could accept this challenge. I could not accept the harassment and the unjust treatment. I felt no attributions from this immature man for good. He never felt I would ever amount to anything. He often called me names and belittled me. He did a great amount of harm emotionally. This was relieved at a later time in my life. I truly pity this person and regard him with disgust. I try to understand that he had problems too. He had no right to hurt a child. I had to continue with his abuse until I was sixteen years old and finally left home to avoid it. This significant other is considered a negative in a great sense. I, too, can see some positive things that happened. I learned to grow stronger and lean more on myself. Most people tattled anything. I sought answers to questions and he interpreted this as a threat to him and his good name and I was beaten again. Thus more confirmation that I could not trust anyone. I had to keep everything to myself.

The abuse continued into her teenage years:

When I was thirteen years old, my mother and stepfather sold the ranch and moved back to the city. The drought had driven most of the farmers and ranchers out of that area. I did not want to leave Nevada because I would have to leave people I loved. We moved to a poor part of town. I hated the area. I could hardly wait until I was old enough to leave that part of town. My stepfather returned to a job as a drag line operator and my mother to nursing. I resumed the same responsibilities in the household. A good meal with desert was always on the table each night. I really did well. Still-no praise. Something was always found to be wrong. The severe beatings and abuse continued by my stepfather. I was maturing faster emotionally and physically than most of the other kids. In fact, I felt I was born thirty years old. I was greatly self-conscious, super sensitive and very confused as to what was happening to me. I started my period when I was thirteen and handled it calmly. I was alone. I was baptized when I was thirteen. I remember seeing my first TV when I was thirteen. I made friends fast. Because of my religious training, I could not participate in a lot of things the other kids did. Most of the time, I did not have time because of my home duties. I did not mind the hard work. I resented the hostile atmosphere and the continued beatings—the constant upset. There was no security.

A divided self crystallizes. On the one hand, there is the Rebecca who performs well at school and is admired by her teachers. On the other hand, there is the Rebecca who so enrages and infuriates her stepfather that he beats her and calls her nasty names. Throughout these years of severe abuse at home, Rebecca gained positive support at school from teachers who were sensitive to her situation and who recognized her abilities. She mentions, in particular, her sixth grade teacher.

> As a result of our long talks and sharing secrets she became one of the first persons I could trust and a life-long friend. . . . This woman had problems of her own, but never too many to help me with mine. She treated me like an adult. She shared with me good grooming and inner peace. She expected me to do well, to achieve high grades, to excel in sports, to excel in art, to build a good life and turn bad things into good. I achieved all her expectations, and did excel by always being on the honor roll.

This teacher fostered Rebecca's confidence. At the same time, such emphasis on achievement facilitated a "workaholic" type of maturing. In such cases, the person feels she is only acceptable and worthwhile as long as she is performing at an optimal level.

Rebecca's seventh grade teacher combined respect for Rebecca's abilities with an understanding of her emotional pain:

> My seventh grade teacher . . . knew of the cruelty of my home life. I did not have to tell her. She had heard it elsewhere and found it in her heart to be sensitive toward me. She never treated me as if there was a big problem. She helped me overcome some of the attitudes I was developing about myself because of the situation. She believed in my abilities and cheered me on. She was a strong person, a busy person and a well liked person. Her husband was superintendent of our school. He helped me also. I was often taken out of class (because I had all my work done and I had top grades) to help in the tax office or in his office. I felt needed and I did my jobs well.

In looking back at the effect of the church on her life, Rebecca found it to be significant. It was a strict church and became her "parent." Legalistic and rigid ties to the world of meaningful cultural symbols (or the "proto-symbolic" to Huertas-Jordas) inevitably have harmful effects on the child's becoming. The church fostered hypocrisy and self-contempt such that no one could live up to all the standards. In addition, they tended to be rigidly hierarchical, sexist, and be characterized by communications that do not seek so much to be truthful as to be "acceptable." Such religious doctrines subtly or directly encourage contempt toward the many other nonperfect human beings:

> It (the church) was full of "thou-shalt-nots" and a set of rigid rules made by man to keep everyone in line. I drank them in for all they were worth. They later were to be a source of unhappiness to me because I could not live up to all that was expected of me. In later years I could reflect back and pick and choose which ones I could accept and which one I could disregard. I feared being a bad girl so much, I tried to be perfect in everything I did. I even slept in the position I should be buried in if I were to die. I was carrying a big load for a little girl. I worked diligently not to be any problem to my parents or teachers. I wish I were that pure again. The expectations of the religious body helped hold my character in principle, but it damaged the emotional element of my life. The constant guilt one feels when they can not live up to the set of strict rules is almost devastating and most undermining of the real purpose of such an organization. I accepted the good that built a strong principle and rigidly moral standard for my life at that time. I was too young and inexperienced to reject those elements that were to hinder my growth as a useful human being. Most of the time the interpretation of the scriptures were narrow and unyielding. The people who were to be the fine examples were great disappointments and forgot to love each other. . . . They often preached one thing and did another. I was really confused. I just existed most of my life (until I was 22) and did not drink, smoke, dance, wear shorts or pants, go to movies, play cards, go in mixed swimming or neck with the boys. Good girls did not do those things. I still was criticized, no matter how good I tried to be.

During her teenage years, Rebecca continued to excel in school and to carry heavy household responsibilities. At age 16 she began to work after school until 9:00 P.M, walking a mile and three quarters home after work. Upon arriving home she was not allowed to use the bathroom for fear of waking her stepfather. Her mother hid her supper under her pillow and she had to study at night with a flashlight under the covers. One night her stepfather caught her studying after "bed time" and beat her unmercifully. Some months after this, at the age of 17, she left home to live with a family from church. She worked in their home and in a downtown store, paying her own way. She found relief for the first time from the tense atmosphere and beatings to which she had been subjected from age 6. Rebecca supported herself throughout her college years. When the couple she had lived with at age 17 later broke up, some of the church elders blamed her, although she really had nothing to do with it, according to the wife.

Rebecca worked while in college. As in childhood, she continued to do what she did best—succeed at work. The first 2 years of college her grades suffered due to the adjustment. However she achieved honors level by the time of graduation. Upon graduating, she started working in a records department of a hospital. She moved back home and paid her rent while working. Meanwhile, she attended special administrative workshops and achieved numerous promotions. Two years later she purchased a condominium in the city, in a highly fashionable neighborhood. This home is important to her since it was the first one she ever felt comfortable in. As she said, "It was mine and I feared no one." As a young professional woman, she did not have any close relationships. She spent most of her time advancing professionally.

Two years later, the wife of a respected church gentleman in the community died of cancer. Rebecca sent money instead of flowers to the church and invited the family to dinner. Following this eventful dinner, Rebecca and the gentleman became inseparable and later married. He was 27 years her senior. After marriage, her image of him as a strong, wise protector was shattered. Rebecca's need for a loving father was not met by this man. She therefore became highly critical of him. He turned out to be weak and dependent on her for strength. Thus she continued the "vicious cycle of contempt" in relation to her husband:

> One of the problems was the older son. He called at ridiculous times every night,—usually while we were making love. This got out of hand and my husband would not correct it. One thing led to another until the situation almost pushed me into the arms of another man. I was not used to his possessiveness. He was everywhere. It reminded me of my stepfather when he would check up on me. I could not live with my feelings. The guilt of having married a man and then finding out I had another child on my hands was too much. He is both father and husband. He is my friend. The depression that developed within my being could not be avoided. He might have been at the right place at the wrong time. I checked myself into a psychiatric hospital, leaving him crying at the back door.

In the psychiatric hospital she was fortunate to have a sensitive and perceptive doctor. She was diagnosed as schizophrenic. The doctor was shocked that she had not committed suicide and was not walking the streets, given her negative early life experiences. Nevertheless, he recognized her intelligence and talent and therefore did not prescribe electric shock treatments, but instead encouraged her to work through her problems through psychotherapy, where she learned to accept herself in spite of childhood difficulties.

After 3 months of treatment, Rebecca was released from the hospital. She decided to try to make a success out of the relationship with this man who she described variously as father, husband, son, and friend. He was very patient with her. They traveled to Europe and Africa together, and bought their lake estate. He established a successful consulting business while in his sixties. They built a new house and did most of the work themselves, planting a garden and an orchard. In discussions of the current relationship, she emphasizes the work they had accomplished together. This commentary focuses on why she should love him, and why *everyone* respects him, but not that *she* does.

> All this we did together. I plow the fields and do a lot of tractor driving. I love it. I can see what I achieve as I work and at the same time I am alone with my thoughts and am getting good exercise. We share household chores. I could not ask for more. This is one fantastic man that everyone loves. He is greatly respected. There will never be another like him. I am very lucky.
>
> I consider myself one of the lucky ones on this earth. What started out to be a terrible experience in life has thus developed into a happy and normal life. I have many to thank for their care and confidence in me and for sharing their lives in such a way that I could live.

Rebecca's improved marital relationship and the way she is caring for her aging mother seem to indicate that Rebecca is moving toward maturity. Yet the ghosts of her childhood pain linger in her bitterness and in her reaction against weakness in others.

Rebecca Today: Toward Greater Maturity and Intimacy

When a first draft of this book was completed, I sent copies of each of the segments where quotations were extensively used to each participant to get their permission for publication and to get an update on their current lives. Of all those written to, "Rebecca" responded most quickly and enthusiastically. She found the interpretations to be accurate and offered the update on her life which follows. She indicated interest in helping others cope with the "ghosts" of their childhoods through their writing. She said this was the first time she had expressed in writing the emotions and inner growth that she felt:

> Some phenomenal changes have been made in my life. I think you realize that in spite of the lingering hurts, pains and ghosts in my life, I have always been progressing forward in search of truths to find the real me, a self-worth and a self worthy of approval and love—otherwise I would not have been in your research project. All the degrees of search has finally paid off. You first have to recognize you need help and do something about it. Although it seems ages ago, it was really the entrance into the psychiatric care of a wise doctor that gradually opened the doors of my mind to define and redefine, evaluate and re-evaluate information which would eventually set me free to mature to the point I am today.

I am 49 now and happier than I have ever been. I can deal with life more directly and do not need the crutches of ghosts of my childhood. Yes, they are still there and always will be. But they have turned into a source of encouragement to others who can succeed in spite of their pasts. When you are a person who is considered successful in every way, envied for your position, your confidence and your physical beauty, it is hard to believe that you have traveled such a rocky road to get where you are. However, this is the opportune time to share those ghosts with others who are struggling in order to encourage them to keep on trying.

I have spent a lifetime seeking the approval and love of others in order that I might feel good about myself. I was highly criticized by not only my biological parents (stepparent) but by the religious "parent." There was never a feeling of trust and security. I in turn admit I was critical and resentful of those who seemed unable to achieve the success I had. My success was a way of saying I was worth something. Although I had extreme financial success in my business career, it was only the by-product of my efforts to become a more worthy and loved person. My work was my lover. I did not fail it and it loved me back with strings of successful jobs. It loved me back where relationships could not be trusted. Financial success and possessions were not my goal, it was the achievement. It was essential in my professional training to know the value of profit. It was more essential to me to set and reset creative goals which were to become the very epitome of success.

Rebecca shows in the next paragraph the way she rid herself of the "ghost" of her mother. Where she could not change her mother into becoming the kind of mother she needed, she could change her relationship with her mother, by no longer taking responsibility for her mother's feelings. She also found a "spirit" in the form of an aunt.

I have dealt with the role my mother has played in my life by virtually alienating her from my life as my mother. She is now like any other human being I would meet. I will feel no guilt in her death as I have done all I could to make her proud of me and comfortable in her last years. The "monkey" is now on her back and she can no longer manipulate me into guilt feelings. My Aunt, her sister, had a lot to do in helping me achieve this by stating the fact that my mother had always punished me for being my father's child. I was alienated from my aunt all these years because my mother was threatened by her sister's freedom and happiness. I am comfortable with the situation now and can handle issues without reliving the pain associated with her. The aunt has become a positive significant other in whom I can confide as a surrogate mother.

Rebecca continues to describe the way she became a close and trusting friend of a young couple. This couple have become spirits who love, support, and constructively criticize her. They seem to have taken the place in her life of the ghost of her sister, who is alienated from her life.

Rebecca has expanded her network of supportive others, including a
male co-worker and her 16-year-old goddaughter. She also has continued to enrich and build upon her relationships with her seventh grade
teacher and two nurturing high school teachers. Thus Rebecca has rebuilt a positive "family" for herself out of friends and even her husband
who she sees clearly now as providing a "good father" role in her life:

> I have purposely saved the most significant other until the last. Although I
> remain married to the same man I married twenty years ago—I do not in-
> tend to abandon him—I can realistically accept him only as a father figure
> in my life. I love and respect him and appreciate his friendship as well as
> his patience with me. I also have been responsible for him living at the
> ranch in a very comfortable situation financially and actually while I con-
> tinue pursuing my career. I do not feel guilty or do I intend to as he would
> not have what he has if it were not for my abilities in comparison with his
> procrastination. I do everything I can to make sure his dignity is preserved
> and that he enjoys his life.

Finally, she tells of her love a special man with whom she feels
intimate:

> However, unplanned on either of our parts, is the emergence of the most
> important significant other that I have ever had in my life. One who is here
> to stay and with whom I can eventually plan a future. We have formed a
> mutual support system both personally and professionally. . . . It was not
> until two years ago at a social event that a simple greeting sparked the most
> beautiful relationship I have ever experienced. He is ten months older than
> I and the first male I have let really penetrate the true depths of my heart.
> Our relationship is one of deeply caring, sharing concern, protectiveness,
> and mutual personal and professional respect. To put it bluntly, we make
> a hell of a fantastic team. I truly trust this significant other with my deepest
> emotions—which is mutual. We work as equals. He is the first person who
> has opened my eyes to my many, many talents which I had taken for
> granted all these years. I thought everyone had them . . . his love and
> friendship has made me aware of me. For the first time in my life, almost
> like coming out of a thick fog, I love myself . . . there is that trust, that
> dependability, that encouragement, that understanding and that whole-
> some concern for the other, that keeps the relationship in an interesting
> balance. We are not intimidated by each other's success or careers. I look
> forward with great anticipation, when the time is right, to planning our
> future together. With this significant other I no longer have to prove I am
> good, pretty, talented, or worthy of his love. I am loved and I can love.

Finally, Rebecca comments on her enriched sense of the religious:

> I no longer need to seek guidance from the "religious organizations" which
> exist now as a poor man's club. A church is not the building but the people

in the world who meet to encourage others in the world. The churches today exist in the world and are often alienating themselves because they do not seek out the world but expect the world to succumb to their rigid rules and regulations to be a part of God's world. God didn't have anything to do with their rules. Besides, if I cannot be sensitive to the needs and do something about them for my fellow man every day, sitting on the church pew isn't going to help me to be acceptable to God. I realize there is a super power and upper being, I just do not believe in this person as most do.

Gloria—The Ghosts of a Battering, Verbally Abusive Mother and an Absent Father

Gloria Sewald is a medical social worker working on a master's degree. She is married to a Vietnam veteran, that she met while he was a hospital patient, and has a 5-year-old stepson.

As a child, Gloria was physically and verbally abused by her mother:

> I remember being scolded and hit by my mom a lot. Even at this young age (pre-school) I recall being scared to do anything wrong for fear of punishment. I saw my mom kick my sister in the stomach when I was about five, for what I do not remember. The main characteristic she attributed to me, I think, was that of being a brat. We (my two sisters and I) were always called brats and good-for-nothings, which I definitely internalized for a long time, up until my last few years. My negative concept of myself started at this age.

Loneliness is one result of a lack of empathy on the part of the parent along with inadequate appreciative mirroring of the child's emotions. One can see the roots of an emotionally divided self in such parenting practices. One's own body in relation to important others is experienced as a body in pain, not in pleasure:

> Very well do I remember the touch associated with frequent spankings. My mother did seem to spank us a lot, for various reasons. I do not recall any comfortable episodes of touching, although I am sure there were some. I do not recall much about my early childhood, and have not for a long time. My childhood was a negative one, growing up alone in a family of five is a good description. For this reason I feel I have blocked a lot of my experiences.

Gloria spend third and fourth grades on a military base in Darmstadt, West Germany, where she did well academically, especially in arithmetic. She worked quickly but needed to be more careful about drawing hasty conclusions. Gloria attributed this zealous haste to her mother always telling her to "hurry up." This sense of pressure in relation to time mitigates against authentic appreciation of temporality. Time pressure is related to pressures in regard to inadequacies in the self. Negative attributions are associated with doing things too slowly.

> My mom made me feel that I was never quite good enough, at whatever I did. It could have been just a little better. If I didn't get straight A's, something was wrong, and I should get them next report period. Very little praise was offered, or at least I don't remember very much from her. The attributions I received from this was one of inadequacy, incompetence, being just below par. She wanted me to be perfect, especially in school. She stressed education, but negatively. I never felt that smart around home.

> Another attribution I feel I received from my mom during this period is that of uncreativity. She used to say that I had no imagination, to the point that I believed her, and quit trying to have one. My mind went blank when called upon to conjure up stories about pictures, for I was always very literal and superficial. If I started to daydream about something, I often would not carry ideas through, perhaps because I had unconsciously accepted the fact I was not creative enough to be doing such a thing, at least not as well as someone else. My mother was creative, but I wasn't and I do not believe that I am today.

> As a child, I never was very sick. But when I was, I usually had to do work around the house, regardless of my illness. I remember one time having to iron daddy's shirts and mom's dresses when I was about seven or eight. When in Germany, we became ill with colds. My mother made it clear what a burden it was to clean up after us. But I did incorporate her reaction to illness by complaining even with a little pain. I didn't get sympathy growing up, so I wonder if I'm looking for it now?

As was typical for military families, they moved frequently. For Gloria the saddest move was from Indiana to Georgia prior her entrance into first grade. This was because her grandmother lived in Indiana and, in contrast to her mother, showed her warmth and affection:

> My grandmother was someone I did not see very much at this age, but I knew she loved me and would be glad to see me again. In fact, when we did move back from Indiana to Georgia when I was almost six, I cried as soon as I saw her. She didn't understand why I was crying, but I was so glad to see her. She didn't expect much from me, except to be kind and respectful, but she wasn't strict or anything like that. She had come from a close family herself, and I think now that that was what I longed for. I felt comfortable with her. Already so young in life I would rather have lived with her than my parents.

Gloria says little about her relationship with her father except that it was nonexistent. When he died, she was attending a professional conference, and did not leave it to go to the funeral. She comments about this:

> At the present time I find myself thinking about my father much more than I had, since he died just five months ago. I realize I knew so little of him and he of me, and that hurts me to reflect upon. What really concerns me is that I have incorporated a lot of patterns from my parents that I did not like as a child myself, but at least, I suppose, I am becoming more aware of them with the possibility of changing them. The incomplete relationship I had with my father is sometimes overwhelming if I am in a certain emotional mood. I have not finished with it yet, so I do think about it a lot, more than people realize.

The inadequacy she had internalized from her mother's critical attitude and her lack of connectedness with her father infected her school years. It took a lot of positive commentary from school mates and others before she started to think well of herself. For example, in girl scouts she never really tried to earn badges since she always assumed ahead of time that she could not do it.

In high school, her father was away most of the time, serving in the navy in the Middle East. Her first boyfriend (who she met in high school) respected her quick mind and her participation in social activities at church and school. Although he was a strong influence, she was not able to overcome her low self-esteem. Her mother's effect was far more powerful. Gloria recalls her mother accusing her of being narrow-minded, because she inevitably took an opposing point of view from her mother. She maintained negative feelings for her mother:

> My mom also expected me to love her, which I did not. She would hug me and say "I love you. Do you love me?" To which I would reply "Yes" since I was supposed to. Then I felt guilty for lying, not feeling badly for not loving her.
>
> She also expected me to do what I was told, regardless of the logic underlying the request. For the most part I did, until I got older. She still talks about the fact that I would rebel less than my sisters if asked to do something. But I too usually had some whining or talking back to do. I became very selfish and a loner in my own family. Nobody liked her, let alone anyone else in the house. We all had our individual brand of suffering.
>
> My feelings of worthlessness from my mom again outweighed even John's (her boyfriend) feelings of pride and love for me. I now know I am worth something to myself, as well as to other people, not just because I am a social worker. I am an intelligent person who has feelings for others, and is often very sensitive to them. I also am a good citizen and obey most of the laws. But it took a long time to overcome the worthlessness I had accepted for myself. The guilt I had built up over the years in relation to my

poor relationship with my family and my mom has been for the most part resolved. I'm not perfect, but I sure am a better and more interesting person, more willing to take risks and give of myself.

This feeling of worthlessness pervaded her life, even though she gained considerable recognition from joining numerous school and church organizations. In the process, she developed negative feelings for the church. The church was a legalistic organization that expected a lot from her and gave little in return. Frenetic activity was used to mask the emptiness that she felt. The tragic model of social drama was in place, creating a sense of guilt in Gloria as a teenager:

Since I was active in church activities, I struggled with my own beliefs for a long time. My mother was a hypocrite in my opinion, which began to turn me off to religious beliefs in general, but not severely until after I had left home. I felt I was expected to be a good person and love my mom and dad, but I didn't see them do too much loving of their children. All this did was create confusion and guilt, because I felt I didn't love them, and couldn't. So I got active in the music department at church. Even then, people felt I was a good Christian, and kept telling me so, because I enjoyed the music activities. I felt guilty about being called a Christian, since I did not describe myself that way. Other people believed more than I did.

At age eighteen Gloria went away to college, and worked in the school cafeteria. Her supervisor there respected her work and the speed with which she did it. The supervisor continued to be supportive through several years of changes. Her best friend in college, Sheri, also had such a positive effect. Both Sheri and Gloria's supervisor looked past her harsh exterior and saw her as an extremely sensitive and basically good person. In this way, Gloria started to build important supportive relationships to counteract the ghosts of her parents. This intensified the emotional division within her which came to a head in a relationship with a man:

Another person who played a central role in my life at this time was a man I used to date for about two years. His influence was more negative, because he held me back, or I let him hold me back. I was on my way down to the low point in my life, when I hooked up with him. He mostly dated me for sexual experiences, I think, because we did have a good time then, even though I knew he was dating his old girlfriend off and on at the same time. I even drove by her house and saw his truck sitting out front a lot of times, yet I kept on with him. Looking back, he must have thought I was a fool for all of the crap I put up with for that time. He was a blatant liar, a very aggressive, self-pitying and insecure person, with a bad chip on his shoulder. As far as expectations are concerned, I think he never knew what to expect from me, other than to be his lover whenever he chose. We did live together for six months once. It was a totally unhealthy relationship from the start, although I had the highest hopes I could help him drastically change and everything would be all right. It finally hit home to me what he had wanted when I broke up with him the last time, and told him I was going off of the pill. He was really shocked to think that I would do that—how could we make love then if I had no protection? He had missed the point completely, that I was through with sex for a while, and him. We tried to get back together again, because he wanted to, but this time I was up front. I told him I expected honesty in our relationship, among other things, and that was it. The next day he had left me a note with his key to my apartment saying he could not live up to what I wanted. I felt good that at last I had told him what I expected. I had not lost anything. He had expected me to be loyal, but yet he did not have to be, he felt. It still surprises me how I could have gone against all that I said I had stood for by staying with him, which really shows me how poor my self-concept was.

Such an abusive close relationship will be especially appealing for a young woman with an emotionally divided self. In this case, the relationship was not physically abusive. The sexual contact provided a pleasurable physical relationship that she did not find with her parents. But this newfound pleasure was a trap for Gloria as she quickly found it did not mean intimacy, but a new form of alienation.

Reacting against hypocrisy and rigid bureaucratic institutions, Gloria tried to forge out a different sense of herself:

During this time I was beginning to reject middle class values as I saw them, or at least I thought I was. My idea of society was a negative one, that extended to morals and values about what was right and good. I was tired of behaving like I felt was expected of me. I began to rebel, so to speak, in my own small way. I was ashamed to be middle class, because of this negative attitude I had. During this time, I was picking up where the end of the sixties had left off. I quit wearing a bra, I started smoking, I wore jeans almost everywhere. I espoused some anti-middle class values, such as not wanting to get married, not believing in God. I became a female chauvinist, too, very aggressive and opinionated, and believing all that I was saying. Society expected me to be submissive, to not sleep around, to not cuss, to not smoke, to believe in God, to attend to others before myself. So I did the opposite. I totally overreacted.

Gloria's rebellion led her once again into the relationship with an immature man.

The person associated with this time passage was a man I married when I was twenty-five. He was a drug pusher and an alcoholic, who had just escaped from a Brazilian prison after being incarcerated for four years. All of this I knew before I married him, after knowing him for only five weeks. When I reflect upon my reasons for going through with it, I can only think how desperate to be loved I was. I had again hooked up with a pathological personality, that could only bring me harm. He told me he thought I was a good woman, and that he loved me, and would never leave me nor look at another woman ever. I'm not sure what his expectations were for me, even after he said all of this. He took me for the sucker he probably knew I was, perhaps without knowing it himself. He was a lost soul, reaching out for anything or anyone. I happened to be one of the first anyones he ran into after returning to the United States after almost a ten-year absence.

Well, that relationship lasted about five months, after which he left me in Atlanta to go to California. But before he left for good, he had told me he had no sympathy for people who did not do what they wanted to do in life. It stuck with me, to this day. During the month I was in Atlanta by myself, waiting to go back home to Indiana, I decided to take hold of my life and quit letting things happen to me without my say-so or any protest. I did not want to live to get away from the past anymore. Ken had been right—I had not done what I said I wanted to do, and he knew it by my staying with him, and not leaving first. It was as if I were two separate people, one watching and detachedly analyzing the other's actions. That was the way I felt most of the short relationship.

The positive side of Gloria's divided self reasserted itself after this as she once again achieved success on her job and the respect of a supervisor. Achievement and recognition were to take the place of love:

I was not afraid of strangers, such as store clerks and people walking down the street. This extended to my career, not being afraid of patients' families or the physicians. They were all just people, like me, who were not going to harm me. I walked more erect. A significant person from this time is a supervisor with whom I worked at my new job. She made me feel like a really good physical therapist, which up until this time I was struggling to feel myself, although other people often told me this. As I grew more self-confident as a person, so I did as a professional. She helped me by trusting me, which she had not been able to do with anyone for a few years. Her expectations for me were to help her grow, to guide the shift on which we both worked, to help her as a person who had not many friends.

Shortly thereafter Gloria met a patient, Tom, in the hospital who fell in love her:

He thinks I am one of the most intelligent women he has known, and respects my advice. I am seen as very independent, sweet, and loving by him. He thought I would make a good wife, so he married me. His expectations for me are for me to do what I want to do, especially in furthering my education, and growing as a therapist. This is important to me, and all the more remarkable about him since he is almost five years younger than me, and much less educated. We want the same things out of life, such as kids, a home, travel, experience and close family ties. He does expect fidelity and communication between us, which we have. There is little competition between us.

Tom brought his 3-year-old son with him into the marriage. The son had been abused by Tom's former wife, according to Gloria. In her marriage to Tom, an emotionally disturbed Vietnam veteran, who did not finish high school and was unemployed, Gloria was, unknown to herself at the time, repeating the pattern of selecting an inferior, immature mate. The pattern of her childhood household, where father was absent and uninvolved was also repeated in these relationships. In all three of Gloria's serious relationships with men they viewed Gloria as a strong, competent woman, able to take care of their needs, physically, financially, and emotionally. In return they fed her weak ego with the complements for which she thirsted, and with the gratifications that come from being "needed." While such attachments allow for immediate relief from feelings of worthlessness, they confirm them at a deeper level. Speaking through the overlay of complements and the feeling of being needed, was the undercurrent of being worthy only of an inferior man.

Such a marriage allowed Gloria to repeat the pattern of her childhood at the emotional level. When she was a child both of her parents had such empty emotional "pots" that they could not meet their children's needs. Instead, they met their own needs through the achievements of their children. In her relationship with her stepson, Gloria inadvertently repeated the pattern of "reversal" parenting that she had experienced, where the child is expected to meet the emotional needs of the parent. The boy was pressured by Gloria to achieve beyond his abilities. He was expected to express affection to her and none for his natural mother, of whom she was extremely jealous. When he did not meet these expectations, Gloria became physically and verbally abusive with him. It is greatly to Gloria's credit that this came out in the documents, hinting that she was trying to deal with it.

The first indications of her spouses' inadequacies and her abusiveness to her stepson appeared in her descriptions of the way she experienced the passage of time. In her description of the first year of married life, she wrote of her husband's aunt, "who accused me of child abuse, and to this day does not talk to me, nor I to her." In this account, she writes of the future in terms of fantasy:

I am single, have lots of money and status, good clothes, and can do and go where I want without any question or feelings of obligation toward a family.

In her descriptions of the passage of time during the last year, she recounts a time in July when her husband had a "severe anxiety reaction":

> It got really bad the next day, and I had to make arrangements to be absent from work one day to just be with him. We did get in to see a physician who prescribed some Valium, which really worked well for the time. That's when he started to see a psychologist for help.

The two parts of Gloria's self—the negative voice of her mother's ghost—and the positive attempts to free herself from the pattern, speak clearly in Gloria's diary. Her positive achievements at school, work, and in the group stand in contrast to the emotional ambivalence associated with her marriage and family life:

> My husband was sick today, lying on the couch feeling terrible. It is probably related to his anxiety attacks that started this past summer, but it also could be a bug or virus, since he is nauseated again. I feel so sorry and helpless when he is this way, and also guilty that I can't spend all of my time with him. . . .
>
> September 7: My husband had an appointment with his psychologist, to help him over his latest spell. Sometimes I wish he weren't so dependent on me, so I could be dependent on him at times, but I can't. Most of the time it doesn't bother me, but there are days I don't want to be the strong one or the one who handles the money and bills or the one who works. I always assume he wouldn't understand so I never say anything, because most of the time it doesn't bother me too much. On reflection, I suppose that isn't healthy for me or our relationship, but I'm trying not to put too much on him at this point right now. He has his own troubles to think about, too.

The next day Gloria blames herself for not having a "positive" enough attitude. She expresses resentment that her husband's brother and her husband's best friend come over regularly to use their washer and drier and not to see them.

Gloria wrote continually in her diary about her stepson. She and her husband had filled out a questionnaire in order to have him evaluated at the school for a developmental problem:

> He is unable to follow verbal directions, without being shown first, even for simple instructions. I blame it on his natural mother, who makes me very anxious just to think about her. She did absolutely nothing in the way of teaching him anything or disciplining him as he was growing up. Consequently, when we got him a few days before we were married, he was a little brat who pouted, whined, kicked, tried to bite, couldn't even talk clearly, and he was over $3\frac{1}{2}$ years old. Needless to say, it took a lot of work

to straighten him out from all that, except he has always been slow to understand simple directions. Rote memory is fine. He learned the alphabet finally, after several weeks. But this problem with hearing directions and synthesizing the meaning by interpreting them is an impossibility for him. He just stands there and looks dumbfounded, which used to make us mad until we realized he just didn't know any better. So now here we are trying to get him checked out to see if it's something physical or developmental, and it makes me mad as hell, especially since she comes to see him every other weekend because we moved ourselves physically closer to her (not for her, of course, but because we wanted to come here). I need to get to where she doesn't bother me so much anymore, but I hate her, I think, for the things she did to my husband and to my son. She won't let me adopt him because she thinks if something happens to my husband she will get him back. She is dead wrong! I will never allow that to happen, and neither will my mother-in-law. There is no way in hell that she will ever get him back. So here we are, in an ongoing battle, and meanwhile our son suffers, not knowingly at the present, but in the future?

September 9: My husband picked me up after class today, which I enjoy because I get to see him as soon as I am out. I enjoy the feeling of being a student again, and sensing the atmosphere of a university campus again. Since I have become more dedicated to my profession in the past few years, I really enjoy learning more about it. The class is one which invites discussion, and I participate freely. I remember all too well when I was in undergraduate school how quiet I was in class, even when I did not understand something. My anxiety level was so high that it precluded me from seeking answers openly. But now I can, and I enjoy school so much more now.

And then there's work. It was extremely busy today. What infuriates me is that a young girl was brought in, shipped out to city hospital, only to die later after being hit by a hit and run driver. Her father and sister were already dead. Life is so unfair, so cruel sometimes, and that is the point—life is not perfect. Its reality hits hard. Before the young girl, we had another woman, in her early thirties, who had a cerebral hemorrhage, which will probably kill her, too. She had a baby that was two or three weeks old. And I think I have problems—they certainly shrink in comparison to others' predicaments and poker hands. I felt really drained emotionally after tonight. So much death and despair so close together in my small world. It brought home the fact that I could go any time, too. . . .

On September 10 Gloria met with her husband's psychologist who had seemingly corroborated some of her advice to her husband. Gloria mentioned turning in a grant application that would allow her to cut her work days down from five to four hours. She mentioned the burden of taking nine graduate hours while working full time. Meanwhile, her husband who neither works nor goes to school aggravates her:

I asked my husband to take our son to preschool in the morning, and he almost sounded like he was whining. It made me instantly mad to hear his tone of voice, so I asked him if he wanted to or not. He said he would do it, but I could tell he still didn't want to. I usually am the one to take him because I either have to go to class, or have to study. Only about once a week do I ask him to take him, which isn't much. I'll have to see about next time, if he whines or not, then I'll say something about it.

Gloria wrote on September 11th of her experiences with the group of women, discussing their childhoods:

I talked about my own negative childhood, since it is a subject on which I can expound at great length. I was surprised, almost, to find others who also had some bad negative experiences without permanent damage to themselves. We all survive.

The next day Gloria expresses her bitterness towards her stepson's mother.

September 12: Today I woke up early with the rain. I do love rainy days. My son and I watched cartoons while waiting for his natural mother to come get him. I could feel my heart beating faster just knowing she was coming. She said she would be here at 9, but of course didn't come until 11 A.M. My son had said he didn't want to go with her, so I told her he wanted to tell her something. She talked with him about 20 minutes until she had talked him into going, by bribing him with a visit to his favorite relatives. I told her she should consider letting me adopt him if he continues not wanting to go with her and she replied that she would never do that. So I told her that it would be selfish of her if she didn't, that she was doing it for herself only, and not for my son. She doesn't communicate with me very much ever since I told her off a couple of months ago, and told her she was a sorry excuse for a mother. She certainly doesn't understand what I am talking about, and that's the point. She's selfish and immature, and a liar to boot. I just can hardly stand to see him leave with that bitch.

Gloria's deep concern and commitment to the welfare of her patients comes through clearly in the diary:

September 13: My heart broke today. I was reading today's paper when I saw an obituary for a former hospital patient, who had been transferred here only a couple of weeks ago. She died Friday night. It hit me quickly, and I cried for a few minutes. She was a lovely lady, even living on a ventilator to breathe for her. Her smile was radiant and genuine, and I felt very close to her, as did several nurses who took care of her. Who knows if she was better off dead than on a machine, since she could not be weaned from it? I am certainly glad my life was touched by her. I did love her. I was down when I went to work today. Another nurse I worked with had gone to a funeral of the woman who had the cerebral hemorrhage a few days ago. She was already upset about that, and then I told her about Mary. Not a good day . . .

My son was brought home late again today. This time she (son's mother) told my husband in front of our son that he said he didn't want to come home, and he was standing there shaking his head that he did not say that. So now he knows she is a liar too.

It never occurs to Gloria, apparently, that she may be pressuring the boy to the point to where he may be afraid to admit to her that he really does want to be with his mother sometimes. The boy is caught in the tug of war between Gloria and his mother.

On September 15 Gloria expresses dismay at getting up late and having lost those few precious minutes of time in the morning with her stepson. She also speaks of a trip to the library where she met a lab technician she works with who is attending school to obtain her bachelor's degree in chemistry. She expresses her faith in education as a means for growth.

> September 19: I had a good time with my son this morning, sitting with him while he ate breakfast. I think he did, too. He is always so pleasant and cheerful when he gets up, it's almost fun to get up to see him.
>
> At work today I received a very favorable evaluation from my boss, the Director of Social Services. He also stated that he has not heard anything bad about me, and feels I have been well-accepted. He's proud of me, I think, and so am I. I do good work. Also, I will be getting a raise with this evaluation, starting next Monday. Still not as much as I am worth, but I'll take it for now, until I graduate.

That evening Gloria's husband and his best friend had a fight. At night, after lovemaking, Gloria cried:

> Thoughts of my father who died in May kept coming to me, and of my friend in Arkansas who hasn't written in six months and I feel has deserted me, and of my bad personality traits. Negative, negative thoughts hit me all at once, it seemed. But I kept them in. I didn't want T. (her husband) to know I was crying. He would get worried and I didn't know how to explain it to him. So I didn't. Poor T. I feel sorry for him at times, for what he doesn't know about what I think. Like I was feeling a lack of total love when I was crying. But it isn't his fault I feel that way. I want a perfect love, and there is no such thing. He is a good, wonderful man, and I love living with him. It is me I can't stand to put up with at times.

Here, characteristically, Gloria blames herself for any emotional problems and difficulties she may have. She had just had a day where she had an argument with her husband over intonations of voice. She had been concerned about his problems with his best friend. Her feelings about her husband's continued inadequacies are introjected upon herself.

Gloria writes of feeling tired on September 21. The previous day she had gone to an amusement park with her family, including her mother-in-law and her mother-in-law's fiance. She spoke kindly of her. Gloria is disappointed with her own performance in a class, saying she feels stupid. Of her husband she writes:

> Tom went to the chiropractor today, which he has been needing to do for a long time now. His back bothers him so much of the time that perhaps this will do him good. I know his body will bother him more and more as he gets older. I hope I can tolerate the pain with him.

On September 23 Gloria tells of efforts she had made to help her husband change:

> Tom and I had a good discussion today about ways to change behavior and attitudes, and again I gave my advice about how he could do some changing; make lists of priorities, do more things for himself, talk to people as if they were just plain people. He listened, but I don't know how much he will do. It does take time, I realize that since I had to have time when I did some changing, too. I am proud of him for the changes he has already made. He does care even if he lacks motivation right now.

Gloria writes on September 24th and 25th about the power struggle with her stepson's mother over the son. The mother had called and said she was coming to get her son for the weekend. Gloria said she felt she had won the son, since he said he did not really want to go with his mother, and that even if something happened to Tom, the boy's mother would not get him.

> I feel myself getting nervous about Sally's coming tomorrow to get Johnnie. . . . I just can hardly stand it.
>
> September 26: Boy, I was nervous when I got up today, waiting for the confrontation with Sally (Johnnie's mother). Then come to find out, she had called early in the morning and Johnnie had answered, but he neglected to tell us for 3 hours that it had been Sally saying she wasn't coming after all, since he didn't want to go and she was "sick." He finally told Tom that she wasn't coming. I almost got raving mad at him for not telling us sooner, but he didn't know. I'm glad he isn't going. This is certainly going to age me.
>
> September 27: Tom had another "attack" of anxiety tonight. I thought we were through with those, but I guess not. . . . I just don't know what to do. I get so tired dealing with these problems, but I have to realize that's being selfish. Still, I wish I didn't have to deal with things that I don't feel like dealing with. Doesn't everybody?

On September 28 Gloria once again tries to give Tom advice and serve as his counselor and mother:

We, Tom and I, went grocery shopping together today, which I thoroughly enjoy. I always want to go with him, because I enjoy being with him and because I don't want to be the only one picking out what foods to eat. I sure do love him, that man of mine. He proved again what a family man he is by choosing to not go to the Rolling Stones' concert to be home on Halloween night because he wants to go trick-or-treating with Johnnie and me. I told him he could go, but he said no.

We had a very long talk about his feelings/anxiety about jobs, death, life, goals, how to solve problems, church, heaven and hell. He listens to me, but doesn't always follow my advice. He then told me about an incident in his younger years, about 17 or 18, that he has wanted to tell me about for a long time, and just never has. He had told his psychologist, so decided to finally tell me. I guess he thought he would make me change my feelings for him by telling me, but it didn't. *(Gloria did not say what this event was.)*

Like many women who marry men who are not their intellectual equals, on October 5 Gloria muses about her own abilities and the lack of stimulating conversation with her husband:

I love to philosophize about some things in specific and lots of things in general. My husband doesn't like to, partly, I think, because he isn't good at it. His command of the English language is not that good. I really yearn for that kind of conversation at times, and get mad, silently, because Tom can't do that with me. And then I wonder if I would not have been better off to have married my high school sweetheart.

On October 6 Gloria wrote of her concern for the political problems in the Middle East. She and Tom had gone to the State Rehabilitation Commission to obtain help for Tom in finding a job or training for one:

Perhaps they can suggest a field that would be interesting to Tom, since he can no longer work on jet engines with his arm being weaker since he broke it in two places. But then again, maybe Tom will never go to school. That's a possibility, I suppose, and he doesn't really have to. I will always work in social work, and he can stay home if he wants to. He is a good home-maker, just doesn't like to cook.

In her diary on October 8 Gloria says she is mentally tired because she cannot change Tom and Johnnie. She cannot make Tom more motivated. He has not even taken his G.E.D. (high school equivalency) yet. She is disappointed that Johnnie shows so little learning ability. She feels like she is in the middle of a big circle she cannot control.

By October 10 the intensity of Gloria's dissatisfaction with her marriage seems to be increasing steadily. She continues in her pattern of denial and self-blame:

> Am feeling unhappy today about my marriage. I don't feel I need my husband, and sometimes wish I weren't married at all, to be free of dealing with unfulfilling relationships. I love him—he's very nice, and a considerate person. But my expectations for him are getting restless. I wish he were smarter, more mature, a reader, a thinker. He watches too much TV, and does not spend constructive time with Johnnie. He doesn't read him stories or go over his book on how to teach him to read. My husband is not motivated right now, and I hope I can hang on until he gets there.

The very next day Gloria blames herself for her unhappiness. She puts herself down for being too demanding and aggressive, and for wanting Johnnie to do what she wants, not letting him be free to relate to his mother as he may really want to.

Gloria's diary continues similarly throughout the next 2 months. There is a steady increase in her feeling enthusiastic and competent about her professional and academic work and a steady decrease in her good feelings about her marriage.

On October 13, Gloria has an argument with her husband about all the fatherly things he should be doing for his son but is not, such as, reading, getting him healthy snacks, and playing with him. She also mentions not wanting to make love with Tom.

The next day she writes enthusiastically about her work in the hospital room. She muses on October 15 about trying to talk with her husband about her unhappiness. On the other hand, she did well on an examination at school and feels good about that. The next day she was again feeling happy about her marriage, since her husband had gotten a permanent wave in his hair and had quit smoking. Gloria has a tendency to be depressed and then to deny it. For example, whenever she is not working constantly she feels tired and moody. There is increasing tension regarding Johnnie.

> October 26, she writes: I must not be in a good mood today. I sent Johnnie to bed for not remembering to keep his elbows off of the table after the fourth time he was told. He had almost finished his supper, but not quite. He looked so puzzled. I shouldn't do stupid things like that to him.

Gloria's home life became increasingly chaotic. Her husband's 33-year-old brother Eddie came to live with them. He is unable to take care of himself. He smokes a lot and just sits around the house watching TV and eating and sleeping. Gloria expressed anxiety about Johnnie's docility. Now he calmly does whatever he is told. They gave a wild party which was crashed by twelve strangers from a bar who tried to sell them cocaine and stayed until 4:00 A.M. Gloria felt alienated about the crashers but entertained them until they left! The party actually got kind of lewd, with one of her husband's friends flashing for the group because Tom promised him 5 cents. He was angry later because he thought he was offered $5.00.

The first direct admission that Gloria may be physically abusing her stepson, Johnnie, came in the diary entry of November 2:

> I went to the library this morning after taking Johnnie to pre-school. I hit him for saying "I don't know" to something I knew he knew. Why do I fly off the handle like that? Sometimes I think I am mentally ill, which I may very well be.

Apparently this way of reacting to Johnnie was typical of Gloria, or else she wouldn't have treated it as something she regularly does. If this is the case, it is no wonder that Johnnie is docile and passively agreeable.

Gloria's acute enthusiasm for her work overflows from school. She says in her diary of the next day that she is anxious for a break so that she may read nursing journals outside of those assigned for class. The same day she is once again concerned with the way her hair looks. This concern is a regular entry in her diary. She is also upset about having gained 2 pounds and asks herself if she is being pulled in too many directions.

On November 4 Gloria expresses regret that she cannot do anything monumental to change the life of Eddie. At the same time she praises him for loving Johnnie and laughing at TV with him. She expresses her dismay at her overall situation.

> There are days I feel so much like a loner. I feel I must make decisions by myself and do a lot things by myself, like pay bills. I have formed habits that I probably decided to get into, without being forced into them. But I am not always so quick to point this out to myself. Someday, I have said for so long, I will talk to a counselor or someone who can possibly help me think things out.

Gloria says her day on November 6 was pretty good because the people at work complemented her on her hair. Her ambivalence about her husband shows up in her commentary for she complains of the $16.00 per week chiropractor bills for her husband and yet says she is glad his back is better. She approached her husband about her feelings of being alone, distancing herself from him, and this results in their sex life getting worse. She blames herself for this, because he listened to her. She said he deserves a better woman than she is.

Gloria felt worthless due to lack of motivation on November 9. She came home early from class and was upset that Johnnie's mother had called and said she would pick him up for the weekend and Johnnie had said he would go with her. Gloria was to be off from work and had anticipated having time with Johnnie herself:

> I am very upset. My adrenaline is pumping away—my mood has swung to a shitty one. I want to get at her so badly I can't stand it. I'm using poor Johnnie to do it, telling him what a rotten person she is and how it makes us very sad when he does go away with her. I'm also fed up with Tom and the goddamned TV, Eddie and those nasty cigarettes of his, and Johnnie and his learning problems and me and my selfishness. I want everything the way I want it—Tom to work part time and start reading, Eddie to stop laying around like an old man, eating and smoking himself to death, Johnnie to start thinking (which he can't), and Sally to go fuck off. We will be out of town by the end of summer, and out of the state. Unless I get to adopt him first which will never be, I bet.

Apparently, Gloria had taken her negative feelings out on Johnnie that day, for the next day she states:

> November 10: I got up and took Johnnie to preschool today. He kissed my hand as I was sitting on his bed after I had awakened him, because I didn't kiss him as I usually do. God, he loves me after all I did to him yesterday. I was mean to him. I'm gonna pay for this later on.

Gloria's increasing distress about these things takes its toll. She is starting to loose her confidence in herself as a student, and castigates herself for waiting until the last minute to begin assignments. That same day she gives another, still rather incomplete and indirect, indication of her physical abuse of Johnnie:

> Tom called while I was at work, which was very busy, and said he was upset about the bump below Johnnie's left eye I made when I slapped him last night. Johnnie told him I had done that when Tom asked him where he got the little red mark on his cheek. My adrenaline started flowing because Tom didn't ever like me to slap Johnnie in the face, and I am having a hard time breaking myself of this. I have got to stop it, now.
>
> November 11: Today I just knew Tom would be mad at me for the bruise on Johnnie's face again, but he wasn't. I lay in bed waiting for him to come back and jump on to me about it. My stress level sure is up.

Her husband got a part time job as a delivery boy which started today. She asked her brother in law why he did not do anything but sit around and watch TV. He told her he likes it.

That same day she writes enthusiastically about her job and a session with some of the new social workers about worthwhile community projects. She seemed pleased about this work.

On November 14 Gloria reminiscences about her high school boyfriend, who is now in Law school:

> I heard "Hey Jude," a Beatles song on the radio today, and thought of my first boyfriend, Jim. That song was out when we were dating back in high school. And today is also his birthday. I think of him sometimes, and wonder what I would be doing if I had married him, since I had two chances to do it. He married a day before I did back in 1977, but mine only lasted 5 months. He got divorced, though, about 1 ½ years ago, which I never thought he'd do. When he married, he wanted it to last. Don't know what happened to it. Now he's in law school, being the brain that he has always been. I need and want to call him someday. Perhaps soon.

Some of the pressure she has been putting Johnnie under about visits to his mother is brought up by Tom:

> Tom said he and Johnnie talked a long time yesterday about Johnnie's mother. Johnnie has a good time when he goes down to visit with her, after he gets there, but he'd rather stay here with us. Poor confused little boy.

The next 30 days of Gloria's diary shows little development. Rather than confront her difficulties, she decides to escape instead. She joined the army. The motivation for this came after a discussion with a lawyer where she inquired if she could prevent Johnnie's mother from seeing him. When he said the only thing she could do to prevent it was to move away, she immediately made plans to do this. At the end of her diary Gloria was still living in the midst of the ghosts of the past, unhappy in her marriage to an intellectually and physically inferior man, and abusing her stepson. She hoped that the army would send them to Germany.

Postscript: When I wrote to Gloria, asking her permission to use her narratives as I have in the case construct, Gloria had been divorced and remarried. She offered little information about her current circumstances.

Greta—A Battering Mom

Greta is a black, divorced mother of an 11-year-old girl. At the time she wrote her autobiography and diary, she was a student in a medical assistant training program and working as a resident staff assistant in a hospital. Her daughter lived with Greta's mother in a near-by city. Greta visited them on weekends.

Greta was always extremely tired and expressed anxiety in the group about her ability to stay in the training program with the problems she was having with her daughter and mother.

She could not remember anything about her preschool days. She had a twin sister, of whom she spoke very little.

Greta's first childhood memory is of first grade. She cried the first day because she missed her mother. A sensitive first grade teacher gave her small responsibilities, such as holding on the drinking fountain for the other children, which made her feel needed. Other such chores assigned by the teacher throughout the year increased her sense of being wanted and of caring for others' needs. She had maintained the spirit of this teacher in herself:

> Now that I am twenty-seven, I know when things get shaky, I will make it. When I see friends upset, I try and make them feel comfortable and wanted.

Greta's next vivid memory was of her older half brother, Ned, who used to pick her sister and her up and take them out. She expressed loss of respect for him since he had not saved money for her college as he had promised.

Entrance into her teenage years threw Greta into a state of turmoil. Her parents were constantly bickering, but trying to hide it from the children: "The air was so thick you could cut it with a knife." Greta's mother would frequently say, however: "We never want to argue in front of you, drink or smoke"

Such double messages, which Bateson (1958) found to lead to schizophrenia (see also Bowen, 1960) characterized Greta's home environment. Greta's mother kept her from all social activities with other teenagers, telling her that she would get into trouble if she associated with boys. Then suddenly, on her fourteenth birthday, her mother asked her when she wanted to start "taking company." When Greta did not respond her mother became angry with her. Greta felt that her mother was then taking a contradictory attitude by forcing boys down her throat.

By age 15 $\frac{1}{2}$, Greta became interested in boys herself. At this time, her parents seemed to again reverse themselves, forbidding her to go out on dates. Her father would violently expound upon how he would revenge himself on any young man who took advantage of his daughter. Greta vividly describes her feelings the day she was not allowed to go to an amusement park with her friends:

Howard was wanting to take me to the State Fair. I wanted to go desperately. My brother had gone once before. He described the rides and how pretty it was. I went to my room and closed my door. Layed on the bed and thought how I wanted to leave the house. Tears began to roll down onto my pillow. Laying there wondering why are they so protective of me? All I want is to live life as peaceful as everyone else. Getting to know my friends, going camping with the girls at school, go to a few parties and learn how to dance. Dancing was not allowed in our house and only spiritual music could be listened to.

Also about this time Greta's mother was in a an automobile accident. During and after her mother's 3-month stay in the hospital, Greta took over all household chores. Upon her mother's return from the hospital she also took care of her. Finally, Greta devised a way to get out of the house. She lied about where she was going, saying she was going shopping, and really went to the movies, or shopping, etc. She describes her first sense of relief when she got home and her lie was not discovered:

I did buy a purse so that I would have something to show. The sun was down when I made it home. I was feeling pressure and fear. When I walked in the kitchen door, I was ready for the screaming, but everything was OK. How relieved I felt.

About that time she fell in love with her cousin. She began seeing him regularly. At age 16 she became pregnant. Later they married. The marriage was not a happy one, because her husband was neither committed nor responsible.

Greta was determined at this time to improve her lot in life. She entered a community college and completed her Freshman year. By the third week into her sophomore year her husband demanded that she quit school, which she did. Indications of abuse or neglect of her daughter were mentioned at this time:

My daughter was beginning to have crying spells and pull out her hair. Asking for mama. I could see the bald spots in her head. We finally left his mother's and fathers' home.

The tensions she experienced at the time were due in part to their living with her husband's parents. Even after moving into their own home, their problems continued. Her husband dated other women while pretending to take the daughter on outings. At the time of the divorce, her husband's mother tried to obtain custody. This woman treated Greta badly and made her feel worthless. This experience remains as a ghost in Greta's life even at the present time:

This has affected my way of thinking about people. I am more aware of
them, and I find it hard to be very close to anyone. I want to be but, I always
feel myself drawing back.

Six years after her divorce, Greta met a man to whom she later became engaged. She is hopeful that they will be able to work out their
relationship.

Greta did not write about the physical abuse she experienced from
her mother. However she spoke about it in the group. In fact, when she
went home on weekends, if she did not maintain a curfew, her mother
would beat her. The only thing that had changed in the situation was
that sometimes now she would hit her mother back. At the same time,
Greta expressed love for her mother, because her mother took care of
and supported her daughter, especially since she did not get any child
support from her former husband.

The continued effect of these negative experiences was evident in
Greta's preformance on the job and academically. She was continually
feeling "put upon" by her supervisor and was very angry and upset a
lot of the time about the hassles between students in the program. She
was worried about her daughter, who continued to lose her hair. As a
result, Greta's grades and health suffered. She always seemed to have
a cold or flu when she came to group sessions, and did not complete
her time studies or diaries. About midway through the term she
dropped out of her training program. Her mother said she could no
longer pay for her granddaughter's care and that Greta should let her
former husband's parents adopt the child. Greta would not hear of this
and instead dropped out of school to work to support her daughter.
Shortly after this Greta discontinued attending the support group as
well.

In the case of Greta, one could not really say she was haunted by
ghosts from her childhood. Rather, the problems of poverty, conflict,
and abuse continued in her life into her third decade. Tragically, the
pattern was already profoundly effecting her daughter's life.

Postscript: Greta was about to enter college again at the time this text
was completed. Her daughter was about to graduate from high school
and also planned to enter college.

Conclusions

Rebecca, Gloria, and Greta are haunted by the ghosts of battering
parents and parents who filled their minds with negative attributions
about themselves. At the same time, a lot was expected of them. Each

was expected to take care of their parents emotional needs. Rebecca also took care of physical needs of her parents, cooking and cleaning. Each was also expected to perform well at school, attend church, and present a good appearance.

The ghost of the battering parent had carved a divided self within the women. With one part of themselves they were aware of the pain of abuse and rejected it. But the other side identified with it—it is a part of their being which they unconsciously felt must be there in order for them to exist. Gloria and Greta admitted to continuing the cycle of abuse. Rebecca has had a difficult time accepting weaknesses in others including her husband.

Gloria possessed what Miller calls "narcissistic pride" and the "vicious cycle of contempt" and illustrates the way these tie in with child abuse. These are likely to occur when a child does not receive adequate empathy. Rather, the child is pushed to meet the narcissistic demands of parents who are contemptuous of failure to meet their high standards. Gloria was driven to achieve both professionally and scholastically. Yet she felt self-contempt if things did not go well. Her competitive attitude in regard to her stepson's natural mother, and her unrealistic expectations for him, given his limitations, were both frustrating to her pride and threatening to her self-esteem. The little boy's expressions of love for his natural mother were interpreted by Gloria in an immature manner as taking away from love that was her due. She lashed out at him emotionally and physically.

Greta's experience clearly illustrates the extent to which a low-resource context and a continued cycle of abuse can tragically engulf a family. Greta's family suffered from the overall effect of being working-class blacks. Greta became pregnant and married a young man who was not yet able to provide adequate financial or emotional support for a family of his own. Greta's mother was both loving and physically abusive, alternately severly restrictive and encouraging of Greta's sexual involvements. Here an overly rigid church structure came into direct conflict with overall societal pressures toward sexual expression. The continued pattern of physical "acting out," "hypochondria," and "paranoia" took a heavy toll on Greta's ability to function as a resident aide, student, and mother. She again became a college drop out. Her high degree of perseverance demonstrated in the attempt to re-enter college years later illustrates the unfathomability of the human spirit. There was nothing in her background or environment which could explain her strength against the odds she faced.

Rebecca, Gloria, and Greta were all negatively affected by religious institutions. For Rebecca, an overly rigid and righteous church filled her early years with guilt. After her marriage to a recently widowed church member, the church members ostracized her. Gloria was disillusioned by the hypocrisy of her parents' religiosity. Greta experienced the conflicting expectations of a strict church, her mother who was alternatively strict and encouraging of her sexual acting out, and peer pressures. Table 5.1 summarizes the parenting practices in these three case constructs as presented by the women in their narratives and discussions.[1]

The battering parents in this study illustrated all of the elements of "immaturity" in their relationships with their children. Parents who physically abuse their children also emotionally abuse and neglect them. The parents expected and received nurturance from their daughters. This is "reversal parenting" that is prevalent among physically abusive parents. The parent is inevitably disappointed by the child who cannot fulfill the parents' needs for nurturance.

Rebecca's bond to her mother was ruptured by the mother's insensi-

Table 5.1. Summary of Parenting Practices Experienced by Rebecca, Gloria, and Greta[a]

	Rebecca	Gloria	Greta
Primary bond	Fractured	Fractured	Fractured
Mirroring	Inadequate	Inadequate	Inadequate
Style of parenting	Double image	Projective	Projective
Communicative stance	Blaming	Blaming	Blaming
Defenses	Psyc/immature	Immature	Psyc/ immature
Attributions	Negative	Negative	Negative
Expectations	Positive	Positive	Mixed
Temporality	Stressful	Stressful	Stressful
Dramatic form	Tragic	Tragic	Tragic
Moral development	Surv/good	Surv/good	Surv/good
Ethical level	Resent/indul	Resent/ indul	Resent/indul
Child's self-integration	Divided	Divided	Divided

[a]For an explication of the terms in this diagram see Chapter 4, pp. 81–97. The terms in this chart are abbreviated as necessary to fit the space. For example, "resent/indul" refers to resentment and indulgence as the ethical level of these parents as described by their daughters. Psyc = psychotic and surv = survival.

[1]It must be kept in mind that the parents of the women may see the matter quite differently. No claims are made throughout this work that any of the parents of the women in the study actually acted as described. This study is about parent practices as they are seen by the adult children.

tivity when she allowed her husband to physically abuse Rebecca. The mothers of Gloria and Greta physically and verbally abused their daughters. Therefore their bonds to them were contradictory and hence "fractured." The caretakers of these girls did not empathically mirror their children's emotions, but imposed their own. The style of parenting was double image in the case of Rebecca. Her mother projected negative qualities on her because she was her natural father's favorite. She also used "reversal" parenting in that she expected Rebecca to take care of her needs. Both Gloria and Greta received projections from their parents who did not empathically relate to them.

The parent–child communication was characterized by blaming, indicating that the parents did not take responsiblity for their own emotions. Rather they expected their daughters to fill their empty emotional "pots." These parents projected negative or confused attributions and expectations on their daughters. As individuals, they used immature defense mechanisms, from psychotic denial of what was going on (in the case of Rebecca's mother) to dissociation, to acting out. Each experienced time as stressful rather than meaningful. There was little joy in shared family activities. A tragic form of sociodrama took place in these homes, with the girls as the victims. The heroine in each tragedy is the adult woman as she struggles to face and then exorcize these ghosts from her childhood.

The moral and ethical levels exhibited by their parents was survival to goodness. Rebecca's mother's choice of an abusive second husband and her tolerance of his abusiveness to her daugher indicates that she must have had survival needs invested in him. A "goodness" kind of morality pervades all three homes, as the parents strive to be thought acceptable in the eyes of their churches and others in the community. The parents in these homes had not achieved self-control, artistry, or love which Weinstein sees as essential to being ethical. Rather, they harbored resentments and acted out in self-indulgent fashion as they either abused their daughters themselves (Gloria and Greta) or tolerated the spouse's abuse of the daughter (Rebecca). The pervasive immaturity in these parenting patterns led to an intensely divided self in all three women.

Ghosts of Sexually Abusive
Fathers—Janet and Delores _____ 6

Introduction

This chapter is about two occupationally successful women who, as children, had difficult relationships with their fathers. While neither one may have actually been a full incest victim herself, both had fathers who had incestuous involvements with other daughters. Because of the strong social reactions against incest, both of them may have had full incestuous experiences themselves which they did not totally reveal in this context. Janet and Delores both also were haunted by the ghosts of the sexual abuse they experienced. As Justice and Justice (1979:184) indicate, frequently women who experience incest have difficulties in relationships with men in later life.

"Delores" expressed concern and dismay about her father's direct attempts at sexual involvements with her, however she insisted that she was able to consistently ward them off. Her sisters were not able to resist. When she was just entering high school, her parents separated due to her father's incestuous relationships with her sisters. In addition to the struggle with this family problem, as a child she had to deal with the extreme poverty of Los Angeles' Hispanic ghetto, and as a teenager she dealt with a traumatic move to Mexico. Today, she is a successful medical technologist and student. Her diary expresses distress with her marital relationship.

Socioeconomically "Janet" was brought up in a well-to-do family. Her father is a surgeon and her mother a former debutante. Her mother is also the adult child of an alcoholic mother. Her mother was habituated to the caretaker role and conformed to the pattern of protecting her emotionally disturbed husband who physically and sexually abused her three children. The ghosts of this neglectful mother and immature father still haunt Janet. Fear of the anger within herself has kept her from wanting to have children. The ghosts of her father, intensified by her experiences with her former husband, led her to prefer the company of women in close relationships. She is still extremely angry about both the physical and sexual abuses she suffered. A victim of the vicious cycle of contempt, Janet perpetuates this cycle in her relationships with her clients as a Child Protective Service Worker.

Delores—The Ghost of a Seductive Father

Delores was the youngest of four sisters. As a child, she grew up in extreme poverty, living in a high-rise tenement building in Los Angeles. She vividly remembers the cockroaches climbing the walls in the small, one and a half bedroom apartment. She and her four sisters slept in a small alcove off the living room, behind a make-shift curtain made from a blanket brought from Mexico. A kindly woman came early in the morning to stay with her, since her mother had to go to work. Overtly sweet, this lady was orderly, but cunning; she manipulated Delores to care for her comforts. Delores was forced to be a good example for her older sisters, who resented her for being "Miss Goody-Two Shoes." Her memories of living in the Los Angeles Hispanic ghetto when she was in first grade are vivid:

> My eyes open to a crowded one and a half bedroom apartment with shades somewhat bent and sun rays pouring in and reflecting on the sheets. I would then go to a brighter kitchen that was crowded with a table and appliances everywhere and rats and roaches roamed in the night.
>
> Smell milk boiling over and burning on the stove and deodorant aerosol and perfume coming from the bathroom. The room is muggy and damp but the kitchen begins to smell as boiled eggs are peeled and made ready to be eaten. Stairs smell as someone forgot to go to a bathroom and instead urinated there. Garbage accumulation outside in the alley decomposes and reaches the top floors with its nasty smell. Cold, sticky bannisters, tried not to handle them, and then dirty door handles you had to push to get out. Smells fresh outside until you get to the main avenue where fumes started accumulating since early this morning.
>
> The streets would be vacant in the morning but crowded by the time I got to go home. Throughout my walk many buildings were passed that were high and touching one another in which you could climb without any difficulty. All was made out of bricks and very few trees and grass. People would sit around in the corners and on the stairs with some fashionably dressed and others in worn out jeans, sneakers and caps. Many young ladies wore a dark red lipstick, tight skirts and very high heels shaking as much as they could and chewing gum and smiling. Bored with the day I would go to sleep early to return to my dream world which I considered very realistic.

Fantasy provided a welcome relief from the slum environment. This dream world included a fantasized significant other. She was her "Fair Ballerina," who danced in her music box. Fair Ballerina was dressed in pink, with her hair neatly tied up in a bun. As the music played she danced perfectly without error. Fair Ballerina was perfect in every respect. If Delores did not turn out that way she would only have herself to blame, she thought.

Even the pressures of the ghetto environment should not inhibit her success. Unlike most children of this age, Delores had strong images of death. The dangers of the city environment had a profound effect on her in this way:

> I thought about death every time I was alone or away from most of the people. Saw myself being taken by a thief, assaulted and then let to die without anyone ever finding me. Most of all I didn't want life to end because there were too many things to do and mostly because I wouldn't be next to my loved ones. I feared most of all seeing myself in the coffin, viewing my family and unable to get out and touch and talk to them.

Subtly, she felt that her baby sitter, and her parents, wanted her to meet their needs. Delores was clearly in a situation of reversal parenting and received inadequate parental mirroring. She expressed the feeling that she was not allowed to be herself, or to express her concerns in her own way. Later when she writes of her desire to have her own child, she says she "needs" this child to fulfill her desire for being loved and appreciated. Thus she unwittingly repeats this cycle. The use of a child to meet one's own needs was carried to the brink of incest by her father:

> When I was seven, in the first grade, my father used to go to work later than my mom. I used to go to bed with him so I wouldn't be alone. One day to my amazement, he did a sexual pass which at that moment made me think is this normal or his way of showing his love? Deep down I knew something was wrong and resisted and made the excuse that I had to get ready for school. During the whole day I didn't think of anything else and stated to myself he would not do that again.

The way in which a girl's father becomes a model for all men is made clear in Delores' response:

> At that time I though all men were like that and couldn't trust them anymore, especially alone. I thought he expected me to fulfill his desires at that moment but I knew that wasn't what I wanted to do and rejected him being close from that moment on, and also decreased the confidence I had toward others, especially strangers now that I couldn't even trust my parent.

Constant quarrels between her parents created a tense atmosphere in the home. However, in spite of this, Delores felt that her parents loved her.

It became apparent to Delores during her school years that she lived in a male-dominated world. At church she learned to be "dainty," avoiding involvement in rough games. She learned that if she did not follow these rules about being a "good" girl she would be sent to hell by "God, another man."

She was a good student, and had one male teacher in school who expected her to achieve, "even though" she was a girl. He was the only man she trusted as a child although she avoided being alone with him. At the age of 13, she did poorly in school, because she daydreamed about a teacher she had a crush on. Her father punished her for the bad grades by making her stay in the house and iron or clean:

> Another means my father used this punishment for was to get close to me but I would always put him on the spot and keep away.

Unlike most young girls in this position, Delores had the strength to keep her father at arms' length, if her diary and autobiography are truthful. She never mentions having told her mother about her father's conduct, however. Her sisters were not so fortunate. When she was 15 her mother divorced her father, having found out about his incestous relationship with Delores' sisters. Her mother took her children back to Mexico for a year. Even then Delores expressed love for her father:

> I realized I loved both my parents but something was wrong with my father and it was best for us to separate and find ourselves again and maybe he could too.

Entering high school at that time in a strange country was viewed by Delores as a challenge. As we saw in the case of Rebecca, such determination to prove oneself without needed assistance often leads to a sense of resentment:

> I was willing to make the best of it to succeed and prove we didn't need a man around to do just that.

Returning to Los Angeles at the age of 16, Delores entered college. She had skipped two grades early in school because of her ability to learn rapidly. She fell in love with a young man in the ROTC. and became totally emotionally dependent upon him, only to become disillusioned with how badly he treated her. Was she unconsciously repeating her relationship with her father in this first serious love affair? His over-all attitude to her was cold and unappreciative, viewing her as an object to be at his beck and call:

> I tried to be sincere with him, as my most intimate companion. In return I would get lies and hurt. It made me see how vulnerable I let myself get and to learn again not to trust men.

The college itself was male-dominated. Deciding to prove that she could compete with men at their level, Delores joined the Army ROTC. She distinguished herself in this effort, but was sharply criticized for it by her fellow students, both male and female. She strove to become strong and capable, so as not to be vulnerable to others. Delores, as is frequently the case with young girls who are victims of incest, or of incest attempts, felt a pervasive insecurity and vulnerability for which she tried to compensate.

With the help of the ROTC, Delores completed college with a degree in medical technology. For a while, she worked in the medical field, but did not feel up to the challenge. She then entered the Air Force as a way of gaining greater experience.

Meanwhile Delores had met and married her husband. At the time she married, she viewed the past as one where men had taken advan-tage of her, and now she was ready to distrust and take advantage of them. Her musings about this illustrate a "survival" level of ethics and a spirit of revenge:

> The past had been an experimental process of hurt and despair but now I was going to use every situation to my own advantage. I would often recall circumstances when I would be challenged or put down by the opposite sex.

In her marriage Delores was willing to sacrifice personal liberties in order to have a companion. She was not happy about her husband's expectation that she would take care of all the household tasks, shop-ping, and cooking in addition to working full time. Of this Delores wrote:

> I would not accept his negative behavior in not taking his share of the housework and meeting my needs for recreation also.

She felt that if she did not fight with him about these issues immedi-ately she would have to accept them indefinitely. These issues remained unresolved, however.

After 3 years in the air force she decided to return to the university. In order to do so, she had to be temporarily separated from her husband. He encouraged her to go ahead. She took a job near campus to pay her expenses. Learning to trust a man was not easy:

> I experienced insecurity but as time passed I accepted it could be possible to trust another individual (even a man). . . . I wasn't getting more socially involved because I was married and not because I had school work to be done. I wanted to succeed but this time at my pace and fulfilling my needs as they came along.

Their marriage stayed intact in spite of the separation. At age 26 she insisted, above her husband's objections, on having a baby. She perceived the baby as meeting her needs. (This is what de Mause calls "reversal parenting." The child is viewed as a means of meeting the parent's needs, instead of vice versa.) As Delores said:

> My husband was partially right, it was not the best time to have a child, but he didn't understand that I needed someone now to be close to and even maybe to give me an excuse to take a break from school.

Her husband made it clear that she would have to carry the primary burden of caring for the child. Delores went ahead anyway, giving birth to a daughter. After the child's birth, Delores felt a sense of despair and bitterness.

> I've thought about my death very often especially after our child was born and when different ailments come to my body. I see myself dying alone somewhere and no one finding or coming to see me. It scared me because so many things were yet to be done, but most of all of how little I felt I had been appreciated in my lifetime.

In her mothering practices, she once again expressed the "reversal" reaction to her baby. She writes of how her caring for this baby taught her discipline and to control her outbursts of rage:

> Our baby has made me realize not to demand extensively with rage or outbursts because all it will result in is disapproval from others, discontent and fear to express one's true feelings.

It is clear here that as Delores is taught to understand and control rage by her infant, instead of the other way around that she is experiencing reversal parenting. Apparently her husband's warnings about the tremendous demands of caring for an infant came true. When the baby was 6 months old, Delores took her to stay with her parents for a semester while she attended school.

After that semester, Dolores took her daughter back home. She made the point that parenthood had to be learned and that her husband needed to help her. The following week, her husband gave her a surprise birthday party, which greatly pleased her. In spite of this, Delores' diary reflects that they were having continued marital troubles, since they frequently discussed possible separation.

In her discussions with the other women in the research project, Delores learned to view her husband and his friends as "traditional" men. This domineering type of role is expected of "Latin" men. Her husband took an interest in the research and her discussions in this group. When she related to him her insights concerning "Latin" men he vehemently denied that he fit that stereotype. Remarkably, for the first time since they were married, he stated that he was going to prepare breakfast and lunch that day without being asked!

On the other hand, it was not until their daughter was over a year old that her husband had assumed sole responsibility for his baby's care for one 24 hour day. Delores had to work a night shift. He expressed dismay at how little he was able to accomplish since the baby's care took so much time.

In the next few weeks, Delores' husband did the laundry and helped her regularly with household chores. Even these acts were interpreted by her in a suspicious manner: "I thought he may have done it out of fear of losing me."

A visit from her sister, who still lived in Los Angeles, filled her with anxiety. She was afraid her sister would be critical of the way she was caring for her daughter. Delores felt the need to discuss with her sister the incest situation that had occurred in their home when they were children. At that time, her sister was in the process of trying to adopt a child. She spoke of all of the children from troubled homes who were not being adopted. Delores was upset that her sister said she would not consider adopting a child who was the result of an incest situation. Delores could not confront her sister with the possibility that her sister could have borne a child from her father who would likewise never have been adopted.

Delores felt that her inability to express what she really felt with her sister was reflected in her inability to express herself with her husband. On Valentine's day her husband spoke with her about separation:

> He said it was not the right time for us to separate and I said when would it be for him. I said I was tired of giving and getting nothing in return,

and it was high time he gave. I wasn't going to give anymore unless he demonstrated sincere giving and sharing.

Although Delores' diary provides little detail, one wonders whether she was not expecting too much from him. She seems to have a general feeling of resentment, and does not feel appreciated even when her husband displays caring. Perhaps it is just such a resentful attitude that is one of the legacies of her mistrustful relationship with her father.

Delores reflected upon how little time her parents had spent to care for her, and how much she hoped that she would not make the same mistake with her child. Meanwhile the conflicts with her husband intensified. One day he stated that he wished that she would behave in a more feminine fashion, namely, speaking more softly and being more accepting. She felt that to do this she would then be taken for granted and ignored. She went to bed in an unhappy mood. The next day she stayed in bed all day with a stomach ache. Even then she felt she had cause to resent her husband, because he did not take care for her as she does for him when he was sick.

On their anniversary she gave him a card. When he did not give her one in return she felt cheated and taken for granted. She wanted to hurt him back so she told him that she did not mean what she said on the card.

When she attempted to tape some of their conversations at home for the research she said he sounded fake and untruthful.

Delores' thoughts about the future are tinged with the same mood of fear and distrust which she expressed as a child:

> I see the world of constant violent crime, inability to sleep due to fear of being hurt or robbed of your essentials.

Delores' case study illustrates the interaction between a low-resource context - a ghetto neighborhood, a sexist family and cultural milieu, and personal difficulties.

Both of her parents were so preoccupied with meeting the immediate physical needs of the family that they had not the luxury to be concerned with their children's maturational needs. Instead, they felt it their right to expect the children to care for them. Delores had her baby to meet her need for release from academic pressures and to fulfill her emotional needs. However, when she realized that her infant daughter demanded that her needs be met, Delores went into a rage and sent the daughter to her parents for a semester. The result of this is the continuation of the pattern.

Delores is making a courageous attempt to break away from the pattern of the past through education and is trying to establish an egalitarian marriage. She still feels despair and resentment, as images of death are still reflected in her diary. Her relationships with her husband and sister lack intimacy.

Janet's Anger

Janet Brown, now 35, was brought up in a strict, fundamentalist family, the youngest of three children. Her father, Dr. Joe Brown, a neurosurgeon, came from a poor family. Her mother, Sarah, a former debutante, met Joe in college and was attracted to his independence, masterly personality, and intelligence, qualities which the artistic, sensitive woman found lacking in herself. When Joe returned from a stint in the navy she used her inherited "allowance" to put him through medical school.

While the family was comfortable materially, Janet recalls being frightened and lonely as a child. Janet's mother made sure that the whole household centered on the father's career needs and everyday life comforts. When Janet and her older brother and sister were preschool to school age, their father's roles in the family, when at home, were drill sergeant, preacher, judge, and jailer. Dr. Brown grilled the children about their grades, and their achievements in music and athletics. When they failed to meet his standards he punished them with extra chores like cleaning the dog kennels, no television, or enforced study halls or practice sessions. As "preacher," Dr. Brown read to them at the dinner table from the Bible or religious tracts. He punished them severely for the slightest infraction of his rules. They were told to strip below the waist in an upstairs bedroom and wait, in the locked room for an hour or longer until he came up and whipped them mercilessly with a belt. As his anger intensified, they would be beaten with the buckle as well. The punishment was humiliating because they were all punished together. Janet writes about this in her autobiography:

> I remember coming home from school in first grade and riding a bus. I used to think all the way home—I wonder whether Daddy will notice that I have not cleaned the dog kennel. Will we all get whipped again tonight? On the bus, a boy, Charlie (a friend of my big sister Alice) would tease me— "There's that fat cheeked Janet" in a nasty tone of voice. His voice was so sure and deep and he was tall and good looking. I knew he was right. I was very ugly. All the other kids laughed when he said that. I thought then that my father was also right for all the punishment.

That night we were lucky, my grandma was visiting. She was my mother's mother, the rich one. Even though she was always drinking and saying silly things, I would relax the minute I saw her big white car parked in the driveway. Daddy would be sure to leave us alone. After all, it was "Nema's" (my name for my grandmother) money that put him through school and made the down payment on our big house. . . .

Some days we were not so lucky. The worst was when Mom would be gone—to a meeting or something. He'd always find something to punish us for. One day my brother, Rick, was really in trouble. He had left some model he was working on on top of the coffee table. The glue was not dry. It dripped and stained the finish. Dad had had his usual two or three martinis after work and was already upset that Mom was not home. . . .

He yelled. He called me lazy and rotten and my sister a "filthy slut." My brother was a "worthless s.o.b." *(not abbreviated)*. He destroyed my brother's model airplane kits and threw down the television and smashed it on the floor. Then he ordered us all to go to the third floor bedroom and strip. We knew we could not even have our underwear on when he got up there or it would be worse. We waited in the dark room, all huddled together as usual. He came up and beat us with his belt, telling us we were all "worthless vermin in the sight of God." Rick got it the worst. He had welts all over his back and still has some scars. That night he vowed to run away as soon as he got the chance.

When each of the children reached sexual maturity they were punished alone. At this point the punishment included forced sexual intimacies. Janet's mother dealt with all of this by denial and disassociation (immature defense mechanisms). She had always served as the caretaker for her alcoholic mother and emotionally cold father. Her disassociation took the form of frenetic activities, many of them socially valued. She was president of the P.T.A., active in the Junior League charity functions, on the symphony league, and a church elder. Ironically, the topics of child neglect, abuse and sexual abuse were periodically addressed by these organizations, possibly at the very time when she was neglecting her children and her husband was physically and sexually abusing them. When not busy with these activities she was at aerobics or oil painting classes. Janet's mother also suffered from anxiety for which Dr. Brown prescribed Valium.

When Janet's old sister, Carry, (5 years her senior) went away to college, the situation worsened. Following the loss of her first serious boyfriend, Janet's sister attempted suicide and was hospitalized for psychiatric care. An astute social worker uncovered the truth. Carry could not maintain a normal sexual relationship because it reminded her of her father's incestuous and sadistic treatment. The hospital called Janet's mother, forcing her, for the first time, to face up to what she really suspected and could have known about for some time. Her brother, already in the navy, called his mother after hearing from Carry and told her of the father's sexual as well as physical abuse of him. Mrs. Brown and Janet entered psychotherapy. At the time Janet was 15. She began sleeping with a baseball bat next to her bed:

> When I was fifteen my sister told my mother about Dad's involvement with her. This was when she was at college and was in the hospital following a suicide attempt. I felt so badly for my sister. But I knew what she was going through. Shortly after she left for college (and I was entering the 9th grade) my father kept inviting me to his photography lab at the back of the house. He said he wanted my help. At first I was pleased, thinking he was finally starting to respect me. The first few times he just showed me how to develop pictures. One day he said he had some "special" pictures to show me. He said I was becoming a woman and needed to know the "facts of life." The pictures were of naked women and men. Then he exposed himself to me, explaining that this was the best way for me to come to know about men. After that evening I dreaded his telling me to come to the dark room. He would announce his plans at the dinner table to my mother and I right after he said grace! . . He would say "Jan won't be helping with dishes tonight—I need her in the dark room." I would protest that I had homework. He said he would help me with it later. These visits had progressed from fondling to his forcing me to have oral sex with him. He would always threaten to beat me if I told mother or anyone. He also made me feel guilty and ashamed.

Following her sister's suicide attempt Janet told her mother about these episodes:

> At first my mother did not believe me. She got angry with me and my sister for lying about Dad! Only after my therapist sat down with her did the pain he caused me become real. Meanwhile I began to do things which still frighten me. I began taking my frustrations out on my dogs! I feel guilty about that until this day. I won't have pets or children because of this.

Six months later Mrs. Brown filed for divorce.

After graduating from high school, Janet worked as a salesclerk in a department store and studied at night to become a commercial artist and photographer, turning down her grandmother's offer to send her to college in the east. Two years later she became the assistant manager of a beauty saloon and began working toward a degree in social work. She hoped to work with perpetrators of child incest and abuse. Janet finished her social work degree 6 years later and did begin working in a child protective services agency. Shortly after this she had another unfortunate experience with a man:

I had known the guy for over a year, casually and in passing . . . he lived in the same apartment complex. We saw each other in the laundry room at various times. One day we were doing our laundry and he asked me out. He was an active Christian and even spoke of going to the seminary one day. We went to a movie. Shortly after this I started attending his church. One month later we became engaged and six months later we married. He then insisted that I quit school (I had begun graduate school at night) and spend my evenings in church-related activities. He would go into rages if the supper was not on time or if the house was not spotless. His constant exercise of what he called "husband's rights, wife's duty" often amounted to what I now recognize as marital rape. As my job started to yield success and my income exceeded his, he began to physically abuse me. I was once again in the living hell I had been in as a child. I was afraid to leave and afraid to stay. Only after such a severe beating that I ended up in the hospital did I leave him.

After a year of separation Janet obtained a divorce. Since that time she has never again had a close relationship with a man. She limits her close relationships to women:

Two years later I met an older woman where I worked. She was really kind and we had lots of similar interests. One thing led to another and we started living together. The three years with her were the happiest of my life. Then her mother became ill and she had to leave the state to care for her. I would have gone with her, but she did not think her mother could handle the shock of learning that her daughter was homosexual. Linda (my ex-lover) and I still write and see each other occasionally.

The ghosts of Janet's childhood still haunted her at the time of the study. She was having difficulty establishing a lasting relationship (which she wanted) with her female companion. She also showed an alarming tendency to dislike her clients and co-workers, especially if they happened to be men. In this way she continued the cycle of contempt and resentment that was initiated by her abusive father and emotionally neglectful mother.

In the follow-up to the study she offered this update:

I feel I have grown a lot since the time of the study. Now I am supervisor for Child Protective Services. It gives me great pleasure to help bring charges against abusers and perpetrators, the majority of them being male. I'd personally like to see all of those suckers locked up for good and their kids put into decent homes, or institutions. I meet with these men in group therapy (which they are forced to attend or go to jail). I force them to face up to the scum they really are. In my group with the victims I can speak from personal experience about the long-term damages done by men against women in our society.

Summary

The nature of parent–child relationships in incest exemplifies each of the aspects of immaturity delineated in Chapter 4. These aspects are summarized in Table 6.1 below.

The primary bond to the perpetrator of incest is ruptured as the child is not cared for and protected, but becomes an object for use. The primary bond to the mother was also flawed because she failed to protect the child. Incest fractures the bond of trust (if it ever was established at infancy) in an especially insidious manner.

Incest confounds pleasure and pain. The pleasure experienced by the adult is accompanied by pain in the child. Pleasurable physiological sensations may be experienced by the child concomitantly with the physical and psychological pain. Intense physical closeness is felt along with the violence of the greater power of the perpetrator. Physical and sexual closeness for the incest victim is forever associated with the ghosts of the perpetrator. Feelings of powerlessness and worthlessness instilled in the victim reinforce the vicious cycle of contempt.

The perpetrator relates to the victim in double-image fashion. The unconscious projections of "sexiness," "provocativeness" and guilt are vested onto the little girls. At the same time, the perpetrator demands that the little girl take care of him, instead of the reverse (reversal parenting). The communicative style of the perpetrator vacillates between blaming and placating the child. The mother's communications move between irrelevant and blaming stances (Satir, 1983).

Table 6.1. Summary of Parenting Practices Experienced by Janet and Delores

	Janet	Delores
Primary bond	Fractured	Fractured
Mirroring	Inadequate	Inadequate
Style of parenting	Double image	Double image
Communicative stance	Blaming	Blaming
Attributions	Negative	Negative
Expectations	Positive	Positive
Temporality	Stressful	Stressful
Defenses	Psyc/immature	Psyc/immature
Dramatic form	Tragic	Tragic
Moral development	Survive/good	Survive/good
Ethical level	Resent/indul	Resent/indul
Child's self-integration	Divided self	Divided self

The attributions and expectations of both parents in incestuous families will be negative or contradictory. On the one hand, the child is debased and blamed for the degradation. On the other hand, the child is often expected to prove her worth by high achievements in school. Sexual abuse thus provides a strong foundation for an emotionally divided self. Both Delores and Janet experienced time in a stressful manner. Delores was often literally afraid for her life, due to their impoverished living conditions. Janet too lived in constant fear of the next attempt by her father to molest her and/or shame her in relation to her mother.

Sexual acting out is an immature (adolescent level) defense mechanism and this behavior in relation to one's own children is a "psychotic" defense because it necessarily involves a denial. It is questionable in the cases of both Janet and Delores whether their mothers were aware of the abuse. To the extent that they were aware, the mothers must have been using primitive to immature defenses such as denial or dissociation.

The ethical level in their homes and projected upon Janet and Delores was that of survival with aspects of goodness (Gilligan, 1982). In Delores' case, the extreme poverty she also experienced reinforced the survivalist approach to life. True caring in Gilligan's sense was not in evidence in these homes. The perpetrators of incest show little or no ethical self in Weinstein's sense. Their lack of control of their sexual desires greatly interfered with the becoming mature of Janet and Delores. The ties to the "protosymbolic" realm were greatly distorted in Janet's case. Her father presented himself as an extremely religious man. He said prayers at the dinner table. His physical abuse of them was under the guise of the "just" punishments of a father carrying out his religious obligations as a father. The thoughts of a person who perceives himself as especially religious, and yet physically and sexually abuses his children are wrought with intense contradictions.

Janet and Delores have intensely divided selves. Delores is unhappy in her marriage and cannot wholeheartedly devote herself to meeting her child's needs. Janet has not exorcized the ghost of her father as he haunts her personal and work relationships.

Michelle and Barbara—Rebelling Against the Ghosts of Poverty and Neglect _____ 7

Introduction

Michelle and Barbara experienced the childhood adversities of poverty, abuse, neglect, and sexism. Both of them rebelled against the ghosts of parents. Michelle's father, an alcoholic, was verbally and physically abusive. He expected Michelle to take care of his needs and to contribute her meager earnings to the household. While Michelle's mother was kindly, she was also "nervous," as is the case with most battered wives. Both parents were emotionally distant. Michelle rebelled against these influences by working her way through college, and finding a marriage partner who did not drink or smoke. They established "open" communication with their girls. Michelle's was a success story, which the others in the group found hard to believe. She consistently advised them on how they could follow in her footsteps and break out of the patterns established in the past. Michelle's documents almost brush aside her father's physical abusiveness. It is difficult to say whether Michelle was intensively denying her reality or whether her "success" story, as presented, was accurate.

Barbara gives a mixed picture of her parents. Her mother was critical and rejecting. Her father favored her while she was a young girl, but rejected her when she became a teenager. The ghosts of her rejecting parents continue to the present day.

Michelle—Reflections on Poverty

The story of Michelle as she told it is a remarkable one, for her reflective self-awareness and independence of mind began when she was just a child and has continued consistently throughout her life. Michelle not only knew what sacrifices and decisions she would have to make to achieve her goals, but she made them. She grew up in poverty, as a coal miner's daughter in West Virginia. Currently she is a professor of English at a private university. She has been happily married for nearly 30 years and is the mother of two grown young women.

Michelle was the third child in a family of four girls. Her brother was born when she was 6 years old. Since her three sisters were quite a bit older than her, her little brother became her primary companion. Since the home was small, she shared a room with him, even through her teenage years.

While Michelle had adequate food, clothing, and shelter, she received little companionship from either of her parents or from her older sisters. She remembers her mother, Joyce, as loving, caring, and protective, but nervous. Because of this nervousness, she left the discipline of the children up to her husband, who was strict and domineering.

Since they had little money, Michelle's toys were handmade items. Her mother was creative in teaching her children to make interesting play things out of scrap household items. She made toys from strings and buttons and a musical instrument from a comb and a piece of waxed paper.

Michelle felt that the few times her father took the children somewhere, or played with them were rare indeed. Her father came home from the mines each day black from the coal. While he paid some attention to family needs, he drank heavily, as most miners did. While drinking, he could become verbally and physically abusive to his wife and the children. He read the newspaper daily and stressed the importance of the news on the children. Neither parent offered her much guidance and encouragement. At a minimum, they expected her to obey them in doing her chores, do well at school, and keep out of trouble.

Michelle's extended family was extremely large. Her mother was from a family of twelve children and her father had eight siblings. As a consequence, weekends were often hectic, with get-togethers involving lots of relatives and activities which centered around family and church. Michelle withdrew from this hub of activity, preferring to observe quietly or retreat into her own space to play by herself. Her tendency to be independent and reflective started early in life. Living across the street was a playmate, Susan, whose family was Greek and whose father had a barber shop in their home. Michelle loved to play there because they could play house in the barber shop.

When Michelle was 6 her mother became pregnant. Her mother was happy to have a son, and seemed less nervous. Her father was elated. Michelle learned very quickly that she must have been a disappointment to her parents when she was born because she was the third daughter. Her father spent a good deal more time with his son then he did with

Michelle. Although they were always short of money, they always had alcoholic beverages in the house for her father.

Michelle's tendency toward reflectivity was intensified by the birth of her brother and her parents' reaction to it. Michelle felt that her parents were negative toward her. This caused her to withdraw to a large extent from the hubbub of family activities. Consequently, she read more and became more introspective.

In spite of her jealousy, Michelle became friends with her brother and played with him a lot. She also enjoyed girl scouting and her special friend Jean. Another friend, Sally, walked a mile each week with Michelle to the library. She also attended Sally's protestant church and observed her quiet family life as an only child.

When Michelle entered high school her mother went to work in a weaving mill. This increased Michelle's independence. She too began to work as a baby-sitter and house cleaner. All of her earned money had to be contributed to the household budget. Michelle resented this and vowed that it would be different for her own children. Remarkably, Michelle was able to take the negatives in her childhood life and ensure that they were not repeated with her own children.

Michelle's life seems to be modeled on the negative, such that much of her upbringing represented things that she rejected and attempted not to repeat in her adult life and with her own children. She experienced sexism in her family; her little brother was favored emotionally and financially. She was neither adequately mirrored nor communicated with by either parent, both of whom seem unreal by her description. Her alcoholic father was more concerned with his own needs than his children's.

Michelle always knew she wanted to be a teacher. She hoped to go to a nearby teacher's college, if only her parents could afford to send her. Her parents gave her no help, however, since they said they had to save all their money to send her younger brother to college, even though he was not interested in going. Michelle bitterly resented this. She also felt rejected by their cold general attitude toward her and their indifference toward her future. While her older sisters were primarily concerned with finding husbands, Michelle, once again observing and analyzing this pattern, knew she did not want it for herself. Relatives had her dubbed as the typical "old maid school teacher." Michelle preferred to be alone with her own thoughts, and took long walks:

> Noncommunicative parents allowed me the freedom to develop my own mind and evaluate myself throughout these years—a positive result for me.

Although her mother thought her hopes to be a teacher were good, she nevertheless hoped that Michelle would marry a well-to-do man, preferably a doctor. This attitude on the part of her mother made Michelle all the more adamant not to marry just for the sake of marrying.

When the time came for Michelle to attend college or obtain a full-time job, her father had a better job working for the State. Still, her father would not help her financially. She made a deal with her father that if he would only let her save her tips from a job as a waitress she could save enough for her own tuition. Remarkably, this is just what Michelle did. She completed her teacher's training while living at home and working as a waitress.

Upon graduation, Michelle was expected to find a job at the local school, while continuing to live at home, and turn over her increased income to her family. Michelle decided against this and instead left for New York where she took a teaching position and worked on her master's degree as a part-time student. She lived at the YWCA Women's Residence, taking advantage of the concerts, plays and meeting interesting men. She dated an airline pilot, a psychologist, and a lawyer, but was not serious about anyone. She was sure that each of them was not what she wanted.

After several years of working in the city, Michelle moved to western New York. While on a skiing trip, she met John; she knew immediately she would marry him. John was a businessman whose values were similiar to hers. He did not drink or smoke and was health-conscious.

Michelle and John had two daughters, six years apart. Michelle portrays their family as close, with open communication. This was very unlike the home atmosphere in which Michelle grew up. The feelings of rejection and coldness from her parents continued after Michelle's marriage, however. Since she was married in the Methodist church instead of the Catholic church, they did not recognize the marriage for 7 years! Finally, for fear they might die without meeting their granddaughters, they invited Michelle and her family to visit with them and had a reconciliation.

At the present time, Michelle is completing her doctoral degree in education while teaching in a junior college. John has been continually supportive of her educational and career goals. Michelle and John have had normal parental problems with their girls, who rebelled against some of their values. The older daughter began to drink and otherwise abuse her health. At the present time she is married and is slowly accepting her parents' values.

Michelle's father died several years ago of a ruptured blood vessel. Her brother died tragically in a car wreck last year. At the time he died he was married and the father of two children. Michelle is currently enjoying a warm and communicative relationship with her mother for the first time in her life. They talk on the telephone for at least an hour every other week. Her best friend is a divorced mother of three, living on welfare, who keeps in touch with Michelle through her mother.

Michelle's only indications of trouble in this paradise were her daughter's alcoholism and her parent's rejection of her marriage. In group discussion, Michelle consistently presented the image that she had completely overturned these childhood influences. She had a happy, egalitarian marriage. Hopefully this was the truth, although I consistently heard from other students that she could not be trusted or believed. When others in the group spoke of problems with parents, children, or spouses, Michelle would advise them that these could all be handled, for she always had an answer for how others could function better if they could be more like her.

Given the way she did not discuss the physical abuse she suffered from her father with the emotions one would have expected, it seems that "denial" may have been a consistent defense for Michelle. Michelle presented her idealized version of life for the group to emulate. Some in the group had difficulty in believing her success story.

Barbara—The Ghost of Overly Critical Parents

Barbara, 42, is divorced and the mother of a 16-year-old daughter and a 12-year-old son. She has been divorced for the past 3 years, and is completing a master's degree in accounting. Her diary projects a current situation of lack of fulfillment and constant hassles.

Barbara was the middle child of five, with two older sisters and two younger brothers. Her father was a car salesman in a middle-sized town in Arkansas. Barbara remembers her early childhood as happy, because she was her father's favorite. Her mother, on the other hand, was critical of her, for being hyperactive and a tomboy. Barbara did get into trouble as a child, falling out of trees, into ponds, and riding her "kiddie car" down the stairs. She also remembers blowing up a gas stove.

While Barbara says her childhood was happy in many ways, in actuality she gives the impression that she felt rejected by her mother and favored by her father. However, a scandel involving her father in her early teenage years caused her to become disillusioned with him. Barbara's ex-husband reminded her of her mother, for he too was always critical and rejecting of her. When asked to reflect on her past Barbara says that it was unpleasant.

The critical attitude her mother had toward her was mirrored by the attitudes of her teachers. In kindergarten she remembers being the only child who did not get popcorn in her basket and had to ask for her share. In first grade her teacher slapped her face for forgetting a song. School continued to be traumatic, with teachers generally having negative attitudes toward Barbara.

Barbara's play activities were active, such as cowboys and Indians. There were no female roles in the games, and she was usually the only girl in the group. They played hide and go seek and ball. As a group, they spent a good deal of time roaming in the woods. These outdoors activities instilled an early love for nature in Barbara, resulting later in an active interest in environmental issues. Barbara could hike and fight as well as any of the boys. In fact, the mother of one of the neighborhood boys complained that Barbara had beaten up her son. Barbara's mother made her apologize to the boy.

When Barbara reached puberty, her father insisted that she stop associating with the rowdy boys and stay home:

> He called me in to the house and slapped me across the face and informed me that I was to "stay away from those nasty little boys." Later in adult life my face would sting when I was in a difficult situation. I finally resolved this with psychiatry.

Barbara was not permitted to date until the age of 18. At that time, she felt herself to be socially retarded, so she started dating younger boys.

Her father was involved in a scandal of exploiting customers. This, along with his having an affair and deserting the family for 3 months, was made public on the front page of the local paper. This greatly humiliated Barbara, making her feel even more unworthy socially. She withdrew from social contact. Meanwhile, Barbara's relationship with her mother worsened. She associated Barbara with her father, thinking she was like him. Barbara reacted by trying to eradicate all aspects of her personality that were like him. In the process, she also lost some of his good qualities. As hard as she tried, she was never able to please her mother.

Dating several men before she married gave her greater self-confidence. Unwittingly, she married a man who was as critical of her as her mother had been. Even though prior to marriage they had agreed that they would have children immediately, when she found herself pregnant after 3 months of marriage her husband took her to have an abortion. At that time, abortions were illegal and dangerous. The abortionist inserted a tube into her uterus and left it there for a few days. When nothing happened, he removed the tube and scraped her uterus without administering anesthetic. This was extremely painful.

After that event, Barbara began to wonder if her husband was having an affair. She became anxiety ridden and lost a lot of weight. She dropped out of graduate school to obtain a job so that she could pay for psychiatric treatment:

> The psychiatrist was a kind, gentle person. This was the best relationship I had had during my entire life. For once I was accepted the way I was and not required to change. This relationship helped set my value structure; it helped me to learn to care more about others and gave me more self-confidence.

Following this treatment her marriage improved. She and her husband began to take dancing lessons together and enjoy relationships with the other couples. In retrospect, Barbara thinks that she became happier mostly because of these social occasions, rather than because of an improvement in her marriage:

> My husband seemed to be critical and I often thought that he didn't really think that I was very important. Since our marriage seemed better on the surface we planned to have children.

Barbara became pregnant and needed a Cesarian Section. The amount of care the first baby required came as a surprise to Barbara:

> I had not realized how time consuming it was to care for an infant. I was unable to nurse, and I spent hours each day sterilizing bottles and making formulas. Friends told me that it took all day every day to care for a new baby, and it did.

Barbara's second pregnancy occurred during the Vietnam war. At first critical of war protesters, she later realized they were right. She lost all respect for Bob Hope, her childhood hero, because he supported the war. She was upset about the actions of the Chicago Police who used physical violence against the protesters. Barbara blamed the Vietnam war for all of the bad things that subsequently happened in her life.

With this second pregnancy, Barbara's husband again insisted that she have an abortion. She refused and filed for divorce. Soon she realized that she could not make it alone—pregnant and caring for a small child—so she withdrew the action.

Her son was red-headed and hyperactive. He was very much like Barbara had been as a child. It was not until he was 3 years old that she was able to sleep through a night. At this time Barbara was working on a master's degree in psychology at a nearby university where most of the professors and students were male. The university was so male oriented that the restrooms did not even have tampon dispensers.

While her children were young, Barbara became active in the League of Women Voters, the National Organization for Women, Planned Parenthood Society, and several environmentalist groups. She became a local officer of several of these organizations, coordinating activities and making trips to Washington, D.C.

Meanwhile, her husband became more and more critical of Barbara. When her children were age 6 and 10 she got a divorce. At the time of the divorce Barbara's mother became ill and died. Barbara's grief over her mother's death was intensified because she could never please her.

Barbara had great difficulty in finding a job. Finally, she obtained a job as a caseworker at a welfare department. Barbara felt that the job was demeaning both to workers and clients since she was required to ask personal questions about their love life and whether or not they received money from men. Her clients were AFDC (Aid to Families with Dependent Children) cases and were comprised of mostly female single mothers with children. She had a caseload of 365 and could not adequately handle them all. She was only allowed 20 minutes to interview each client, verify the information, and put it into a statewide computer. She was always behind in her work. She worked in the worst part of town and frequently was verbally assaulted by clients or by people on the streets.

After her separation, Barbara, at the age of 45, went to a singles' event with a friend who was 10 years younger than her and was greatly insulted when a man asked her if she were this friend's mother. She learned quickly not to frequent such events because they were attended by many more women than men, and consequently, the men were arrogant. Experiences with her three divorce attorneys also led her to a depression:

> One said to me, "Why don't you beg your husband to take you back? There is not much demand socially or in the work world for women in your age bracket.

Finally, Barbara's divorce was settled. Having received a little money from the sale of property, she decided to quit her job, work part time, and finish her master's degree. Barbara expresses the feeling that she is going backward. When she was younger she had better jobs and lots of dates.

Barbara has an artistic eye. It is her moments of aesthetic appreciation which seem to provide her with the most solace:

> In the morning I go out for the paper, usually it is dark. Sometimes the stars are brilliant, and I linger to enjoy them. By breakfast it is light and I look out the window at the flowers in bloom. When my children come to the table I look at their fresh young faces; they seem so innocent. Both have large blue eyes with long dark lashes and turned up noses. They are pretty children. They depart for school in a large dark green van. I leave for work in a small gray car, that is designed to be aesthetically pleasing. When I arrive at work I see rows of cars. In the distance is the contemporary college; as I walk between the handsome buildings I come to a beautiful court yard with fountains, gardens and a windmill. Ivy covers the west walls. Asian jasmine grows in the beds which are interspersed with the aggregate walk-ways, throughout the courtyard. I approach another elegant contemporary building and walk on carpeted floors until I reach my windowless office. Time stood still when I related the beauty of the buildings and the court-yard. I was uncomfortably jolted awake when I arrived at my dull looking office.

Barbara's diary reflects a feeling of being overburdened and unful-filled. Already, in the first week of classes, she expresses anger at being overworked both at home and at school:

> 9:00—Watched "Dynasty", mindless program, I guess I enjoyed vicariously their sexual escapades and their social events. My life is so boring. School work, yard work, house work, etc. I don't have a great deal of time to be with friends and I never meet any interesting men.
>
> Next Day: "No school. Went to work and thought about another job. I like the people where I work but the job is generally boring. I should be in a better job. I feel like a failure. I don't feel assertive or competitive.

As a single mother, Barbara's workload is very hectic. On Saturdays she got up at 7:30 A.M. She ate cereal and juice, read the paper and then made pancakes for her children. She took them shopping for school clothing and supplies. That afternoon she worked in the yard for several hours, then stopped to talk with a cosmetics consultant. The rest of the day she cleaned house and cooked dinner. After dinner she bathed, washed her hair, and read some old news magazines. Later she watched a movie on the public television channel and did mending. Following the movie, she spoke with her daughter who was feeling anxious about not doing well enough in school.

The next day she went to church, cooked, called her brother to wish him a happy birthday, and worked on health insurance claims forms. Sometimes Barbara feels guilty for going to church on Sunday because this takes time away from her housework and studies.

During the week Barbara takes her children to school. She also attends school and work. She drives her children to various doctors appointments and other activities. She must grocery shop, or if the shopping is already done, rush home to cook supper. She then helps her children with their issues and concerns and mends or sews. When all of this is completed, she begins her studies.

Meanwhile, pressures mount, Barbara's son is having some difficulties and is seeing the school psychologist. Sometimes when Barbara talks to old friends she feels inferior because she is not successful in a career, nor does she have an ongoing relationship with a man.

In spite of these problems, Barbara reads the daily newspaper and also news journals and bulletins. She keeps up with some of her political and environmental issues. One day she commented that reading the Sierra Club Bulletin made her sad because she longed for a trip out of doors.

Barbara decided to relieve some of the pressure and sadness by taking her children on a weekend camping and canoe trip. She tried to get several friends to go with her, and finally succeeded in finding a friend who has several children to join her. This trip was one of the highlights of her semester.

> After getting lost on the bayous for a while we saw another boat and asked how to get to our Island. They gave us good directions and soon we were there.
>
> The entire area was incredibly beautiful. Pine trees cover the high areas of land and cypress draped with strands of Spanish moss grow in the wetlands and in the lake itself. In places hundreds of water lilies fill large portions of the lake. We traveled by slough and bayou to avoid motorized boats. The Island appeared eerie in the late day almost as if it were haunted. We hurriedly set up our boats and prepared dinner before it became dark. Later we sat by the fire talking. The two boys had set up their tent in the interior of the Island. That night we could hear the sound of owls.

While on the trip she developed bronchitis and had to stay home for several days that week.

In spite of her tight schedule, Barbara accused herself of not being more systematic. One day she muses about dropping a class and says:

> I could probably handle twelve hours of courses (full time), read to children, drive, car pool and work half time but I just can't seem to get organized. I need to have some fun.

When invited to a friend's party on Saturday night she wonders if there will be any single males there in her age bracket. However, as it turned out there were not; she still had a good time.

The day she needed the car repaired became a major disaster. She had to rent a car in order to get herself and her children to school and to work. By the time she added the cost of the repair and rental she earned so little that she felt she should have stayed home.

Barbara does all of the housework, cleaning, shopping, yard work and cooking by herself. She assumes that this is the way it should be, never thinking that her 12-year-old son and 16-year-old daughter should, or even could, help:

> Woke up at 6 A.M. on the one day when I could have slept late. Skipped church and studied most of the day. Cleaned house and did laundry also. The kitchen paint was finally dry so I replaced all the dishes and pots and pans in the cupboards. The children came home again so I had to go the store for groceries and then cook dinner.

At times Barbara's plans were thwarted because of unexpected illnesses or activities of her children:

> My son fell off his skateboard last night and was not wearing his knee pads. He stayed home from school today because it hurt him to walk. I had planned to spend the day in the library, but instead stayed home and worked on an abstract and fixed food and drinks, etc. for him. I went to my evening class feeling very depressed.

When Barbara saw a television show about the genetic basis of depression she expressed relief. She said she had felt for some time that there was something in her chemistry causing depression. Barbara does not specifically deal with her difficulties as a child in relation to her problems later in life so a biological explanation for her feelings may have been comforting.

The burdens of being a single parent were extensive. The next week she had to take her son to the school psychologist because he had had a "personality change":

> The next day I had to miss work to take my son to the school psychologist. He used to be outgoing and now has become withdrawn and has developed an irrational fear of kids beating him up. Last year all of his teachers and the school counselor called to say that he had had a personality change and I had noticed it too. I assumed some of this was that he was approaching puberty. He doesn't want to be macho but I told him if kids pick on him to go ahead and slug them and I'll handle the problem with the school. He worries constantly that someone will beat him up. Apparently other children sense this and pick on him. I'm really upset and can't talk to my ex-husband because he says there's nothing wrong. It is impossible to deal with him.

Barbara found it especially difficult to deal with her son after he had been visiting with his father:

> Last night my son said "when you and dad remarry . . ." I said, "we won't remarry." He said "I know you will because you are still in love with each other:" I said "that is not true and we can't get along with each other." God will this ever end. I feel like I'm being punished for something I didn't do.

Throughout the course of her diary, Barbara writes about trips to visit her son's teachers and appointments with the psychologist. At times, especially after visiting with his father, the young man would have temper tantrums. Between these difficulties and her daughters' activities, Barbara spends a good deal of time driving:

> I'll now have to pick my son up at school and drive him to the psychologist each Thursday. Then I'll have to return to the school to pick up the rest of the car pool children, dropping each one at home. Following that I'll have to come home and take my daughter to her piano lesson, drive home, and drive back to pick her up at 8:00. I don't know how I'll do it!

By the time Barbara got finished she was exhausted, only to spend the evening cooking, doing dishes and refereeing fights between her children. After weeks of sessions, the psychologist informed Barbara that her son was seriously disturbed..

Throughout all of these difficulties, Barbara perseveres, and continually tries to help her children and others. On Thanksgiving day she invites an acquaintance whose daughter died within the last year of a disease which was the result of an undetected birth defect. Barbara's keen sense of aesthetics come through in the delight she expressed in her discussion of their drive to see sculpture in the nearby metropolitan area:

> We enjoyed the day and after dinner we went downtown to see all of the contemporary sculptures. The Court House has an abstract muscular structure in marble and another sculpture floating on a pond. The building itself is very unusual. The top slants away from the base so that the upper stories are in effect cantilevered on each descending floor. We've enjoyed these for years but this year there is a new sculpture by a West Coast Artist. It is eighteen feet high and extends at a perpendicular to the building wall.

The details of Barbara's daily existence reveal a woman still haunted by ghosts of cruel and neglectful parents. The voice of Barbara's rejecting and critical mother continued in that of her husband. The aftermath of extricating herself from this bad marriage left her with a disturbed teenage son. She had little sense of hope for her future.

Conclusion

Michelle and Barbara represent the divergent ways that women can rebel against ghosts of childhood rejection and neglect. Michelle consistently strove to direct her life away from the influences of her parents. Barbara attempted to find the love and acceptance she did not receive as a child from a man who was just as critical of her as her negative mother. Michelle tended to deny and underplay her problems. For example, she does not seriously discuss her son's drinking and drug problem. The members of the group found Michelle's continual presentation of her marriage and her life as perfect in spite of her childhood privations difficult to believe. Was Michelle so much the victim of past ghosts that she had to deny the reality of their effect? Barbara, on the other hand, tends to deal with her problems directly.

The effects of sexism were evident in Barbara's life. As a child, her naturally physically active nature was sharply curtailed by her father when she entered puberty. The ghost of a father with an abusive side and sexist attitudes may have effected her choice of a husband who was similarly cold and rejecting. Barbara's experiences with male divorce attorneys and with singles groups activities reinforced the sexist notion that a woman of age 45 is too old to be desirable. Overall, the behavior of their parents as they described it was more "immature" then "mature." The dimensions of this are summarized in Table 7.1.

Both Michelle and Barbara had stable, but weak primary bonds. Michelle's mother was disappointed that she was not a boy and seemed to ignore her most of her life. Her father was an abusive alcoholic. Barbara's mother was consistently negative toward her. She did have a close

Table 7.1. Summary of Parenting Practices Experienced by Michelle and Barbara

	Michelle	Barbara
Primary bond	Stable	Stable
Mirroring	Inadequate	Inadequate
Style of parenting	Reversal	Projective
Communicative stance	Blame/irrel	Blaming
Defenses	Immature/neuro	Immature/neuro
Attributions	Negative	Neg/mix
Expectations	Mixed	Mixed
Temporality	Stressful	Stressful
Dramatic form	Tragic	Tragic
Moral development	Surv/good	Surv/good
Ethical level	Resent/indul	Resent/self-control
Child's self-integration	Divided self	Divided self

relationship with her father until she reached puberty when he began to be cold toward her. Neither Michelle nor Barbara received adequate mirroring from either parent. These parents were too wrapped up in their own emotional and financial problems to be empathic. Instead, they projected qualities such as "responsible" for Michelle, and "clumsy" for Barbara, onto their daughters. Michelle's parents communicated poorly or not at all, their communicative stance typically blaming or "irrelevant". Her father's "acting out" in the form of alcoholism and violence was an immature defense mechanism. Michelle's mother seemed to exhibit some neurotic level defense mechanisms, such as sublimation, in her religious activities. At the same time, she may have also been dissociating from a bad situation.

Both Michelle and Barbara received negative attributions. Barbara also received some positive ones, mostly from her father. They also received mixed expectations. They were expected to achieve, but it was not clear how, or even if it would be possible. Their experiences of temporal events was stressful. Michelle especially dreaded family holidays because she thought they were too hectic. The dramatic form in both homes was tragic, with their daughters as the victims. The moral development of the mothers was somewhere between survival and goodness. Both were concerned with what others thought of their children (goodness) and neither were able to be free enough from their fears and anxieties to relate to their daughters in a caring way (survival). Their ethical levels were somewhere between resentment and self-control. Some degree of artistry was exhibited in both homes. One indication of this was the creativity of Michelle's mother in giving her make-shift toys out of household items. The overall low level of empathy, poor communication, negative attributions and immature defenses in these parent–child relationships ensured that both Michelle and Barbara would develop emotionally divided selves.

The Death of a Child's Parent—Shelly and Karen _____ 8

This chapter tells the stories of Shelly and Karen, who, as children, suffered the death of a parent. Shelly, now 56, lost her mother when she was 12. Karen's father died when she was 11. Both of them exemplify a principle first articulated by Freud: We deal with the loss of a loved one by taking on that loved one's characteristics.

The death of a parent brings into radical relief the strains and pressures of being a single parent. Death of a child's parent taxes resources for care and sustenance. The problems of inadequate social supports become acutely evident in these examples. The stress of loss of a spouse is likely to mitigate against mature responses, at least immediately, by the remaining parent. Of the various forms of adversity experienced by the women, death of parent did not impact as severely as maltreatment such as physical, psychological and sexual abuse or neglect. The deceased parent continues to play an important psychological role in the family system. The mature or immature practices of this parent continue to effect the child's becoming.

Shelly and the Death of Her Mother

Shelly is the wife of an insurance company executive and the mother of two sons. One of the sons, age 28, lives at home and attends the university. Shelly, trained as an elementary teacher, is currently a university student majoring in nutrition.

As a child in a small town in northern Colorado, Shelly was the daughter of a minister. She had four brothers, two older and two younger. Her family life was stable and harmonious, stressing caring for others, music, and education. However, all was not easy for them:

> Our family moved to another small town. . . . the depression was in full
> swing. . . . my father was earning $25.00 a week as a minister and choir

163

director for a small church. . . . I was in the third grade. We were very poor. Our bedtime snack consisted of one slice of jelly bread. The seven of us lived in a small frame house next to the church.

Here I saw the first "dead" person I had ever seen, a neighbor, laid out in the parlor. This was significant to me. I was frightened and also curious. I was six years old.

I had my first real "pet." She was a little brown and gold colored chicken. She hatched a week out of order from the rest of her group. I took care of her. I named her Chicken Little. One night she froze stiff, but I found her in the nick of time, put her in an old sock, and then into a strawberry box. I placed the box on the back of the coal stove. She slowly thawed out and lived for many months. She followed me around the yard. She was significant to me in that she taught me to care for "life."

We moved again when I started fifth grade. It was a better church for Dad and included a parsonage with a bathroom.

Shelly faced a stern and competitive school situation where she learned early about inequities between men and women:

My teachers became a positive significant influence in my life for the next four years. I feel that I learned the most in those four years than at any other time in school. My eighth grade teacher, Mr. Smith, was very stern. I do not think he liked me. I studied very hard, especially history. He was grooming the class to compete in an all county eighth grade test. He bragged each day about the intelligence of Calvin, a classmate. This stirred up my sense of competition. I studied many extra hours. My efforts paid off. I made the highest grade in the country on the test. I would say that Calvin was significant to me. Because of him, my determination to score above him, I became a strong competitor. I still have this quality. The combination of Mr. Smith and Calvin revealed to me the first glimpse I'd had of the inequalities of women in our society.

When she was just 12 years old she had two experiences with death:

Before Christmas that year one of my classmates, Gilbert, lost his mother. I can remember Mr. Smith telling the class about Gilbert's mother's death and explaining that Gilbert would be absent for a few days. I was anxious for him to return to school. I expected him to look different. I never talked to him, but I stared at him and felt sorry for him. I thought he would change. I couldn't imagine a person not having a mother. Shortly after the County test was over, my own mother was taken to hospital. She died a few days later. I was crushed. My life crumbled.

The last few years before my mother's death she was very significant to me. She was a loving mother, tolerant, a good homemaker, and kind to all around her. She loved our family. She told me that Amelia Earhart was her heroine. She told me to train to be an elementary teacher so that I could work and still be home with my children in summers.

At my mother's funeral in church I heard whispers of "it's all for the best. She's in God's hands now." To me, that is the most idiotic statement ever made. No one can tell me that leaving five children motherless is "all for the best." From this experience I learned to doubt the so-called "do-gooders."

Shelly also learned early in life that persons could feel so strongly about their viewpoints that they could be harmful to those who held different ones. Some of the church elders were upset because her father spoke about "venereal" disease in a young adult study group. Shelly's father had rebuilt the parish hall, graded the lawn, planted shrubbery, kept records, taught classes, and served as superintendent of the church school leaving little time for his family. Shelly felt deeply about the unfairness of these small-minded persons. She learned to watch out for them in the future.

The summer after she became 13 her father returned to college for his master's degree, coming home only on weekends to check up on the family. Shelly had full responsibility for all of the cooking, cleaning, and laundry for herself and her four brothers. She also had to pack the entire household for the move to a town 60 miles away where her father had obtained a new position. Of this experience, Shelly writes:

I hated it. I began to blame all this work on my mother's death. I cried a lot. I was sure that had she been there I would not have to work so hard.

Shelly clearly remembers the drive at night to the new town, with her eldest brother driving the moving truck. Arriving there, they had no electricity, only a kerosene lantern. That fall, she mourned her mother's death:

I cried every night in my bed, grieving for my mother. No one ever talked to me about mother.

During Shelly's freshman year in high school, her father hired a woman to do housekeeping during the week. In her sophomore year, a friend who was then a senior in high school, moved in with them. Kathy was popular with the town boys and Shelly also became interested in them. Shelly was not allowed to date, and her brothers were very protective of her:

I knew nothing about sex, except that babies formed inside the mothers and somehow got out of there. I had no idea how the pregnancy was initiated. Later, I can remember Dad telling me very briefly, and with no explanations whatever, about the sex act. He gave me the plain facts in about ten words.

I sensed that I knew very little about it, and kept very quiet. Kathy and I never talked about sex. We talked a lot about boys in general, chasing them around, trying to attract their attention, and all that, but never sex.

When Kathy graduated from high school and left home, Shelly took on full responsibility for the household:

> My school days were difficult. I had to get breakfast for the family. It took time to build a fire to cook. I hated my clothes, with good reason. I hated my hair. I hated my bowed legs and skinny body. I knew the boys at school didn't like me and I was sure that none of them thought I was pretty. When I had menstrual periods I would hide it from my brothers and my Dad. I can remember lying on an old black leather davenport, having severe cramps and crying by the hour hoping no one would see me.
>
> Each summer Dad insisted that we plant a big garden. We all had to hoe and weed. All the extra food had to be canned and stored for the winter. By fall, we usually had about 400 jars of vegetables put away and 150 jars of jellies and jams made up. Dad expected me to do this canning and preserving. My brothers helped, but I carried the responsibility.
>
> The laundry was unbelievable. Dad wore all white shirts. His shirts had to be washed, dried, starched, dampened, rolled, and then ironed. My brother, in college sent his shirts home to me to wash. I often had 30 shirts a week to iron. I learned to iron with my eyes shut. It was so boring. I hated it. My Dad expected me to do all this laundry.
>
> The cleaning was the same deal. We had no electric vacuum. Everything had to be swept with a stiff broom. We had several linoleums to be washed and waxed. These chores were mine too. Whenever company came for a meal I was embarrassed because I felt that I did not know how to cook. One time my older brother invited a friend to stay for the night. His friend was the big jock at the high school, admired by all the girls. I was expected to cook his breakfast. I'll never forget that morning if I live to be one hundred. I planned to fry some eggs. With my brothers and the friend watching, I cracked an egg into the skillet. The egg was so rotten that the embryo of a baby chick landed in the skillet. The boys all laughed. I was totally embarrassed. I knew this story would make the rounds at school
>
> I was on the girl's basketball team. It was probably the most fun I had during my high school days, but it all ended that third year in high school. The superintendents of the state schools voted to eliminate girl's basketball. Reason: Basketball was too strenuous for females. I was disappointed with my Dad. He was at the meeting. He should have prevented this from happening. I became a cheerleader. Disgusting!

Shelly spent many nights at the home of a girlfriend next door. This friend's mother wanted to be a teenager. Shelly felt that neither of them really had a mother. She and her friend, Joyce, often talked about boys. Shelly was also active in church, where her father directed the choir and sang solos. Even her Saturday nights involved household chores:

My Saturday nights were often spent darning socks. It was a matter of pride with me that my brothers and dad have an unholy (sic) pair of socks for church the next day. I copied this idea from my mother.

Shelly also had the responsibility of seeing that her two younger brothers bathed twice a week in a galvanized wash tub placed on two chairs. After heating water on the cook stove, Shelly had to haul it into the back room. Shelly's description of her high school years contains the recurring themes of feeling the brunt of sexist discrimination both within her male-dominated household, where she was the household slave to her father and five brothers, and at school, where she was also beginning to feel the negative impact of being a female. These two themes are intensified by her not having the help and support of a mother through these troubled years. The years were also marked by having to live on a minister's salary:

Winters were rough. My little bedroom had an outside door and one small window. I can remember snow blowing in through the cracks around the door and forming little drifts near the foot of my bed. I was never allowed to have my door open to the rest of the house. We never considered heating any bedrooms. I piled all my blankets on my bed and added a couple of overcoats on the extra cold nights. I put throw rugs on top a few times. I had a little tunnel under the pile of blankets and slid into it at night, laying there shivering until my body heat warmed the bed. I made up little stories in my head, closed my eyes, and acted them out. Usually I would be going out on a "date" with the greatest guy in the world. I imagined what it would be like to be hugged and kissed. I entertained myself with these little stories until I fell to sleep.

The three years in this town have mixed memories for me. On the inside I was constantly crying and mourning for my mother. On the outside I had a lot of fun with Kathy and Joyce. They taught me to laugh at the world.

After her junior year, Shelly's family moved again to a small river town in southern Colorado. She hated to leave Kathy and Joyce and make the change during her senior year. While they had moved to a nicer house with central steam heat, she was still expected to cook, shop, clean, can and preserve, launder, iron, and to excel in school. She hated it:

River towns are notorious for being tough and this town was no exception. It was common to see a bulge the size of a whiskey flask in the hip pocket on some of the boys at the school. This roughness caused my brothers and Dad to draw the security net tighter around me, their female. I was a virtual prisoner. The girls that lived nearby smoked and sat around on the street corners. I could never join them. As a result, I played a lot of baseball with my younger brothers and their friends. I earned the title of "tom-boy."

At that time her father devoted his whole life to the church, rebuilding the facilities, working "tirelessly and endlessly." She resented this in many ways, but did not feel it was wrong at the time. In retrospect, she feels he should have spent more time paying attention to the needs of his family:

> I feel that my dad made the mistake of treating me as a small child as far as social development was concerned, but insisting that I accept the responsibilities of a person many years older. This conflict was never solved. I never accepted this treatment. Inside I was angry. I feel I should have been taught about sexual things, should have had some help to get me through the tragedy of mother's death, should have had more attention paid to my needs in general. Had these things been taken care of I may have been a happy teenager. From these years I developed a strong dislike for housework. This created a problem for me that carried over into my adult life.
>
> I needed someone to hold me in their arms, give me an old-fashioned hug, tell me that I was pretty, care about my hairstyle, my shoes, and my dresses. All human beings need positive forces at work in their lives. Every child that loses a parent needs some special counseling to get the event into proper perspective for the remainder of his/her life. Dad failed me in these respects. In all fairness to him I don't believe he ever knew it. I loved him very much.

Shelly learned important lessons during those years. She gained a belief that one could accomplish a task, no matter how difficult, if one was determined. She learned how to work hard, to be thrifty and to "make do." Shelly also felt the brunt of sexism in her family:

> The differences between being male or female became very acute to me during these years. I am referring to the manner in which the two sexes are directed socially. Dad allowed the boys almost total freedom. On the other hand, I was guarded constantly. I did not accept this treatment easily, because I felt that I was the one that had the most responsibility and work around the house, but was the one with the least freedom. I was angry.

After high school graduation, Shelly, her father, and her two younger brothers moved to a parsonage on a farm in southwestern Missouri. In this house there was no electricity or heat. Shelly had a happy memory of her father laughing as the two of them tried to wallpaper the ceiling:

> With arms in the air, he tried to get the strips to stick at one end. Before he could continue very far across the plank the strips would let go and fall back and wrap around his head and over his neck smearing him with paste on the way. We started to laugh.

Then came the war. Shelly's father took her to be tested as to what jobs she could perform in the service. She became a clerk-typist for the Air Service Command. During this time she spent her evenings at the USO, dancing with the service men, and playing ping pong. One young man became her friend, and she started dating him. Her landlady did not allow young men into the rooms. Shelly later found this to be a blessing in disguise for he was actually married, with a wife and family in New York. Shelly found that she was unprepared to deal with such experiences, because of the way she had been sheltered by her father and brothers.

When the army offered her the opportunity to be certified as a teacher if she would teach for them at a military base for 2 years following her training, she was pleased and took up the challenge. She had wanted to be a teacher, but her father could not afford to send her to school after high school. Her mother had always told her she should study to become an elementary teacher. Shelly also had a desire to learn more about her mother's illness. She needed to study biology to be able to answer this question. She also felt the lack of adequate knowledge about sexual matters and thought she might learn more about the subject in her developmental psychology classes. The concentrated teacher's training program she entered was difficult.

> The training was rigid. There was no time for frivolity. Our studies were difficult and time consuming. The discipline was strict. Each of us was allowed to spend one night per week away from the dorm, and on returning were required to bring in a signed statement from a parent explaining where we had spent the night. No exceptions were made. Rebelling against the rules resulted in expulsion from the program.

> Shelly devoted herself to her training and became an elementary teacher specializing in the sciences. She felt that the male professors (and they were all male) were notoriously condescending to them.

A co-student became her best friend. They discovered that both of their parents were lonely. So they introduced them to each other. A few months later her father married her friend's mother. Her father's new wife had five children. Shelly felt that her father had transferred his affections from her to his new stepdaughters. He became more critical of her. She felt that he did not adequately appreciate the way she had taken over for her mother all of those years.

After graduation, at age 22, Shelly moved in with her father and stepmother, and drove to the city each day to teach. Her father asked her to move out after several clashes with her stepsisters. She moved in with an older brother in Chicago for the summer, then went to Ohio and moved in with her old friend from high school, Kathy. Kathy was married and had several children. This was a happy time, although she felt lonely for lack of a special relationship. Her career as a teacher went well. Her two nun administrators and two male principals lauded her work.

At age 24 she met a young man, a student, who was home for summer vacation. They became inseparable and married after a few months:

> The young man that I married came on the scene quite unexpectedly. He was all I had ever hoped for. He loved me from the first time we talked together. He taught me that I was desirable. I have enjoyed accepting this idea.

Although they moved often because of Joe's education and career, they enjoyed setting up housekeeping each time. After her husband graduated from college they had a son, and she enjoyed being a mother. She continued to work until after her son was born:

> My husband was influential to me because he made me feel loved as well as needed. For the first time since mother died I felt that I had found a "haven." Many times, at work, when I was exhausted and the children were being especially "testy," I would force myself to remember that soon the work day would end and I would be back with Joe. This could have been a dependency but I have never comprehended it as such.

During the 30 years of her married life, Shelly always put Joe's career first. They moved several more times. She took full responsibility for the children and their activities. Joe worked long hours and traveled a lot. She felt that her husband was more considerate than her friends' husbands. When her three children (two boys and a girl) were in grades 3, 5, and 7, her husband entered an MBA program. This necessitated that she return to work as a teacher:

> My days were long and difficult. Joe was in class all day and needed to read and study most of the night. He took care of the yard and the automobile. I had the responsibility of the house, shopping, cleaning, laundry, and getting the children around to the various activities in which they were involved.
>
> I became more and more tired. My days began at 5:30 A.M. and ended whenever we could get everyone settled at night. Central City Elementary School was a center for problem children and a training base for new special education teachers. I carried out the duties of a circulating teacher. This involved filling in for ill teachers and helping train the student teachers in dealing with discipline problems. At the same time I was responsible for

setting up and running all the biology laboratories at the school. Frequently tempers would rise and students and sometimes teachers would act out violently. I witnessed some extremely upsetting situations.

While I was working at Central City Elementary the welfare of my sons became a constant concern. The drug pushers were beginning to move into the area. The Vietnam war was underway.

I was nearing my 42nd birthday when I began to have chest pains. Several doctors examined me. Heart trouble was suspected. However, an elderly physician took time to talk to me. He determined that I was merely too tense and needed a break from my hectic schedule. I was in bed for about five weeks and never returned to work as a teacher.

Following this, Shelly's husband took a job as an insurance executive in a northern state. During this time Shelly trained as an income tax consultant and helped set up a teenage center. She gave up work at the center, being unable to cope with the teenager's behavior. Shelly dreamed at this time of being an elementary teacher in a small private school. She recounted a recurring dream in which she was a teacher and made a serious mistake involving a laboratory experiment set-up. She interpreted the dream in two ways. On the one hand, she thought it meant that she had made a mistake in giving up her teaching career, and wished to be involved in it again. On the other hand, she thought that going into teaching at all was the serious mistake, implanted in her mind by her mother and grandfather.

Shelly feels retrospectively that they should have worked out a better way for her to pursue her career and that her husband and children should have had to take more responsibility for themselves and the household:

> My husband was a success-oriented person and it seemed that the more successful he became the more I felt the opposite.

After their latest move, Shelly reentered the university, planning a new career in nutrition. She seems to be satisfied with this endeavor. However, she continues to have full responsibility for cooking, cleaning, and other household chores for herself, her husband, and her 27-year-old son. Shelly comments:

> At dinner table I explained to my husband and son how I organized 21 meal menus on file cards this afternoon. I plan to select out seven cards and shop for all items to keep myself ahead of the rush. I told them I've always not liked having to constantly decide what they're to eat. My son gave suggestions but no actual help. . . . I've had someone to cook for since I was 13 years old.

Shelly felt "motherly" toward the younger students in her nutrition class, especially an oriental and a black young lady who did not seem to understand what was going on in the support group. Shelly commented that she thought the book *The Women's Room* by Marilyn French was "too hard on men." The next day she worries about being behind on all of her housework. The irony of it is that this was one of the points made in the book.

> September 17: Spent the entire day cleaning the house. Hate bathrooms. Worked non-stop until 4:00 P.M. Important conversation: My husband very calmly told me that if I wanted to get some outside help with the housework I was free to. I said not at the present but I would see how the semester goes. My son suggested a cook-out and pool party for Sunday. He named about 22 people he wanted to invite. I agreed, knowing I would have to cook and clean all the more, but I enjoy all the persons he mentioned. Also, I want him to make good friendships here.

Shelly spent the entire next day shopping and cleaning in preparation for her son's party. The next day she cooked all day until the guests arrived:

> September 8: Have been reading on into *The Women's Room*. Am changing my opinion of the book. . . . My English Lit. class in the afternoon is studying *Beowulf*. It never ceases to amaze me how much cruelty and wickedness takes place under the guise of religion. True there is a lot of Paganism in *Beowulf* but cruelty and so-called Christianity hangs in there. Between *The Women's Room* and Old English *(Beowulf)* my head may never return to normal.
>
> September 10: One student was explaining how her friends have changed toward her since she returned to college. She feels bad about it— guilty—that she doesn't have time now for former acquaintances. Others agreed. I made the point that a woman going to college doesn't exclude her old friends any more than a woman working—so why feel guilty???It's just that working in middle age is more acceptable—Several people said "good point" I was pleased.
>
> . . . Was late getting home as I had to stop for milk and realized as I came into the house that I had made a big mistake. I'd forgotten that my husband had a Thurs. night planning meeting at 5:30 and I needed to have his dinner ready at 4:30. It was 4:45 when I arrived. He was boiling a hot dog. (He hates hot dogs.) I felt guilty for not being home. (I had a good dinner planned of Oriental Pepper Steak with Rice.) He didn't say anything. I said I had forgotten and was sorry and quickly found some other items of food to accompany the hot dogs. He ate and left hurriedly. I sat down. In a while I decided that I wasn't going to worry or think anything more about it. After all, in 32 years I have cooked a heck of a lot of meals ON TIME. And even before marriage I had to cook for my Dad and brothers.

On September 11, her 32nd wedding anniversary, Shelly's husband took her out to breakfast at MacDonald's. She was delighted. Then she came home and did laundry, cleaned the kitchen, cleaned out the refrigerator etc.:

> I rushed around full speed thinking about a million things I had to do. Suddenly, my vision blurred (similar to migraine.) I laid down on floor with feet on couch, covered eyes, and tried to relax. Then I went into the tub and took a hot bubble bath. My husband gave me a pair of beautiful earrings and three red roses for our anniversary. He really does love me and always has. It is a good feeling.
>
> I feel that I'm speeding up on some of the mundane chores I have to do. I'm looking for ways to cut corners and to speed up.

Shelly comments on trying to write her autobiography:

> September 14: Found it very difficult to remember significant others. After a couple of hours I caught up to the time of my mothers' death in 1938. This was undoubtedly the most significant event of my life. I would venture a guess that as a result of her death my life was changed for many years to come and in almost all aspects. I became sad and had to leave the typewriter.
>
> September 14: Had a very good conversation with my husband about the things we've been talking about Mira, the woman in *The Women's Room*. I would say it could be the most "open" conversation we've ever had about men and women's roles.

Shelly continues to work on her autobiography each day and to feel that the process is exhausting:

> September 21: feel that my innards have been stirred around.

Early in October Shelly strained her back and continued to have problems with the pain throughout most of the semester. In spite of how busy she was, and her pain, she took the time to help a friend who is having difficulties with her teenaged daughter. She and her husband also spent time with a visiting friend who is going through a divorce. She talks with other women students who are having similar problems:

> Went to lunch with a friend. She is over 40 and will be 44 when finished with her degree. She likes the program. She's rather strange in that sometimes I feel she's sort of in a dream world. Another older student sat with us. She is having problems making time for the whole bit; school, home, family, driving, etc.

My husband had another late meeting. He works too hard. Sometimes I resent this but the pay is good.

November 3: Seems more difficult to keep up with housework. Am discouraged about this. But with my bad back I can't do more.

November 13: Feel bad because our dogs haven't been taken care of since my back trouble began. Wish John (son) or Joe (husband) would work on them, but they are busy, busy.

November 20: This was a great day. I took three ladies (two very young) and myself to the mall to shop. All day. We enjoyed the Christmas Store. Arrived home exhausted. Joe never minds when I take a day to "goof-off." He is very considerate of me.

Shelly went to a literary club meeting on November 23rd where a book about a local murderer was discussed. She was disgusted with herself for giving time to discuss such a "heel."

Thanksgiving Day: "Spent the morning cooking."

After having Thanksgiving dinner with a group of friends, Shelly and her family stopped to pick up a little 8-year-old girl who was going to spend the night with them. Shelly enjoyed the company of this little girl. Shelly's diary breaks of abruptly on December 5th after a day of cleaning and trying to read.

Death of a Father as a Child–Karen

Karen, the baby in a family of three children (with an older brother and a sister) was the apple of her father's eye. Her father, a physician able to afford the trappings of success, did not support the life style with investments and insurance. His death, when Karen was just 11 years old, left the family impoverished.

Karen was not a planned child. Her mother became pregnant with her in her mid-forties, with the other three children already in their teens. Karen's father was extremely jealous, accusing her mother of having an affair and of carrying another man's child. Nevertheless, Karen and her father were extremely close:

I'll tell you at the onset that my father has always been a central figure in my life. I worshiped him ever since I can remember. One of my earliest memories is his going off to work in the morning. I would sit on the curb and just cry and cry. I loved both my parents, but my daddy was more special than I can tell you. He idolized me and I did him. My favorite thing was going to the yacht club with him, especially when there were races. I always felt very special when I was with my daddy. Together, we seemed invincible.

Karen's mother was tolerant, and did not discipline her at an early age, although she did when Karen was older. As a young child, she was treated like a "princess." Her mother made her feel like it was a joy to be around her. In contradiction to the accusation he made to her mother about her not being his child, Karen's father told her she could do anything because she had "inherited his brains." He told her that she could become anything she wished, such as a singer or a movie star, however since they were "cheap" professions, she should not do that. Of course, since she was a girl, she could not hope to become a doctor or lawyer.

Until age 5 or 6, Karen and her parents lived in Boston. They did not have a car. She remembers the snow, big trees, and squirrels and the old buildings. She remembers not wanting to leave Boston. At this time in life she has happy memories of her times with her father. While roller skating after school, Karen feels happy about her father's return from work:

I can see Daddy walking up the block. We don't have a car like most of the people in this town. When I see my Daddy, my day improves a lot. This begins the neat time of day when I feel the happiest. . . . I like to smell Daddy. This must be what men smell like. It's a good feeling when I smell his skin. He doesn't wear perfume. I must smell sweat. His shirts smell good too. I like to sit on his lap before I have to go to bed. He has a good smell about him. . . . My Daddy is scratching my back and it feels so good. I feel nice when I am on his lap. He feels solid.

I was really the apple of my father's eye. He liked to come to the most expensive stores and dress me and Mom out for Easter. He would let the models parade in front of him while the sales staff kept him supplied with a full drink, and he bought and bought. We also had a large yacht. Daddy and I would sail in various races up at Cape Cod. I could see that we had a lot of the things that rich people had and did lots of things that took money. However, it didn't seem real to me. Real as in really wealthy, genteel, high society. It seemed to me that it was a facade like wearing a mink coat over dirty underwear. We weren't for real.

I wanted to be two things when I grew up. One was a ship's captain and one was a doctor. My father said nobody would ever use a woman as a captain and a woman doctor was out of the question. I remember thinking how unfair that seemed, but I believed everything my father said. He treated my mother like a slave, but when he wanted to show off, he loved to buy her the best clothes, the best shoes, and take her out. He must have had the idea that women were possessions and nothing more.

At this time of her life, Karen's family plans a move to Tennessee; it was a primary memory:

> When I was in the first grade, we moved all the way from Boston to Nash-
> ville, Tennessee. I can remember crying as we pulled away from our old
> house. It wasn't because we were leaving, but because we were entering
> the unknown. I have never liked to leave anywhere since. I hate good-
> byes—I mean I HATE them. When we left, my father took a plane and my
> mother and I brought the dog and bird on the train. My older sister and
> brother were in college.

This move brought about many changes and adjustments. For example:

> I'll never forget trying to sit in the urinal in the boys' restroom. I can see
> people going into the restroom. When I go in, the arrangement is kind of
> funny looking. There is something that looks like a toilet on the wall. I don't
> know what it is. When I come out I see people smiling at me. I realize that
> there are restrooms for boys and restrooms for girls at this school.

Karen was aware that her Daddy would not always be with her:

> My parents are older than most of my friends. My friend Mike's mother
> looks like a teenager. My mother 48. Most of the things we do are long and
> dull for me. I get very tired. They like to play cards and I go along and try
> to feel comfortable at a strange house. I'd rather be at home. My sister
> doesn't want to baby sit all the time.
>
> My Daddy says that when I graduate from high school like my sister just
> did, that he won't be around to see me. He says he won't live that long to
> see me grow up, but my mother would. I know it's a long way off, so I
> don't really believe what he says. Still, I can imagine in my mind's eye how
> my parents looked as my sister graduated and then envision my mother
> sitting alone as I walk across the stage like my sister did. I feel sad thinking
> about it. I don't understand death. The only thing I understand is that it
> means you go to heaven. My Daddy says he will be dead before I'm grown
> up. I remember when my dog got run over and I hope he didn't hurt.

Karen was not allowed to carry a purse with a shoulder strap or get
her ears pierced because her father said that was only for prostitutes.
Her father had to sanction everything she did. Even at age 12 she was
not allowed to cross the street by herself or ride in a car with an adult
under age 21. She felt like she was in a cage, not even being allowed to
ride a bicycle.

Karen always felt that her mother loved her, although her mother
had the responsibility for her discipline. She liked her less than she did
her father:

I more-or-less observed my mother. I don't remember feeling very attached to her. She expected me to grow day by day, and all of us in the family did my daddy's biddings. That was our life—to do what he wanted.

Because of the overt trappings of their life style, and because her father was a doctor, people thought that they were wealthy. In reality, her father was a big spender, and had no savings and many debts.

Karen excelled in school. She became aware of class distinctions, and how they related to money, academic achievement, good looks, and not being handicapped. She remembers a friend of the family saying that she would go the farthest of the children in their family. However, since her older brother was already a physician she could not imagine this being possible:

> I can honestly tell you that I have never really envisioned myself as doing anything in a profession other than the sailor or doctor stuff. I don't know what I was supposed to grow into. I guess a wife and mother—but that was something I really didn't drool about. (Now I know why!)

Karen's father's prophecies about his not being there at her high school graduation came true. He died when she was 12. She vividly remembers the months before his death:

> For several months before his death, he was in ill health. He worked and everything, but he just didn't feel good. He loved to sit at the dinner table and tell me about how soon he was going to die. I always ended up in tears—in fact, my table memories have to do with crying with a mouthful of food. Consequently, my family never sits down to a table to eat.

> Then, shortly before Christmas of that year, he died: One, night, December 21st it was, my father watched us decorate the tree. He said he felt like he had a cold in his leg. That night, he became very short of breath and kept saying he was going to die, he was going to die. And he did. Mother was calling the doctor and wringing her hands. I held his head in my lap and he just gasped a few times and then got cold very quickly. My mother was hysterical, the dog was hysterical, everything was falling apart. I remember that night so well and it's not easy to relive it for you today. I became an adult that night and really, I've never ever been a kid again since. I took over immediately—went out and got a neighbor to stay with my mother, made some calls to family and friends, tried to get some part of my life back to normal. My sister was out of it—more a child in her grief than I would allow myself to be. They talked of taking the tree down—I just couldn't imagine doing such a thing. I had come to believe that Christmas transcended everything. Nothing could diminish it. I think I still feel that way. So my brother moved the whole big tree into another room so it wouldn't be inappropriate in receiving visitors. Everyone expected me to be a child and cry and carry on.

Karen had "grown up inside." Indeed, she did not cry about her father's death for several years. Sensing that her friends felt sorry for her embarrassed her and made her feel different. She did not feel shattered by the death. Rather, she felt marked, as if others viewed her as different and to be pitied.

A severe economic crisis for the family followed her father's death. Because of his weight, her father did not have any life insurance. Although her mother had a college degree in nursing, at that time it was thought that she was too old to begin a career. Her mother took a $1.00 an hour job in a restaurant. They had to sell their home and her father's office equipment and books in order to pay off her father's debts. They then moved into a tiny apartment owned by a friend of her mother's. Although all Karen really owned of her own at that time was toys, she felt badly about selling them:

> It hurt to have to part with everything that had been my world forever.

It was at this point that she gained weight (Karen has had a problem with weight since then.) As in the case of Shelly, she took on the traits and responsibilities of the lost parent.

Her mother had to cut down hand-me-downs for clothes for her and they looked "tacky." The new things her mother picked out were too loud for her taste—electric blue, bright yellow, etc. She did not feel comfortable until she received a school jacket at Christmas time:

> When I was in the eighth grade, more than anything in the world I wanted a school jacket. They cost about $13.00 in those days, and that might have been a million to us. I can remember wanting one so much, it just burned inside to think of it. That first Christmas morning, after the year when Daddy died, I opened up my last gift, there it was—the coat. To me that coat was everything. I felt secure in it! It made me like everyone else. . . . Kind of an equalizer. And it covered up my body, fat, clothes and all. I considered it part of me.

Although she would have liked to be a beauty queen in high school, she was popular. She was elected president of various clubs. She had a couple of good friends. Because of her sense of humor and her outspoken nature, people felt comfortable with her. Her self-image in this sense has remained much the same since high school.

While in high school she also was very aware of societal expectations; to learn to sew, cook, and look for a husband. After graduation from high school they moved again. Her mother had remarried. She did not like her new home because she had no friends. Karen left home and moved in with her older sister in another town. She attended junior college. She bleached her hair blonde and had a nice tan and was now a "beauty queen," with all the dates she could handle.

As a sophomore in college she experienced "love at first sight." She went up to him and told him she thought he was really good looking. They soon began dating. When he was drafted into the army her world fell apart. It became clear in the course of their correspondence that he was not going to come home and marry her. She feels that in a way she still loves him, even though she has not seen him for 15 years.

Her parents gave her the distinct message that it was time for her to find a man and settle down. She either had to go to a more expensive college away from home or go to work if she did not marry. Since she did not have the money for college and she did not like traditional kinds of jobs, she decided to look for a man:

> One day this nice, clean-cut person walked through the door at the store where I worked and I thought, "Now there's the kind of guy I need to get me." I struck up a conversation, got myself a date with him, and he asked me to marry him the very next night. Two months later we were married. In my mind, I knew that you were supposed to love someone you marry and I told myself I really loved him. I can see that I was acting out a role. I really do love him now, but I was in a play then.

Her first year of marriage felt like "playing house." She detested housecleaning and her husband developed an unstated disdain for her because of it. This unspoken disdain affected her self-worth which was interconnected with the way she kept house. Her husband was embarrassed about the way the house looked if people would drop in.

> The most important thing about this period for me was that I was devalued down to practically nothing. To build myself up, I figured the one thing that I could do for redemption would be to produce a child. So I went on a campaign to get pregnant. The business of taking care of a baby would excuse me from keeping an immaculate house. People don't expect things to be perfect when you have small kids. So I had found a way to raise my status somewhat without having to become Mrs. Clean. I also worked at a job, but that didn't excuse me enough. Those were the days when women worked just to help out in the finances, so a job was really considered an extension of volunteer activity. Housework was still expected to be done by the wife regardless of how many hours she put in on the job.

Having become pregnant, she worried a lot about how they would pay the doctor bill. Somehow, they managed. Being pregnant radically changed her status with her husband:

When I was pregnant, my husband treated me like a saint. More like sacred vessel of his seed, rather than St. Mary. I definitely took back seat when the baby arrived. You'd have thought he invented fatherhood.

Karen was definitely not enamored with being a mother:

My thinking about young motherhood is that society takes a woman who is a living, breathing person with a distinct personality and makes her into a stereotypical nothing. You either see a super neat, cutsey mother with her little darling all clean and neat clustered in and around a stroller, or you have the harried slob with several dirty youngsters and a baby on her hip (with dirty diaper, of course). Somewhere in one of those images the woman is lost.

She was bored with the conversations and concerns of the other young mothers concerning toilet training, feeding, etc. Therefore, she believed that the other women saw her as one who should never have become a mother:

I'd get comments like, "It's a shame you can't enjoy your children more." I love my children, but they aren't my entire life. There is more to me than meets the eye, please.

She felt like a prisoner in the home when her two sons were toddlers, since they did not have the money for a baby sitter. Her husband resented that she did not take her children with her to the grocery store, like other mothers. Instead, she waited for him to get home and then went by herself. She needed a break.

As her husband progressed in his career, they were able to move into a nicer home. This made her happier, primarily because she thinks that people judge one's intelligence on this basis. Having moved to the new house, they joined a church and made new friends, most of whom were professionals. She joined a music group with them, singing and playing guitar. Two of the group were attorneys. They talked about law all the time. She was awestruck and found it interesting. Inwardly, though, she felt inferior to them because she was the only one without a college degree. Her husband was jealous of her involvement with these people, particularly since some of them were men. She had to constantly reassure him. She loved the interaction with this group:

With all the hunger and heartache in the world, here was this group of people contemplating anything and everything. I loved every minute of it, but felt a little guilty for being selfish about them. We were big talkers, but didn't do much to help the human condition.

A few years later they moved to an even nicer home in another town. She felt even better and got involved in local politics. She also decided to complete her college degree. After entering college she and her husband had a marital crisis. She decided to define herself once and for all. Her husband still expected her to do all of the housework, while condescending to "help" once in a while. She resented this deeply and feels that they still have much to work out. She also resents the stereotypical attitude that many persons have about the women who attend college after having children:

> I read a passage in a book once that said that when women don't want to work at a job, they either go into real estate or go back to school. Then to add insult to injury, I read somewhere also where women who return to school typically study psychology or sociology. Sometimes I feel that I have to defend myself for going back. My own brother told me he wouldn't go to a school to be anything but a doctor or a lawyer. One of my friends told me that she thought that people that were "professional students" couldn't function in the world outside school. She said that a person ought to put college behind himself and go on. Even college teaching seemed to be an extension into the retreat from life to her. I fight off people's opinions like that . . . I wish I could get more positive feedback from friends and family. It burns inside sometimes to know that some of the people closest to me disapprove of what I'm doing. I just have to shake it off and keep on going.

Still, Karen remains highly motivated to achieve:

> I think of the 25–30 years that I have left to be in the job market instead of the 4 or 5 that I'm spending in school. I want to strike while my motivation is high. I hope that someday it will have been worthwhile.

One can hear the spirit of Karen's father in her desire to achieve, just as one heard his ghost in her belief that as a woman she must get married and have children. Another aspect of her father's ghost is her continued struggle with weight:

> I know that it seems crazy, but it's the way it is. My weight has a great deal to do with how I see myself. I know I talk about it too much, joke about it a lot, and really give it too much power over me. When I am on a gaining streak, I see myself as hopeless. Bound to always be fat, kind of neutered, and generally down on myself. When I stay the same or lose weight, I feel on top of the world.

At the same time, she recognizes that the "fix" she gets from food cannot be replaced by anyone:

It carries so many meanings for me that this comfort is extremely difficult to abandon.

Karen's struggle with the ghost of her beloved father is also the struggle to become herself as an extremely talented woman. For it was not just her father's attitudes about women that Karen had to fight, but those of the society, represented not only in her memories of his injunctions, but in their the attitudes of contemporary society. The battle for self-realization for many women presents itself as the battle about housework. Karen wrote the following in her diary:

> September 9: My oldest son and I had "words" about his laundry. He came down and asked if I had washed his jeans so he'd have a clean pair to wear tomorrow. I feel like my family is abusing me! My husband always says, "no one does the yard work so why should I do household work?" It seems grossly inequitable to compare a once per week job to a series of daily chores such as washing, folding, clothes, doing dishes, vacuuming, etc.
>
> I need to get organized somehow. If we had unexpected company, I'd die of embarrassment because the house is so cluttered and dirty. Yes, I know my husband and kids should share the work, so why should I be ashamed? The fact is, it stays this way and I am ashamed. I still really feel crummy when my house isn't presentable because so many women I know keep their homes very orderly and clean. The shame still is on the women. Times haven't really changed so much.

Meanwhile, she continues the struggle with weight and dieting by joining a diet center. Her husband objects to the cost, saying she should diet on her own.

The spirit of her father's financial success, and the respect of the community for his status, reveals itself in Karen's concern for gaining the respect of important persons. As a result, she was continually concerned with her wardrobe, appearance, and the impression they made on elites. She comments on their recent attendance at a local high school football game:

> As I look toward the future and see the types of community involvement I want to have, I know I'll have to know many people and have lots of contacts. But you see, all the big shots were sitting in the reserved section and we were in general admission. Plus we looked like bums since we were late getting off. I wonder how far I can go without support from my husband. It's still a "twosy" world. Also I wonder how far I can go if I don't start dressing better and polishing my appearance.

Weeks later at another game they sit in a friend's reserved seats. She comments on how it is almost embarrassing to sit in the general section:

I wish it didn't bother me, but I guess it does. Status is important to me. Life would be simpler if it wasn't.

Karen continues to be bored with marriage and family life in many ways. While she loves her children, she knows that she could do quite well alone. Frequently she is irritated by their fighting. She finds most television shows dull and prefers to read. Indeed, she is a voracious reader of both fiction and nonfiction. One evening, when she wanted to have sex but her husband watched a football game instead she said:

I'd like to kick the TV screen in. It dominates our lives!

Sundays passed typically. After church, Karen does grocery shopping and laundry:

I was bitter while doing the laundry, ironing, etc., at my husband because he really thinks its a joke that I have to do it. No one irons my clothes for me, dammit! I wonder how much money I'll have to make to equalize our relationship. Will I have to equal his income in order to free myself or just make enough for him to know I'll have enough to make it on my own?

Karen received little encouragement from her husband for her education. She was about to finish her baccalaureate degree in anthropology, and spoke of wanting to finish a master's degree just for the sheer joy of it. Her husband reacted violently to this, saying he would like to do a lot for the sheer joy of it too, but could not. Karen's enthusiasm for education was extraordinary:

When I mention school work, etc, it always surprises me when people say they couldn't motivate themselves or discipline themselves to go to school. Its like they think the work is boring and they'd have to force themselves to do it. I can remember feeling that way when a friend of mine went back. A job in a grocery store or bank—now that I'd have to force myself to do!

She continues also to be involved as a member of citizens community improvement organizations. Her enthusiasm for this is not shared by her husband:

I tried to show my husband the reaction center plans, but had to compete with a TV show (a movie he'd already seen). Why bother?

Karen had strong feelings against divorce. Therefore she put up with a lot. However, she did think about it. One day her husband ran out of gas on the way to work and had to walk back home for the gas can. He blamed her for not filling the tank after driving it the night before. After a fight about this she wrote:

> I guess if I had the courage, I'd leave, but I don't know how really. What do you do without a job or any money? Where do you go with two kids in school? If I kicked him out, who pays 550 ($) for house payments and 200 ($) for utilities, and outrageous gasoline bills and all that?

Later Karen went to the library and checked out a book titled "How to Get Out of an Unhappy Marriage" and left it laying on the mantle. The give and take involved in marriages where the wife is involved in a process of self-development is exemplified in Karen's diary:

> My husband told me he wishes I'd hug him more, I think my affection seeking has diminished as I've come further along in school. It is as if I was saying "please love me even though I don't measure up." Now that I have more self-confidence, I find that I don't hug and fawn over him as much. I think he must be feeling insecure with my independence.

The back and forth aspects of the marriage were clear throughout Karen's diary. She wrote of his outbursts of anger, where he would slam doors and blame her and their sons for his frustrations. When things like this happened she contemplated divorce. The opposite reaction came about when he was gone on a business conference and she missed his coming home in the evenings. She became jealous at his stories of a woman who had become interested in him at the conference, telling him about her recent divorce. Karen reflected on her being overweight and her fear that some slender woman would "turn his head." She wondered whether he would have outbursts of anger with some other woman, continue to complain about his health, and have such a low sex drive as he does with her. A couple of days later, when he remarked that the week at the conference was the best of his life she wrote:

> I felt like I'd been hit in the stomach. He said he's glad they don't have these meetings but every three years. It made me wonder if it will be a new set of girls who will find him attractive at 41, and if the same three years will find me even less so. Isn't it funny how gray hair makes a man look distinguished and makes a woman look old?

After the conference their sex life improved. Karen wondered if it were not because of the stimulation provided by the woman at the conference. She comments insightfully on the sexual dilemmas women face:

I was thinking about all the times I've wanted to have sex and he didn't, and how pleased I am when he is interested in it. For a woman, if she wants to have sex with a man, she has to wait until he's ready. But if the man's ready, they do it whether she's ready to or not. Oh sure, she can say no, but what I'm saying is that its a damn shame she has to be subject to his whims. Since my husband isn't one who is wanting sex very often, I don't ever say no, because I feel that I have to get it while I can whether I'm in the frame of mind for it or not. And in spite of abstinence, some times are more conducive to sex than others. But "gather up rosebuds while ye may" doesn't a poem go like that?

Karen speculated on why she hesitates to have an affair:

To me it would be fear, I think. Fear of losing everything. Sometimes I daydream about being with other men, but I don't know for sure if I'd ever act it out even if I had the chance.

After a party, Karen's husband told her he was afraid she would leave him after she obtained financial independence. She told him not to worry since that was a long way off. She felt that some of the other wives at this party were "standoffish" to her since they found out she would be graduating soon.

Commentary

Both Shelly and Karen suffered the consequences of sexist institutions. For Shelly, her whole life was centered on doing slave labor for her father and brothers. The labor would have at least been shared with her mother if her mother had not died. At the same time, narrow and rigid educational systems cost Shelly's father the loss of a job, and the overall economic conditions that the family faced were worsened by the depression.

Shelly's thwarted desire to play basketball as a young girl, and her lack of freedom in comparison with her brothers taught her at early age about the unfairness and losses in opportunity suffered by women. Shelly's household chores continue as she cares for a husband and grown sons even though she also has worked and is currently a full-time student. Shelly's husband's career has always taken precedence over hers. As a result, his career has flourished and hers has stagnated.

Karen suffered from her father's sexism. Although Karen was "daddy's girl" she still was viewed as an object to be controlled and displayed by her father. When her father died, sexism and ageism made it impossible for her mother to get a teaching job. Sexist attitudes in society, and those held by family members prevented Karen from continuing college until recently. She had to struggle for recognition and acceptance of the validity of her continued education from her husband, brother, and friends. Both women benefited from generally positive attributions and expectations from their parents. However, these were to some extent negated by sexism.

Neither Shelly nor Karen received adequate emotional support following their parents' deaths. Both had to instantly take on the parenting role for themselves and others, even though they were still children themselves. "Reversal" parenting was forced on Shelly who had to take her mother's role in the family. Neither Shelly nor Karen received adequate support or help in handling the enormity of their grief.

The death of a parent is a circumstance which imposes aspects I have labeled "immature" on the parent–child relationship. The way these worked out in Shelly's and Karen's case is summarized in Table 8.1.

The death of a parent brings about a rupture in the primary bond. When one parent dies, the tendency often increases for the remaining parent to become emotionally dependent upon a child to make up for the loss of the spouse. Death is such a threatening event that the surviving parent is frequently unlikely to adequately mirror the child's emotions. Reversal parenting is likely, as the child tries to fill in for the missing parent in the remaining parent's life. The tendency to deny death makes congruent communication by the remaining parent unlikely. Death is a tragedy in the family system, and is guilt inducing. The stress

Table 8.1. Summary of Parenting Practices Experienced by Karen and Shelly

	Shelly	Karen
Primary bond	Fractured	Fractured
Mirroring	Inadequate	Inadequate
Style of parenting	Reversal	Reversal
Communicative stance	Objectivistic	Irrelevant
Defenses	Neurotic	Neuro/mature
Attributions	Positive	Positive
Expectations	Positive	Positive/mixed
Temporality	Meaningful	Meaningful
Dramatic form	Tragic/comic	Tragic/comic
Moral development	Goodness/care	Goodness/care
Ethical level	Artistry	Artistry/love
Child's self-integration	Divided/inte	Divided/inte

of death causes survivors to regress to more primitive and less mature defense mechanisms, such as denial or acting out.

The child who suffers the death of a parent is more likely to develop an emotionally divided self. In this case there is the part of the self which takes on the characteristics of the dead parent, in order that the family system may adjust to this traumatic loss. As the child's grief is not adequately mirrored by the remaining parent, the child will feel all the more alienated, alone, and guilty. Shelly and Karen both had remaining parents who exhibited "goodness" or "caring" as well as "artistry" and "love" in their approaches to others and life. These qualities balanced the life situations of both women toward the positive side. Shelly and Karen have moved toward integrated selves in recent years.

Social welfare institutions provide few if any services for widowed parents or children who lose their parents. It is evident from these case studies that such services are needed if partially orphaned children are not to be forced by circumstances into taking on emotional burdens they should not have to face.

Pam and Rhonda—Mature Parents _____ 9

Introduction

This chapter is about Pam and Rhonda, both of whom had "happy" childhoods. Both had parents who exhibited many qualities of maturity in relation to their children. Pam and Rhonda received warmth and affection from their parents and enjoy their support at the present time. Neither Pam nor Rhonda were abused, incest victims, neglected, or lost a parent through death or divorce. Pam was working through a difficult marriage during the course of the study, and indeed instigated a divorce. Rhonda had already been divorced, but was struggling with her ex-husband over custody of their teenaged son. What is striking about their diaries is the way they went about dealing with these problems and the overriding sense of confidence they portrayed. The level of maturity exhibited by their parents allowed for Pam and Rhonda, in turn, to become mature in their relationships with their children. The maturity they demonstrated is especially high, given that they both were under stress at the time of the study. In addition, they seemed to truly enjoy life, in spite of the problems they faced.

Pam and Rhonda experienced "happy" childhoods by comparison with the other women presented in this book. According to accepted societal norms, they were loved and well cared for. They were not victimized, abused, or abandoned by their parents. Both became wives and mothers eager to fill the expected roles to the best of their abilities. Both have done this well and with maturity. Because their families represent the culturally approved of norm, or "ideal," the problems inherent in these norms stand out more clearly. These stem from immaturities in their parents and the inadequate social context of sexism embedded in family, school, church, and workplace.

The tendency of parents to project their own narcissistic needs onto their children was apparent in Pam's case. Pam was thought to be

189

"cold" and thus not wanting affection by her mother. She was expected to be a helper to the mother in taking care of younger siblings. Pam's father demanded outstanding achievement, for which she was capable. The guilt fostered in Pam by her church caused her to take on the motherhood role intensely. Sacrificing her own intellectual growth, she mothered her three children and her husband. As her husband approached his maturational adolescence, he wanted to be free from Pam, his mother substitute. The sexism of family, church, and school bore down heavily on Pam's experience. In spite of this, she has exhibited extraordinary maturity and strength through the crisis of divorce and in the care of her adolescent children.

Rhonda's loving parents provided her with a firm and stable platform from which to launch her own career as wife/mother. She fell wholeheartedly into the role, and enjoyed the "romance" stage of her marriage as long as possible. Her own abilities and ambition throughout her life, for example, her will to become an engineer, were thwarted by sexist family and educational institutions. In spite of these significant setbacks, Rhonda has launched a career, and is a mature role model for her two adolescent children.

Pam—From Young Love to Midlife Crisis

Pam was the oldest of seven siblings, growing up in an Italian Catholic family, the daughter of a respected businessman. From her earliest memories, her parents thought highly of her and expected the best from her. Pam's father was proud of her precocity and her reaching developmental milestones before the expected time. He thought her to be exceptionally bright, inquisitive, and independent. Pam felt that her father expected her to be perfect, and she indeed tried.

Pam's mother, thought her to be beautiful, verbally gifted and responsible. By the age of 6, she was already helping her mother to care for her two younger sisters and baby brother. Pam's young mother involved her in reversal parenting, but to a lesser degree than in the case of Shelly (whose mother's died), Karen (whose father died), and Rebecca (who took on her mother's role). For short periods of time, she babysat for them. Her mother said that Pam resisted cuddling as a small child. Pam seemed to disbelieve that explanation, implying that her mother projected a tendency to be cold onto her. Even though she had younger sisters to play with, Pam's favorite companion was Lonny, an imaginary playmate. This playmate did not have any special expectations of her and perhaps provided a relief from the feeling that she must always be responsible. Through fantasy, appropriate for a young child, Pam provided herself with an essential significant other. This significant other's positive regard was unconditional.

As a preschooler, Pam attended church and Sunday school. She felt that the power of the church and of her parents were awesome. She developed an air of defiance toward parental power at an early age. Pam remembers well this time of her life:

> Daddy's voice is loud when he yells at me to get up. I jump out of bed real quick. Betty and Dorrie, my younger sisters are snoring; they don't have to get up yet. They don't go to school yet. I'm excited about school. It's so much fun. Our room is painted all bright pink and there's a built-in closet, dresser, and desk my father made for us. It goes all across one wall. I keep my toys in the closet next to the window. My red-haired doll sits on the shelf.
>
> The covers on my bed feel so warm and soft. I hate to get up. The floor is cold, so I run to the bathroom where it's warm from the heater, and I stand on the soft bath mat. Then I run to the hall and stand over the floor furnace. The heat rushes up and fills my nightgown like a balloon. After I'm dressed, I go play with my baby brother. His tiny hands and feet are soft. I run one foot against my cheek, and he laughs out loud.
>
> When I go in the kitchen it is all white, except the floor which is big, black squares. Mommy's cooking bacon and coffee. Of course, I don't get to drink any coffee. "Stunt your growth," they say. When I get big, I'll drink all I want.

Pam remembers her years in primary school with much delight. Her birthdays each fall were very special—her own time. Her mother made a birthday cake and whatever she wanted to eat for dinner. Soon after her birthday came Halloween. Her parents' caring was evident in the way they handled this holiday:

> Mom let me dress up as a Gypsy, using her jewelry, clothes, and make-up. It got cold and Dad made me wear my coat. I cried because it covered my costume, but soon my disappointment was lost in a growing sack of candied corn, bubble gum, homemade cookies, popcorn balls, and a big red apple.

Pam remembers the company they always had at Thanksgiving and how they enjoyed her mother's corn bread dressing. Starting at Thanksgiving, they would begin to mark off the days on the calendar until Christmas:

> It seemed a magical time of year. At school and at church I participated in the Christmas pageant as a wise man and an angel. I made special colored-paper gifts for everyone in my family. My maternal grandmother sent a box

with gifts for each of us. She crocheted a beautiful hat and cape for my red-haired doll. She even included a huge slab of bacon and a ham. Even now the smell of bacon cooking makes me feel good.

After the holidays Pam remembers the cold, short days leading into Lent. Then came extra church services and giving up candy. (This was hard for her to do as a child.) But these days ended in the joy of Easter:

> At the end of Lent came Easter with a new dress, Easter egg hunts, waking up to find a bright colored basket with decorated eggs and candy I couldn't eat until after church. I was to make my first communion. I felt beautiful in my white dress with a veil draped over freshly curled hair. The church was transformed from the purple of sorrow to glorious white. Huge baskets of white lilies rested on altars which were bare only the day before. Organ music and my mother's lovely voice filled our small church.

Summers brought the promise of endless days of freedom; bare feet, swimming, and drive-in movies on Saturday nights. Pam did her chores early in the morning during summer. After that she was free to play—exploring tree houses, digging in sand, playing house and school. On Wednesdays, her mother would bring her a new paper doll. Saturday nights, her father took the whole family in the car to a drive-in movie. Pam especially enjoyed when she got to go with her father to the snack bar for cokes and popcorn. Unlike girls such as Rebecca, Pam's responsibilities were alleviated by times of joyful play.

Summers also brought with them vacations trips. Sometimes these trips were out of state to visit grandparents in Wisconsin. She loved these visits, although the car was crowded and her father demanded silence in the car. At summer's end, Pam anticipated with excitement the beginning of each school year. She would get several new crisp cotton dresses each year, new shoes, and fresh school supplies. She loved the smell of the new clothes and books, and the freshly cleaned school rooms. The beginning of school signaled a fresh start, a renewal of the cycle of her life.

Pam's father continued to think of her as intelligent and strong willed throughout her school years. He expected the highest academic achievement and absolute obedience. Thus he exhibited what Alice Miller (1984) writes about as "narcissistic pride" of a parent who places undue performance pressure on the child. At the same time, he was extremely supportive and helpful to Pam in these efforts. For several years he had Pam and her younger siblings come to his office after school where he provided training in speed reading and comprehension. No matter how well she did, she always felt that her father expected more. Perhaps this was part of the reason for her rebellion as a teenager. A certain amount of "family pride" on father's part was apparent here.

Her mother saw Pam as helpful and mature—a necessary partner in the overwhelming job of caring for six younger siblings. Since her mother was small and delicate and she was tall and strong for her age, her mother called her "sis." Pam felt that she had to live up to her mother's expectations. She felt that she could have benefited from more warmth and personal attention from her mother.

Happily, the family's solid middle-class financial status somewhat alleviated the burdens on Pam. They were even able to afford the help of a maid for many years. In some ways, Pam resented the presence of this maid, because she cut into Pam's authority in the home.

In the neighborhood, there were mostly boys of Pam's age. Consequently, she competed with them for the role of Tarzan in the games. (Jane, Tarzin's girlfriend, never got to do anything interesting, she thought.) Pam's first understanding of class distinctions came about when she brought girls home from school to play who had no other friends. Her parents discouraged many of these relationships.

By the time Pam reached the age of 15, she was already taking care of her six younger siblings over weekends when her parents had to leave town. Her siblings expected her to be a leader and to advocate for them with her parents. Perhaps, if anything, Pam was given too much responsibility.

At this same age, Pam made friends with a young man at school who was having academic trouble. By the time she was 16 they were dating steadily, much to her parents' disapproval. Her sense of independence and defiance led her to continue in this relationship. At the same time, her boyfriend became more adamant and demanding. She felt pressured from both sides. Pam so excelled at the caretaker–leader role that she took on this role with her boyfriend as well. Like a parent, she was supposed to meet all his needs.

Pam regarded the values of her high school peers as shallow, yet she was afraid to openly reject them. Her friends saw her remoteness as strength and looked upon her as a leader. She did some writing and confided in no one. Her parents were preoccupied with trying to make a place for themselves in the community. Pam wondered if this "community" was worthy of her parents.

Her boyfriend's and her own unmet needs for warmth and affection literally pushed her into the role of mother. While a senior in high school, Pam became pregnant. She finished school at mid term and they married. She and her young husband, Roy, left their small home town in disgrace. She decided she was not worthy of her parents and felt she had brought shame upon them. They moved to a large city, with $400 and a used car that Roy's parents had made the down payment on. The past seemed like a harbor of safety.

Pam and Roy moved into a small apartment with an asphalt lawn next to a freeway. The noise of the rushing traffic was strange and constant. Their apartment resembled a motel, with imitation Danish modern furnishings, a gold and orange commercial carpet, and loud flowered orange drapes. There were framed prints on the walls. To Pam, the sights of the city were awesome:

> Blinking neon signs and huge billboards offered every product or service imaginable. The streets and shopping centers teem with people—all strangers.

Pam got a job immediately at the telephone company. The sounds of her clicking typewriter competed with those of the forty men working in a giant telephone bay connecting wires. Once a week her boss allowed her to make a long-distance telephone call to her mother. Her mother's voice was like a lifeline.

Three months pregnant when they arrived in the city, Pam experienced morning sickness:

> Never has my sense of smell been more acute. Everything made me sick—food, my make-up, cologne, hair spray. Every day we drove by a bakery on the way to work and every day my stomach turned over. Grocery shopping was a nightmare. I could just about make it to the check-out counter, and my husband would have to take over while I ran to the car and the bowl which became a permanent fixture there.

The situation made Pam feel dependent on Roy:

> Waking in the morning nestled against Roy's warm body, I felt secure and loved. Leaving him to go to work was agony, and that was the only time we were apart. We physically clung to each other, holding hands wherever we went, as if letting go we might drown.

The most significant event of that year for Pam was the birth of their daughter:

> She was magnificent, perfect in every respect. At Christmas we took her home to meet her new grandparents and many aunts and uncles. They were enthralled with her. My father took picture after picture of her. I cried when we left there, as I would do each time for many times after.

When the baby was 5 weeks old Pam went back to work, this time at the university where her husband was enrolled. When her husband was not attending class, he watched the baby. Otherwise, Pam took the baby to a neighbor who also had an infant. When not at work they spent their time housekeeping, shopping, and taking care of the baby together. Due to limited finances they took their baby to parks and museums, wherever there was no admission fee. On Sundays, Roy would drive Pam to church and wait for the service to end. Their main treat of the week was an ice cream cone after church. At this time Pam's image of the future was depressing:

> Ours was such a hand-to-mouth existence that it was difficult to imagine not having to struggle for survival. All my hopes rested on my husband's finishing school and that was not going well. I had ceased to imagine accomplishing anything myself. I defined my role in life as that of caring for my children and husband, and providing inspiration for him to succeed. That I continued working was a financial necessity, and, as it turned out, a salvation of sorts. I was accomplishing something. I was learning and growing.

Roy viewed Pam as hard-working and often emotional at this time. He liked her emotional dependency. This was the closest they had been. Two years later they had another baby, a son. Two years after that they had a second daughter. At just 22 years old she was the mother of three and their primary caretaker. She also was still the main breadwinner in the home, although it now looked like her husband would never finish college.

Her role as mother was to be a natural carry over from her role at home in taking care of her younger siblings. She felt that she and Roy were not giving the children all of the emotional support that they may have needed, because their life was such a struggle. All of their leisure time centered around the children. They spent no leisure time as a couple.

Roy saw Pam as encouraging and supportive of his career, now that he had taken a full-time job. He thought she analyzed things too deeply, and was too demanding of him. Roy also thought that Pam was not totally accepting of him. He was right. At that time Pam's mother and siblings, especially her four sisters, continued to be her source of emotional support and encouragement.

When Roy joined a men's service organization, Pam joined the women's auxiliary. She felt out of place at the meetings, since she was the only one working. At social events, she preferred to talk with the men, for the women's discussions about children and housework were not interesting to her.

At the present time, Pam's daughters are 19 and 15 and her son is 17. Her son just recently has started relating to her in a positive manner, since he had pulled away totally in the prior 2 years. Pam's 15-year-old daughter hardly talks to her, but does seem to communicate with Roy. Pam's boss thinks of her as a protege to mold into an outstanding "woman manager." She has no interest in becoming one, however.

This is currently Pam's second semester in her freshman year as a university student. She continues to work nearly full time as well. Pam loves school and plans to major in journalism. Meanwhile, her husband says they have nothing in common nor do they want the same things. Indeed, Pam is trying to discover herself at a more profound level:

> All of my ideas about society are now in a state of change. The church, men and women's roles in a relationship, marriage, all my ideas acquired through response to stimuli, conditioning, etc., are changing. Perhaps they are not really changing, but I am just now beginning to understand what my ideas really are. I seemed always to be at cross-purposes with what I perceived as expectations of me. I can't believe how optimistic I feel in the midst of all this chaos. My husband wants to leave me, my children are pulling away and I am in school and loving it!

At the start of this semester, Pam was enjoying her classes. In her diary kept throughout the course of this semester, Pam reflects on the dissolution of her marriage:

> Only the second day into my journal and I have to write that my husband wants to leave me. Why don't I feel devastated? But I do. We talked and talked and talked. Then he told me. All I can think of is that we finally talked! For more than two years I've tried to get him to do that—just talk to me. I knew it wasn't just his job or all the other things he said were bothering him. I knew there must be more; he's been miserable for so long. He says he thinks he's having a nervous breakdown. I wish I could help him not to feel so bad. He won't hear of counseling. I'm afraid for him. Life has always seemed such a burden for him—the kids and their demands, money (there's never enough), the job (he can't tolerate less than perfection there), and the wife (how am I to be objective)? I'm too verbal, I think. I want to read and read and talk about everything I've read. I want to debate politics, religions, philosophy. He says I overanalyze things. I tried not to. For years I read only dime-store novels, cookbooks, and women's magazines. I watched T.V. I wouldn't think of going to school. I quit writing. Then I had a mid-life crisis (trite but true). I had done all the things I thought I had to do to be a good mother and wife. In spite of that, he began withdrawing from me. So did the kids, but their's was a natural part of the growth process. They were becoming independent. I plunged myself into

the kind of reading I love, with some self-exploration stuff thrown in. Now I can't get enough. But my marriage is going down the tube, and I can't help wondering if I've done everything I can to save it—or even if I want to.

Here it is evident that Pam's husband had reached emotional adolescence—he was finally ready to pull away from his substitute mother/ wife and explore life, including the opposite sex, and an affiliation with a group of friends. Ironically, this occurred for him at the same time as for his teenaged children.

The next day Pam had to keep running to the bathroom at work because she had to cry. She talked with a doctor at work who said that maybe a separation might help. Pam worried about how they could afford to maintain two households since it takes all they have to maintain one.

The weekend seemed to stretch interminably before her. She felt like she aged greatly in the last few days. Her husband had told her that he had had an affair with another woman and acted like he may explode at any time. Actually it was not the affair (which he said was over) that concerned him, it was how miserable they both felt. Pam thought that life is too short to be miserable.

That evening Roy went out with "the guys." She did not care if it was the truth or not, she just hoped it would relieve his tension. Pam was worried that he may follow through on his threat to quit his job and leave town. She thought that he could not live with the guilt if he did this.

That Monday, which was a holiday, they went to Pam's sister's house for dinner. Her sister and her brother-in-law had guessed that something was wrong. Pam and her sister went up to the study after dinner. Her sister said she always thought of her marriage to Roy as unshakable but that it lacked depth of feeling. She said they seemed to be together out of a sense of fierce loyalty and commitment to duty. Pam admitted that life had been a struggle for them:

It's like planting seeds in rocky soil, the plant will have strong roots and stalk but no flowers. We started off at eighteen and nineteen years old and pregnant. We didn't think we had any choices at the time. We determined to do the "right thing." Funny, I remember thinking it was a fitting punishment for my sin to have to give up my dreams of college and a career. I felt resolute—I would be a good wife and mother. I would be the woman behind the successful man, just like my mother. It never occurred to me that he might not want the same things I did, only that he might not know how to get them, and I could show him how. College was the first order of

business. I would work so he could study. I would also be a good Catholic
girl, and so we had three kids. He wasn't Catholic, but he never even suggested contraceptives. At the time I thought he was merely respecting my
beliefs. After the third baby I began taking the pill, but not without considerable guilt. At the end of five years it was clear he would never make it
through college. He took a job and I decided never to mention college again.
But here it is, all the old baggage, and I'm writing it down.

At work the next day, Pam felt that her co-workers were treating her
as if she had been sick, all being especially gentle. At school she felt that
her English honors class was moving too slowly—it reminded her of
high school. With the crisis at hand, Pam felt sometimes that time went
by at a maddeningly slow pace. Even at this time of crisis, she had the
inner strength to experience the beauty and solace of nature:

> Fall is the best of seasons, and today its promise filled the air. It has a special
> fragrance and an electric crispness I can feel on my skin and in my hair.
> Thin clouds are stretched across the sky. All my nerves feel taut, stretched. I
> want to walk, no run somewhere—anywhere. I want to run until my breath
> comes in huge gasps. I want to fall on the still-green grass, roll onto my
> back, and then watch the dizzy clouds dazzled with sunlight and floating
> above me.

The next day her slow English class "took off like a rocket." She was
pleased about the challenge it would now present. Some days seemed
almost normal. She spoke to her husband and there was little tension.
That Saturday, Pam spent most of the day on a long list of errands.
She was alone that evening, the children having gone out. Roy went to
a ball game with two new friends. He told Pam that these friends drive
expensive cars and have a bachelor's pad. He seemed to think they lived
an ideal existence. Pam could not resist asking him if he thought they
may be homosexual:

> He almost choked. He stammered, "Of course not." I bet he thought about
> it all evening. (That was wicked, girl.)

Pam spent the evening curled up with "The Canterbury Tales" and
a wine cooler. When the children came home they talked for a while
and they all went to bed. The last time she looked at the clock it was
3:00 A.M. and Roy was still not home. He arrived shortly after dawn.
Sunday Pam started out by cleaning her daughter's closet. Her sister
came over that afternoon and they enjoyed talking about religion, politics, and women's roles. Pam remarked at how bright and individual
each of her siblings are. They each look at life with insight and humor.

The next day Pam felt lonely and resentful. She saw one of the young girls from her husband's office driving his fancy company car. She saw the girl in her husband's car as a symbol of his middle life crisis, and she was not feeling tolerant about it:

> I looked in the mirror carefully for the first time in a while; I don't like what I see. I see a very grim face and eyes without light in them. The mouth is becoming set in a hard, thin line.

Pam's inner resources frequently came to her rescue throughout her current difficulties. One day she "escaped" from home and spent the day off by herself, walking, reading, and finally getting her hair cut short. This was indeed a symbol of breaking free and being herself. (Roy had always wanted her to keep long hair.) Of this day she says: "Imagination can be a wonderful thing—a salvation of sorts." In her classes as well, Pam's imagination was an asset. When asked to describe herself as Chaucer would have done, using his form of rhyme and meter, she found it easy and fun.

The next evening Pam visited with a friend she had been avoiding. She did not want to tell her about her problems with Roy. This friend had been divorced 2 years ago after an unhappy 18-year marriage. The friend was extremely bitter. Pam did not want to have her problems equated with those of her friend because Pam did not feel that Roy was a "bastard" like her friend's husband was.

That Saturday Pam bought herself a new outfit. She said that with her new haircut and clothes she felt a new person. Once again she showed the resources that a person like Pam with a solid, happy childhood behind her can pull together at times of crisis. That evening her daughter lingered and asked why she did not go out and have a good time like her father did. Pam said that she had to study. Pam mused that the children perhaps should be informed about what is going on between their parents. But she did not want to deal with the tensions that telling them would cause. Roy did not return until 3:22 A.M. that Sunday.

The next week brought hard work at the office and school and exhaustion. Pam found the discussion with the other women in the support group that evening to be stimulating. It was an evening when the women had shared memories of childhood. Pam commented on Rebecca, who was a member of the same group:

> Even Rebecca, whose early life was filled with tragedy, lights up with shared triumphs. It alters her whole appearance from a hardness to youthful beauty.

The next day Roy came home and said that he was thinking of taking a job out of state. It surprised Pam when he said that she could come with him if she wanted to. This company would also send Roy to school. Pam was puzzled. She thought that Roy did not want to go to school. She told him that the move would not solve their problem, namely, how to get out from under their financial burdens so that she can become self-supporting and he can leave. He said "I know." The next day, Roy had still another plan:

> I feel like I'm on a roller coaster. Now he's thinking of going into business with a man he almost went into business with several years ago. He's so up, it's almost like there was nothing wrong. He was like he was three years ago, before he became so depressed.

At work the next morning Pam's boss called her into his office. He advised her not to feel like she has to take on new major projects while she is under strain. She broke down in his office. This was the first time in 14 years he had seen her like this. Her boss told her not to feel guilty if she had to coast along once in a while.

Roy continued to plan to start the new business. He intended to keep his current job as well until the note for the business was paid off. He seemed quite nervous and anxious about it. Pam was pleased that he left that evening for an overnight fishing trip hoping that it may relieve some of the pressure.

Unfortunately this did not happen. While on the "fishing" trip, Roy suffered a slipped disc and came home the next day with agonizing back pain. The pain continued for the next 2 days. Finally, they called an ambulance to take him to the hospital. The doctors gave him medication and he was placed in traction.

The same evening that Roy came home from the hospital he left home at 8 P.M. and returned at midnight. He did not say where he was going:

> Isn't it curious, I seem to be only an observer in my own life. I'm watching everything he does as if it has nothing to do with me at all. Would I have been so dispassionately involved a few years ago? I don't think so. What has changed? Well, maybe we both have. It's as though I'm watching my marriage slip out of my hands, and I can only move in slow motion.

With her husband home from the hospital and still confined to bed most of the time, Pam felt overwhelmed with the housework. She had to yell at her son to mow the lawn and at her daughters to help with the house cleaning. She felt that she needed to be at her best to deal with three rebellious teenagers, and she was unfortunately not at her best at this time.

In looking over her diary, Pam is concerned that she has spent too much time writing about her problems with her marriage. She said that she is continuing to experience other things as well, but that the ordinary stresses of them are harder to bear. She is still the primary caretaker of their three children and this is especially difficult now:

> I continue to be concerned about my kids. It requires infinite patience and understanding to deal with their problems and needs. One of the things I wish for most is that my husband and I could be together in how to deal with them and their needs. We are as far apart in our attitudes about child rearing as everything else.

In the group discussion the next night, Pam commented on how disturbed she was by someone in the group dominating the discussion. (Several others in the study commented on this as well.) She dreaded the weekend since it was to be her birthday, and they had to go home to visit her family and Roy's family. She thought they would all be able to tell that something was wrong. That Friday the people at work gave Pam a birthday party, with a cake and a card. This lifted her spirits. Pam's boss took Pam and a friend out to lunch. At home that week end her family also gave her a birthday party:

> My family gave me a birthday party. It was terrific. One of my sisters arranged to have colorful helium-filled balloons delivered. They all sang "Happy Birthday" as the costumed lady handed them to me. Then they brought in a beautiful cake. It was so thoughtful of them and a boost to my morale.

That week Pam's husband started working every night. Pam felt the oppression of the unending housework. She found herself watching TV, a "mindless activity." She placed an order for her son's graduation pictures. She hopes that he will plan to go to college, although he will receive no financial or emotional support from his father to do so. She said that she would do all she could to help him.

Once again Pam spent Saturday night home alone studying. Roy went out with his friends and said he may not be home that night at all. The next day Pam had a confrontation with her youngest daughter who did not do her school work. She and Roy agreed that she should stay at home that week end. The girl sneaked out for several hours that Saturday night. Pam and Roy told her she would be grounded for Sunday, but then when a friend offered her tickets to a professional football game, she begged to go. Roy lost his resolve and said it was up to Pam. Pam's diary is a beautiful reflection of her realization of her role in her daughter's life:

> Roy told our younger daughter that he did not want to get into trouble with me. Then our daughter turned on me and said "it's all you! It's always you." Instead of retreating into defeat again I told her she was right, it was me, and I said no she couldn't go. She screamed and begged, and my husband retreated to his bed and covered his head with a pillow. I stood my ground and when my daughter threatened to run away, I calmly told her that she was fifteen years old and the police would bring her back. Then I would restrict her again. I told her she had better give it careful thought, because there might be something else she would miss getting to do because of her behavior. She cried and went to her room and slept for about three hours, but she didn't leave. I tried to tell my husband that all she wants is for some limits to be set. He always agrees easily but then fails to follow through. If I confront him, he goes into a tirade or walks out. I think I understand finally; my husband doesn't want the responsibility and never has. Nothing I do will ever change that. The difference today is that for the first time it didn't depress me.

On Monday, Roy was home sick in bed with an upset stomach. In her typical manner, Pam came home from work at noon with some ginger ale and soup for him. She continues to care for her husband in a protective way in much the same way that she cares for her children. In reflecting on this, Pam accuses herself of being an emasculating female and a cold fish. She thought that she, as the woman, should be the one to become ill, not the man. She continues to ruminate about why she can't be completely accepting, and then goes on to reproach herself because she thought she should be. Then she says that perhaps she and Roy are just the wrong combination of personalities.

At school the next day Pam is inaugurated into the Journalism Honorary Society. She then was depressed to come home to an empty house with a sink full of dirty dishes.

She woke up depressed the next morning nagged the children and became sarcastic with her husband. By the time she got to work she was on the verge of tears and could hardly function. She reflected that tensions and pressures from school seemed to make the difficulties she experienced at home all the more problematic. She thought that she was correct in waiting to separate from her husband until after they were better able to manage it financially. If her 15-year-old daughter went to live with her father now Pam was convinced that she would not get the supervision she needed and would probably not finish high school. On the other hand, Pam thought that she may be wrong in prolonging the period of unhappy time when they were still together.

Pam's keen ability to cope was demonstrated the next day. She made plans to prepare for her English presentation a step at a time. Her husband agreed to let their youngest daughter work part time in his office.

As this plan began, Pam worried about her strategy with this daughter who was failing in school. That evening Roy announced that he had cancelled another overnight fishing trip and wanted to take the whole family out to dinner. Pam accepted gladly. Meanwhile, the telephone bill arrived with $72 worth of long distance calls made by their daughter to her boyfriend. Roy was enraged, insisting that the bill be repaid out of the daughter's earnings.

Pam spent Sunday alone cleaning and reading. Her husband had spent overnight Saturday night and all day Sunday at his former boss's house, attending the funeral of his daughter. The children were out.

When the work week started again, Pam asked her boss to recommend a counselor. Pam feels overwhelmed in trying to deal with the situation with her daughter. She had spoken with Roy about their telling the children that they were having problems and were thinking about separation. He did not want to call them all together to tell them. He wanted each of them to tell each child individually. Pam felt this technique would only emphasize their isolation from one another.

Pam's classes were going well and she continued to enjoy the work and participating in class discussions. That evening, Pam discovered that her husband had several weeks before told their older daughter and son that they may separate. Neither child mentioned it to Pam. Their older daughter took it very hard and said she did not want to talk about it. Their son said it was "no big deal—lots of folks get divorced nowadays." When he was told he could live with his father as soon as he got settled in an apartment the son said he did not want to live in an apartment.

That Friday night Pam went to stay overnight with a friend. They talked, chain smoked, and ate dinner. Her friend's husband was on a hunting trip in Colorado. They had a good time discussing marriage, Pam's pending separation, raising children, and everything else. The next morning her friend made a delicious brunch and they talked for another 6 hours. She arrived home feeling exhausted but much relieved and strengthened from this good friendship. Back at home Pam spoke with her older daughter who was extremely upset about the possibility of their separation. Her daughter said that in 2 years her mother would have a degree but would have lost her husband. She said her father had several divorced friends and thought it was a great life, but it really was not. Pam told her daughter that the decision to separate was not one they had taken lightly. Her daughter said that her younger brother was extremely upset, even though on the surface he seemed glib about it. This is what Pam had suspected.

In the coming days, Pam's older daughter spoke with her about the separation. She wanted to know if they would have to sell the house. Pam's affirmative answer seemed to upset her the most.

Pam's first session with her therapist went well. He stressed that the only life she could manage was her own. This heightened her feelings of helplessness about her youngest daughter but relieved her sense of guilt. Dr. T. helped her to recognize her anger toward her husband. He said that her husband had not left yet and that actions speak louder than words.

Pam asked her husband to go to therapy with her. He emphatically declined, saying he did not believe in it:

> He was smoldering when he found out how much it cost. He wanted to know how long I planned to go. I told him just until I figure some things out and feel like I can manage on my own. One of the things I need help with is what to do about our youngest daughter; I just can't stand watching her throw her life away and seeing her suffer so. Then I asked him if the reason that he was still living at home was because he thought perhaps we could work things out between us or that I might change. He said he was still here only because of finances; as soon as he had enough income from his business he would leave. He didn't believe there was any hope for us at all, that I made him feel inadequate in every way. He said it might be irresponsible of him but he just didn't want the responsibility of the kids and their problems or the grind of putting me through school. Pointing out the contradictions of his remarks seemed futile. He would only see my logic as confirmation of his inadequacies. To add insult to injury he confirmed that he is involved with a girl from his office—she's only one year older than our daughter!

Indeed, it seemed that Pam was the only responsible parent in a family of four children.

Pam regretted that her parents were coming to stay overnight the next night. She knew they would sense that something was wrong. Pam told them of the situation, feeling that she needed their support. They focused on his infidelity. Pam tried to explain that she saw this as only a symptom. Pam's father wanted to know if she would quit school if this could save their marriage. She explained that in a good marriage both partners should want the other to develop themselves as far as possible. Her father said she should be patient and not press her husband and that he would then come to his senses.

Once again, Pam's Saturday was spent alone. Her husband was at work all day and left at 6:00, saying that he did not know if he would be home. Pam knew he would not. Her children were out, except for the 15 year old who had a friend in. Pam would allow her to go out the following weekend if her counselor agreed.

> I sip a glass of wine and study. It's lonely though.
>
> I woke at 3:00 this morning. It was raining. I went back to sleep and dreamed disturbing dreams about my husband. He kept bringing this young girl around, and I felt humiliated.

Pam read in bed until 10:00 then got up and started the day. Roy came home about 6:00 P.M. on Sunday. They hardly spoke.

Pam's second appointment with Dr. T. went well, but she did not talk to him about what she most feared. This week brought Pam delight in her classes, worry about her son's quiet behavior and hope that she could get through the weekend with the same degree of confidence she feels when she leaves her therapist's office.

Saturday Pam and her husband went shopping to buy her a car. She said that she would never be able to make the payments. Roy said he would help her. This did not seem too possible to her, yet she did need a dependable car. That week Pam had a long telephone conversation with one of her sisters. She was very supportive and offered more time and help. Pam said she had her therapist for that purpose and would not ask her family because they were very close to Roy for all these years. However it made Pam feel good that they cared.

During Pam's next session with Dr. T. he told her she could discontinue treatment and lead a normal, healthy life. He said she should look back at her relationship with her father, because he noticed her tendency to defer to men's opinions, even her son's. He told her that when she took responsibility for herself she would also have to be responsible for her failures.

Pam attended a writer's conference and learned some tips for her own writing. Pam continued to prepare for a group presentation in English class that was worrisome to her. One day she did something she does rarely, she read a magazine from cover to cover—just when she needed most to be studying. She thought that perhaps she needed the escape.

Pam almost missed her appointment with Dr. T . . She mused that perhaps she was trying to avoid confrontation. She knew that she must take responsibility for herself. Dr. T. told her that no one is in charge of her and she must take this step. Furthermore, if her children are important to her it is up to her to take charge since someone has to bring order into their lives. When she got home from the session Pam took action immediately:

> When I got home, I asked my husband to sit down and let's work out a plan. First of all we have to be clear about what we are discussing—divorce. He agreed. It was the first time either of us had said the word. After our talk, I put it all on paper, complete with dates. He will move out by the second week in December. I asked him to read it carefully and see if he agreed or disagreed with any part of the plan. He agreed with it all. Now I have to deal with the children.

On Wednesday Pam had a talk with her oldest daughter:

> I talked with my daughter today. She didn't want to hear, but I told her it was important. Afterward, she cried. I held her for almost an hour. We talked more in depth than ever before. And I didn't censure her criticism of her father. I just let her talk. I think it was good for both of us. I told her we would all work together, and we would be fine—we will be a family.

In this diary entry, Pam shows her extreme sagacity in dealing with the situation head on and being helpful to her daughter. During this week Pam also spoke with her son about the situation. She thought it went well. The children talked to her more than they had in a long time.

Thanksgiving found the family separating. Roy and their son went to Roy's mother's. Pam and her daughters went to Pam's sister's. Pam felt a lot of support from her family on this holiday and had a good time.

Pam wrote of an episode of sibling rivalry with her sister the next day. She got into her "intellectual snob—moralizing parent" routine with her sister. She lashed out at her younger daughter who was fighting with her cousin. When they left, she managed to say some conciliatory words to her sister. On the way home, she and her younger daughter had some dialogue that she thought was beneficial.

That Sunday Pam prepared dinner for her older daughter and son and their respective boyfriend and girlfriend. She enjoyed this.

Her next session with Dr. T. was confusing. She felt she did not say what he wanted her to about the ultimate loss of control. He was harsh with her about intellectualizing her feelings. That night Roy came home and said that the man he was going to enter business partnership with had told him he would not need a partner. Roy had lost their biggest contract. Pam did not have the nerve to confront him that evening with his plans to move the next week.

On Thursday Pam completed her English presentation and was pleased with the results. That evening they put up their Christmas tree:

As my son got the box with the tree and ornaments out he expressed anger that his father had thrown tree, ornaments, and all into the box right after Christmas last year. Some of the ornaments were broken, including the tree-top one. I had forgotten all about that. He remarked that his father was always angry after Christmas. He was right, and I was astonished. I have suppressed so many unpleasant things about his behavior, and often encouraged the kids to do the same.

The next day Pam received bad news from her youngest daughter's school:

I got a call from school today. They said my youngest daughter has been missing her third period class for the last ten days. They are sending a suspension letter. She lied to me. I really thought we were communicating. She said she hadn't missed her classes at all the last two weeks. I'm so worried about what is happening to her.

Pam wrote the next day about her participation in costume at a Christmas party at work. Her fears that she would burst into tears during the show were unwarranted and she enjoyed the party. Pam's final diary entry reads:

I told my daughter that if she was not in school, she would have to get a job and contribute half her earnings to household expenses. I told her that to live here she would have to either be in school and maintain passing grades or have a job and contribute to the house. I told her that everybody who lives here and is part of the family has to live by the same rules. She would have to decide.

This afternoon she went to her older sister's work and told her I kicked her out of the house and told her she had to get a job. She told her that she was really messing up her life; that without a high school diploma the best job she could ever hope for was working in a fast food restaurant; that she was hurting herself and not her mother; and that her parents wouldn't always be around to look after her and what would she do then? My oldest daughter said she didn't answer, but she did listen to her.

Pam's semester ended and so did her marriage. After the home was sold she lived in an apartment with her three children. She continued to work and attend university. She graduated magna cum laude and received a fellowship to a prestigious journalism school. In looking at her past today, Pam says she feels it was an important struggle, "a struggle for understanding of myself, the world, and my place in it." As has been the case since her childhood, Pam has found strength and support this past year from her parents, siblings, and extended family:

This year my birthday was happily celebrated with all my family, including parents, brothers, sisters, their families, as well as my own children, except the one who was with my ex-husband. It was truly a boost to my sagging morale.

Pam's growth and greater maturity is seen in the change in her view toward death. When she was a child she viewed death as a fairy land in a book, a dreamlike place everyone went to when they died. When she was first married, Pam felt with certainty that there was a life after death and that one must follow the rules of the church in order to get to heaven. At the present time, Pam wrote that she had more questions than answers about death. Her thoughts about death are existential in that she is concerned that she have enough time to do the many things she wants to accomplish in life.

When she was in her early twenties, life was such a struggle for Pam that her thoughts of the future were not hopeful. By contrast, today she writes:

> More than ever, I am optimistic about the future. I think that for the first time I truly believe in myself. I know that there are difficult times ahead, but I feel confident that I can at least determine my own destiny.

Pam's diary is a testimony to her successful coping with a difficult situation. She stands as a sterling example of the tremendous personal growth that can occur at midlife. Indeed, it seems that for Pam being middle age is far superior to being younger. The overall good and nontraumatic childhood she experienced certainly provided the basis for such a successful way of meeting a major life crisis.

Pam exhibits the grace of maturity. She was wise enough to recognize her children's maturational needs and provide them. Even her career choice shows a mature defense mechanism of sublimation and altruism. Pam enthusiastically provided a statement for the study follow-up:

> The years since the study have seen much growth and many changes in my life. . . . My years at the university were some of the most valuable and rewarding of my life. I was honored as an Outstanding Senior and received a fellowship to cover my first year of graduate study. I'm now finishing my last semester of school. After licensure examination I plan to join and practice with a well known firm which has already offered me a position.
>
> Of course, a rewarding and satisfying career is only one of the things I've discovered in this beginning of the second half of my life. I've also found a remarkable man with whom to share this satisfying new life. We plan to marry this summer.

My children are grown and making their own lives. Both of my daughters are now married. My youngest daughter has a precious little boy. I am a grandmother! My son lives with me and is working and going to school.

Rhonda—An Excellent Single Parent

Rhonda, age 38, is a divorced mother of a 14-year-old son, Marshall, and a 12-year-old daughter, Linda. She is currently enrolled part time in a masters program in guidance and counseling. Rhonda takes two evening seminars. She also works full time in the student services department of a high school, as a visiting teacher.

Rhonda was born in a medium-sized town in Utah. She had one brother, several years older than her, and no sisters. Rhonda remembers her childhood as a very happy and secure time. Her mother was the closest person to her as a little girl. Her mother had warm feelings toward her, enjoyed taking care of her, and was a loving person. Rhonda remembers her mother holding her and reading her stories. She thought of Rhonda as a good and a pretty girl. Rhonda thrived on these expectations.

Her relationship with her father was also close. She recalls crawling up in his lap and playing toss with him in the swimming pool. Rhonda felt that her father was always pleased with her. She recalls only one spanking from him. Her father trained her to be polite, and to say "please" and "thank you." Rhonda acted out the good parenting she received when she played dolls with her girlfriends:

> We were always good mommies that rocked our babies, fed them bottles, and kept them clean and pretty.

Rhonda remembers her pretty bedroom with white walls and blue and white flowered curtains in the windows with white sheers. The room had hardwood floors that always shined brightly. The headboard of her bed contained a book case where she kept her best storybook dolls. She used to look at them as she went to sleep at night and made up stories about them.

Rhonda's older brother, Bill, was protective and set a high standard at school which she felt she had to live up to. Bill and Rhonda had the normal childhood fights; yet, she has a good feeling inside when she thinks about him today. He helped to get her to play in boys' baseball games. Although she was always the last one to get picked to be on the team, she enjoyed being involved.

As a preschool child, Rhonda had a definite idea that as a girl she would play a greatly different role in life than her brother. Girls were to grow up to be good mothers and wives. Women stayed home, had babies, and took care of the housework. Men, on the other hand, worked, read the newspaper, mowed the lawn, and went fishing. "They did all of the fun things."

As a little girl and on through school, Rhonda had a best girlfriend, Carol. They did everything together, often spending the weekends at each other's homes. Carol was cute and always happy. They made a good pair.

Rhonda's memories of her school years are happy. Her mother used to come into her room each morning and sing her a wake-up song. If it was cold outside (as they had no central heat) her mother would come into her room early and light a small gas heater so that it would not be so cold as she got dressed. As Rhonda lay in bed preparing to get up she would hear the pots and pans rattling and smell the coffee and bacon cooking in the kitchen. She looked forward to the day when she would be old enough to drink coffee. She would hear the water running in the bathroom as her father shaved and she could smell his shaving cream. On cold days as she jumped out of bed, Rhonda remembers the cold hardwood floor on her feet.

Rhonda went to a Catholic school where she remembers the nuns wearing long rosaries on their habits which rattled as they walked down the halls. She remembers the songs the children sang, reciting the alphabet, and laughing at recess. The church bells rang for the Angelas, a noon-day prayer. Rhonda and her friends were curious about the nuns. Sometimes they would see a small piece of hair sticking out from the nun's habit and wonder whether it was short or long.

After school, Rhonda would often smell fresh-baked oatmeal cookies. The house always smelled clean. If her dad had mowed the lawn that day she would enjoy the smell of the fresh mowed grass. When her mother ironed she would smell the freshly starched and ironed clothes. All of these delighted her. In the evening, Rhonda remembers listening to the radio and hearing her favorite scary radio show "The Shadow."

Rhonda remembers the special events that her family celebrated when she was a child. At Christmas one year, Rhonda's mother made her a new blue velvet dress. She loved the color and the way it felt. Each Christmas they opened their presents around the tree on Christmas morning, then went to grandmother's house for a big family gathering with turkey and corn bread dressing. Rhonda's father had seven brothers and sisters who would all come with their families. Rhonda loved playing with her cousins.

Each birthday, Rhonda's mother baked and decorated a cake for her. She often invited friends over to play games like pin-the-tail-on-the-donkey and London bridge. Her mother and father got very involved in these birthday events that made her feel very special.

On the Saturday before Easter they would dye eggs. Rhonda and her brother would leave their Easter baskets on the back steps so that the Easter bunny could find them. He would put chocolate rabbits and jelly beans in them. The Easter bunny would have taken the colored eggs out of the baskets and hidden them all over the yard. Then Rhonda and Bill would have to scamper around trying to see who could find the most. Rhonda always had a new dress for Easter with matching hat, purse, gloves, and shoes. It was fun to get all dressed up that Sunday and attend church.

As Rhonda grew up, she continually observed that boys had more autonomy and power than girls. When it came to neighborhood games, they were the ones who made the rules and the ones who refereed and decided on particulars. While the boys played football and baseball the girls were supposed to take dancing and piano lessons.

Rules were also an important part of life at school. There always were two groups of people—those who made the rules and those who obeyed them. The people who made them were also the ones to punish those who disobeyed, and, in turn, reward those who were obedient. Rhonda learned that it did not matter at all whether she liked the rules, just that she complied. Rhonda obeyed the rules and as a result she was successful within these well-defined boundaries. She was popular, liked by her teachers, and was elected class president several times.

As a young teenager, Rhonda started to notice boys. She had a special boyfriend, Freddie, who became her steady date. Through Freddie she learned what it feels like to be someone really special to someone outside her family. She learned about the importance of give and take in relationships and how to talk things out. She learned to compromise without having heated arguments or losing her temper.

As a teenager Rhonda also came to admire Jane, a nurse who helped take care of her father when he underwent surgery. She was someone who inspires confidence and makes one feel better just by being there. Jane encouraged Rhonda to become a nurse. She said that even if you did not work you could use it at home. If you ever had to work it was a good profession to fall back on. Rhonda listened to what Jane had to say. However, Rhonda loved math and science and wanted to become an engineer. She did not say much about this to her parents, since they were urging her to become a teacher. A chance meeting with an engineer became a deciding factor:

It was a man I really never knew. He worked for one of the oil companies around the Gulf Coast and spoke to a group of us who had gone out to the refinery for a career night activity. After touring the installation he spoke individually with us about what we wanted to do in life. When I said I wanted to be an engineer he got dead serious and spent thirty minutes telling me why I couldn't do it. The reasons were the usual things—work too rough, not open to women, who couldn't mix family and career, etc. and I bought it—hook, line, and sinker.

Today Rhonda regrets having made this decision. She thinks she would have made a good engineer and would have been happier in that field. She would have been more financially secure, now that she is divorced. While teaching did allow her to mix family and career, she could have worked something out with engineering as well.

Crushed ambitions were normal for young women when Rhonda was a teenager. They are still so today. Although she had an normal and loving family life, and went to "good" schools, the sexism of family and school affected her most negatively:

My conception of "society" was still pretty limited. It basically stemmed from school, family, and church. They all had definite boundaries and guidelines. They were all male dominated, had women in subservient positions doing limited things, and showed no signs of changing in the near future. I saw no equal rights or equal pay for equal work. It all looked like I had very little choice to make. It was marriage, children, and housework to look forward to for the rest of my life. Ugh!

Although this did not seem appealing to Rhonda, she felt that, nevertheless, as a girl this was her destiny. When she was 20 she met and fell in love with the man she married just after she turned 21:

Everything was wonderful. He was everything I had ever dreamed about. He bought me presents, complimented me, and was attentive. The only problem in adjusting to our new life together was that he traveled a great deal and I had to become independent. Independent, that is, during the week while he was gone but fall back into the other role during the weekend. I became a master at this and it really didn't bother me.

Rhonda has pleasant sensual memories of her husband when they were first married. She remembers the sexy smell of his after shave lotion in the mornings, and the smooth soft skin on his back:

The warmth from his body while we lay in bed was a close, secure feeling to me.

Rhonda especially enjoyed the feeling of sharing holidays and special occasions with her husband. She enjoyed having him with her over Christmas when many of her family members got together. Easter was very special also. She and her husband visited her parents and her mother made them both an Easter basket, with chocolate bunnies and jelly beans. Her husband seemed to enjoy it even though he thought it was silly. His parents never made much of holidays.

Rhonda's fondest memory of her first year of marriage was her first wedding anniversary:

> My husband sent me a dozen red roses and I was thrilled to death. We went out for dinner at a special seafood place and the meal was fantastic. I remember that I wore a mauve pink suit and I had had my hair done at the beauty shop. That in itself was something special because I never went to the beauty shop. The whole night was special. I'll always remember it.

Rhonda looked forward to a certain future. Her husband would advance in his career. Eventually he would get a promotion and they would move to a different part of the country. They would always be married to each other and always be together. This thought made Rhonda feel safe and secure.

At first, Rhonda thought that they communicated well. Looking back, she realizes they really didn't communicate. Rather, they always did what Jim (her husband) wanted. Rhonda prided herself on never arguing. She thought that she was making things smoother and happier that way. She now realizes that her facile compliance led to the demise of their relationship.

After 3 years of marriage, their first child, Marshall, was born. They had planned for him and he made Rhonda feel needed. He was a good baby and Rhonda enjoyed taking care of him. Rhonda showered her infant son with affection. She longed for more open affection from her husband, but he was not openly loving. Just as she took pride in the care of her dolls as a child, so she took pride in how neat, clean, and happy Marshall was as a baby.

When she was 5 months pregnant, Rhonda quit work and did not return to work for 10 years:

> I stayed home to be a "good" wife and mother. I kept a clean house, played with and cared for my baby, cooked well-balanced meals nightly, rarely complained about the absence of my husband, and thought that that's the way it had to be. I accepted all of the responsibility without question. That's the way it was!

After 2 years Rhonda had her daughter, Linda. Her husband really did not want another child, but Rhonda did not want Marshall raised as an only child. Linda was also a delightful child who Rhonda nicknamed "Little Miss Sunshine" since she always woke up smiling. She would play quietly and gurgle softly in her crib when she woke up before she would ever cry for breakfast or affection.

Rhonda was kept busy by the two toddlers. She loved to watch them play together. Meanwhile, Jim drifted even more toward his job and away from his family. Rhonda spent more and more time with the children. Jim only entered their lives on weekends and then only when he had the time. Over the years Rhonda and Jim drifted further and further apart. They were divorced 2 years ago after nearly 11 years of marriage.

Shortly after Rhonda and her husband had separated, she chanced to meet a former professor. He encouraged her to pursue her masters degree. She was grateful for the little extra push he offered. After 15 years Rhonda has returned to the university. She reflected on her current situation:

> I now find myself in the world of the "swinging singles." I'm a single parent with custody of my two children and about the only swinging I do is on the patio. I hold down a full time job, go to college two nights a week, take care of a house, and do things with my daughter and son as much as possible. I'm very busy and sometimes very frustrated.
>
> Society plays some pretty rotten tricks on single females. Credit for a divorced female is extremely hard to obtain. Single men expect divorced women to be an easy make and, therefore, get highly insulted when I don't go to bed with them. My husband still is doing what he wants to do without any regard for my time or plans.

Rhonda felt that her ex-husband was still manipulating her life through the children. She feels that she is at his mercy when it comes to determining which weekends he will take the children and at what times he picks them up and returns them home. He determines the vacations schedules as well. The most troublesome thing in Rhonda's life at the present time is a pending law suit whereby her ex-husband is trying to gain custody of their son, Marshall.

Rhonda's diary reflects the life of a busy woman who, nevertheless, feels basically happy and optimistic about life. She is able to meet her challenges head on, and still enjoy herself. At work, she is frustrated by a boss who schedules lengthy meetings and still expects her to get a full day's work completed:

> I had a meeting with my boss today. We spent two and one half hours working on revising forms that could have been accomplished in much less

time. My day was already busy and this use of time really made me feel frustrated. She asks for my opinion but when it differs from her's she seems to get upset with me. One of her favorite expressions is "I'm going to come at you like a boss." Another one I heard today is "Mother knows best." I guess I'm too independent to get along well with someone like her. Other then being frustrated by poor time usage my day went well.

That evening Rhonda was served with papers from the court, her husband was also suing for custody of their son:

After reading the suit I became really angry. It was a typical example of Jim's selfishness and how he wants things to go exactly the way he wants them to without any consideration for anyone else. Some parts of the suit are really ridiculous. He made it so bad that I couldn't agree to it out of court even if I wanted to. I tried to talk to my son Marshall about what was in the suit. Some parts he felt were "a little bit much" but I felt he was very defensive of his father's actions. I guess that's to be expected. I'll try to approach him about it at a later date.

A couple of days later Rhonda played tennis with Marshall for a couple of hours in the evening. Rhonda wrote in her diary that she found it difficult to believe that he wanted to leave since he seems to be having fun where he is. On September 6 Rhonda brought up the subject with Marshall:

He says he still wants to go but says he really isn't unhappy here. I tried to logically reason with him about some things but finally (after getting mad) realized that we weren't on the same level. I'm coming from a logical point of view and he's coming from an emotional one. Don't think he's capable of even beginning to understand what I'm trying to say. Don't think I'll try to talk about it any more.

Rhonda does not see that she as well as Marshall was emotional about the issue.

On Friday night Rhonda had a date with a good friend who took her to a movie and dancing. She had the feeling that he would like to be on closer terms with her.

The next Monday Rhonda had to buy new tires for her car and was frustrated by the long wait, making her late for an evening class. There was a new teacher in the class, and Rhonda expressed the feeling that she may not be able to keep up with all of the work. Then Rhonda reported on a meeting with a lawyer:

September 9: Met with B. B., my attorney. Spent two hours talking about what to expect and things that might come up in the custody hearing. He seems to think that we have a very "defensible" case. I sure hope so because its' going to be very costly—to the tune of $2000. We are going to ask that the court makes Jim pay the attorney fees and court cost. I sure hope he has to because I'm not sure where I'm going to come up with the money.

The following work day was hectic for Rhonda, writing notes to forty-seven parents about their children's test results. Her boss called a luncheon meeting, which Rhonda thought had gone well. When she returned to work after lunch, a note that her daughter had called reminded her that she had missed taking her to an orthodontist's appointment. This was an important appointment—the dentist had planned to put her bottom braces on. Rhonda was upset with herself about having done this.

That evening Marshall wanted Rhonda to play tennis with him but she declined because she was too tired. Rhonda found that she had to adjust to her son Marshall's natural desire for greater independence:

I got my very first taste of "dating" with Marshall. He didn't have a date—just several of his friends. After the social on Saturday night they went to MacDonald's for a hamburger then one of the fathers picked them up and brought them home. He got home about 11:30. I guess I'm just not ready for him to be out at night like that unchaperoned. I know I have to gradually let go of those strings and I know he was safe and everything—but it sure was a funny feeling to know that he was out without an adult at 11:30 at night!

The singles night scene was not that great:

Around 8:00 I left to go to a singles' dance at the Marriott. Beth was supposed to go with me but she got sick. The dance was kind of a drag. I met a few interesting ladies and danced quite a bit with a guy who was a good dancer but I really wouldn't want to see him again. I got home about 11:30.

Occasionally, there was a conflict between the demands of her job, her schooling, and her family. Rhonda decided to skip class one evening to attend an open house at her daughter's school. She felt good about it because Linda was so pleased that she was there. The tensions with her boss meanwhile increased:

Boss called today. I was right. She is really angry at me. And now I'm really pissed at her. . . . She also called a meeting of student services at 11:30 today. I didn't get back to school until 2:20. What we discussed could have been done in less than one hour but instead it took almost three. The boss is really disorganized. And we had a hard time getting a direct answer from her even when we asked a simple question like a deadline for the new absences reports to be in. Talk about frustration! Plus she said some things about me in front of the other visiting teachers that was very misleading and totally out of context. I held my temper—but it wasn't easy.

Rhonda's frustrations about her work were somewhat tempered by her liking for her assistant, Joyce, who was extremely helpful and understanding. Rhonda expressed her dismay that evening in her diary about her son Marshall wanting to go and live with his father:

Things are pretty quiet around the house. Marshall and I haven't talked anymore about his going to live with his father. I really have mixed emotions about that. In one sense I can understand how he feels but I also feel hurt that he doesn't want to continue to live with me here at home. I would really like to be ugly to him sometimes, especially when he's asking for a favor or something special. Why should I go out of my way for him when he doesn't want to live with me?

In the midst of her difficulties, Rhonda still is able to break away and enjoy herself for a relaxed evening. She went to a local high school football game with some friends, then went to a party, and ended up drinking beer and sitting in a hot tub.

Rhonda is truly concerned about the students at the school at which she works:

September 22: Big event for today was taking a student to the hospital. She was complaining of severe abdominal pain. I thought it might be a serious problem and I was right. I'm glad I insisted on her being seen even if it meant spending two and one half hours at the hospital emergency room. This girl needed to be seen and her family didn't seem to be too concerned about her. I guess it's really tough having to fend for yourself. I can't imagine being too busy to take my child to the doctor but I sure do run into a lot of parents with an uncaring attitude. And I really don't think that it's that they don't care. I think they're so involved with their own lives that they expect their children to be adults instead of children. It's really sad.

The next evening Rhonda's mother called and said that she and Rhonda's father would arrive on Friday for a visit. The love and support she had received from them as a child was continuing into the present. Rhonda expressed in her diary that she felt extremely fortunate to have such caring parents. She had plans for things for them to do to help her. Her father usually takes care of household maintenance. Her mother helps her with sewing and mending.

On Thursday evening, when Rhonda and her daughter were cleaning the house in preparation for their grandparents' visit, they sat down and had a round table discussion about the alignment of chores. Linda felt that she had an unfair share of duties because she is a girl. This turned out to be the case. Rhonda felt good about their new agreement which takes this into account.

Rhonda's parents arrived the next afternoon laden with good things to eat, including a French dish with crabs and shrimp. On Saturday, while Rhonda studied, her father stripped and revarnished their front door and her mother did mending. On Sunday they celebrated Rhonda's 38th birthday. They sang "Happy Birthday" to her and presented her with gifts. Marshall and Linda gave her a coffee mug purchased with their own money. Her parents gave her some money to buy a watch. Rhonda said she wished that all of her birthdays could be that nice.

During the week she felt the subtle pressure of her mother's disapproval of her rushed life style:

> Mom is about to have a fit. She thinks I'm going to have a nervous breakdown if I don't slow down. I realized it's a fast pace around here but I'm sure it seems faster for her than it does for me.

That week she took a day off to arrange a loan to pay the attorney's fee. She then visited the school Marshall would be attending if he ended up living with his father. She thought the school was very inferior to the one he was attending now. Rhonda did not say anything to Marshall about her opinion of the school since she thought he would just think it was another ploy to keep him from moving in with his father.

That evening they did chores together to get the house cleaned for the weekend. That evening both Linda and Marshall came to Rhonda's room where she was reading. They all sat and chatted on her bed. It gave Rhonda a nice feeling.

Rhonda also continually enjoyed the support of her good friends:

> Got back home around 2:30 and went by a friend's house for a little counseling session. I'm having a little problem handling my feelings about Marshall wanting to move out and I needed some advice. She's always really good about hearing me out and helping me decide what I need to do. I'm really lucky to have the good friends that I have. They really are a good support system for me.

On October 20th Rhonda taught a home economics class about careers and fitting together family and career. Teaching about this made her think that she is making the right choice by limiting her social life and dating in order to spend adequate time with her children. Meanwhile, the custody case dragged on, since her ex-husband's attorney was out of the country:

Marshall still seems really happy at home. I don't understand how he can be so happy here and want to live with his dad. Maybe I'll never really understand. I only hope right now that it'll be over soon and that the judge will decide to leave Marshall with me.

On October 23rd Rhonda's advisor from the university called to tell her she only needed one more course to graduate. She was delighted! On October 24th Rhonda took her children out to eat at a Mexican restaurant. Though inexpensive, the food was good, and they enjoyed their meal.

During the next few weeks Rhonda and her assistant were overwhelmed getting excessive absence letters out. Her daughter Linda needed an appointment with her orthodondist. She spent days trying to set up an appointment only to have to cancel it at the last minute because a Korean student collapsed and had to be taken home. Rhonda also received bad news from the university. The departmental secretary called and said that they had reviewed her transcript and that she needed five more classes instead of one! Rhonda was angry and dismayed, especially after her adviser had initially told her that she needed only one. When she confronted him with this he acted as if it were all her fault.

Sometimes Rhonda enjoyed being at home alone:

> The house was really quiet tonight. The children are at their friend's houses and I'm home alone. It's really nice. I guess this is one good thing that has come out of the divorce. I get to have some time by myself for a change. That's something I rarely had while we were married.

Rhonda participated in a panel discussion in a family living class about marriage. The other three persons on the panel were happily married. Rhonda felt that she always ended up taking an opposing position. She argued that even though children are involved, sometimes it is better to end a marriage then to stay in an unhappy situation. Rhonda learned that there was a significant difference between her marriage and theirs in that the men in those marriages placed a significant emphasis on family and children, unlike her former husband.

Rhonda spent Thanksgiving holiday at home alone. Her ex-husband was to take the children. This would give her a chance to rest and to catch up on her studies. Although they had arranged for him to pick them up Tuesday evening, he called and changed it to Thursday morning. It irritated her that he shortened his time to be with them and once again changed plans. After they finally left, Rhonda got a call from her godmother, who, with her husband and two friends, planned to visit them over the weekend. This ended her week end alone!

On the Monday after Thanksgiving Rhonda had a long talk with her son and daughter:

> Marshall still would like to live with his father and I needed to clear the air on a few things that had happened recently. It ended up not being a real good scene but they need to know that I resent their father still controlling my life through them. I explained as best I could but I still don't think they really understand what I'm saying. Anyway we all went to bed with lots on our minds. I'm hoping that after they think about things it will be a little clearer for them. One thing that really stood out was that they have two sets of rules—one for me and one for their dad and we don't get equal treatment.

In spite of her problems with the custody battle, and being a single parent, her financial difficulties, and trying to finish a degree, Rhonda led a happy daily life:

> I wake up to the sound of the alarm clock buzzing at 6:15 A.M. Sometimes I can hear Marshall in the kitchen already making coffee. He's an early riser and often is up before me. I go to the kitchen and I see my fourteen year old son with his bathrobe on preparing his own breakfast. Later I see a sleepy eyed eleven year old girl with rollers in her hair coming into the kitchen while I'm preparing lunches. At 7:45 I see two beautiful children, well dressed and groomed, ready for another day at school. It reminds me of the cocoon and the butterfly.

> At work I hear the chattering of the students as they pass hurriedly by my door and the periodic ringing of the bell for the changing of classes. I see the bright blue freshly painted room in need of wall decorations. I see lots of students with happy faces darting past my door. I hear an occasional outburst of laughter from the students. Sometimes the laughter is almost contagious and I find myself smiling and being happy inside myself because I'm happy for them. The school I work in is full of happy sounds and it's basically a very happy environment. I see administrators and faculty working hand in hand to try to meet the students' needs. I see a well organized and well run school system. I see a boss that's tired, trouble, and under a lot of pressure. I see an aide that works closely with me that's one of the dearest people in the world.

> At home I see a yard that needs mowing, carpet that needs replacing, furniture that's wearing out, and a budget that won't allow much hope for improvement in the near future. I see two children who are happy both at home and at school. I hear the sounds of my son's and daughter's voices asking "What's for dinner?" "Help me with my paragraph." "I need some more paper." and "Mom, make her leave me alone." I see a family that enjoys doing fun things together like swimming or a game of yard soccer. I see a fire in the fireplace. I see a mother and two youngsters sitting around

the same kitchen table all doing homework together. I see housework that doesn't get done because we'd rather spend the day shopping. And I see a family that pools its efforts to get the chores done some other time. The best sounds I hear are at bed time. I always say "Goodnight and I love you." They reply, "I love you too" and that's really a sweet sound to hear. Especially from my fourteen year old son who sometimes thinks it's babyish to show affection openly. When I turn the lights out at night and lock the doors I hear the quietness of the house. In some ways this is reassuring to me that all is well one more night and that everything is secure until morning.

To Rhonda, a happy family life and mutual love and support are still the most important values. This is the way she lived as a child and the life she provides for her children. She shows that a sense of family and mutual support can still be present in a single-parent home. For holidays and special occasions, the extended family becomes most important:

Easter was spent at my mom's. My brother and his family were there too. We dyed six dozen eggs, had chocolate bunnies, and lots of candy. Easter Sunday my grandmother and some of my other relatives came over for a quick visit.

During the summer we had a big family reunion on my dad's side of the family. All seven of my dad's brothers and sisters were there, all of the grandchildren except two, and all of the great-grandchildren. It was really great. Marshall and Linda weren't too enthusiastic about going but once there they had a good time. In fact they had such a good time they wanted to know if we were going to have another one next year. I got to see relatives I hadn't seen in a couple of years and my children met cousins they never knew they had. I think it was important for them to know that they belong to a larger family unit than just me and them. . . . I have a strong sense of what family is all about and would like my children to grow up with an appreciation of family.

Rhonda feels that time passes by too quickly. She is always in a rush between school, work, and family. She has a positive, hopeful outlook for the future.

The immediate future consists of this year and maybe next. My main goals are to get out of school, find a better job, and keep my children happy. My long range future is a little different. I think of myself being married to a nice man with no financial worries. I'm happy with myself and my situation. We'll have gotten both children through college and we'll be able to do some of the things we've always wanted to do. I know it's all idealistic but it's my dream of the future!

Rhonda's narration exudes feelings of happiness and enthusiasm, in spite of stresses of living, of divorce, and a custody fight. She truly enjoys her children. The calm which underlies the storm of everyday life is Rhonda's personal maturity.

Conclusion

Table 9.1 summarizes the relationships with their parents experienced by Pam and Rhonda. Their parents communicated with them in a predominantly mature manner.

Pam's and Rhonda's primary bonding to both mother and father was stable, stimulating, and continual. The parents showed some capacity to mirror their daughters' emotions, and degrees of ability to empathize with them. Pam's mother involved Pam in "reversal" parenting, for she expected Pam (her oldest daughter) to take care of her younger siblings. Pam's mother tended to project her soberness onto Pam, seeing her as not wanting cuddling. There was more tendency on the part of Pam's parents then Rhonda's to push her to perform more perfectly, moving her more toward narcissistic pride.

Some ability to communicate congruently was shown by both Pam's and Rhonda's parents who were thereby also able to transmit clear and positive attributions and expectations to them. While the families functioned traditionally and hierarchically, the parents in these homes were not tyrants producing highly power-distorted communication. Therefore the children in these families got truthful messages that they could normatively assimilate.

Table 9.1. Summary of Parenting Practices Experienced by Pam and Rhonda

	Pam	Rhonda
Primary bond	Stable	Stable
Mirroring	Mixed	Adequate
Style of parenting	Reversal/empathic	Empathic
Communicative stance	Blame/congruent	Congruent
Attributions	Positive	Positive
Expectations	Positive	Positive
Temporality	Meaningful	Meaningful
Defenses	Neuro/mature	Neuro/mature
Dramatic form	Comic/tragic	Comic
Moral development	Goodness/care	Care
Ethical level	Artistry/love	Artistry/love
Child's self-integration	Integrated	Integrated

The parents of Rhonda and Pam functioned to some extent with mature defense mechanisms. They took delight in anticipation of important family events shared with their daughters, such as their birthdays. They showed altruistic behavior toward them (such as Rhonda's father refinishing her furniture at the present time). These families laughed together. While they experienced stresses of modern life and its time pressures, they also experienced meaningful temporal flow in their shared family holidays and events.

In Pam's family, due perhaps more to the influence of the church, a tragic model of action seems more prevalent than a comic. Here Pam herself became the victim as she dutifully married upon becoming pregnant, and stayed with an unhappy marriage for 20 years. Rhonda also followed what she perceived as her duties as a wife and mother in the traditional sense. While she enjoyed aspects of being a wife and delighted in her daughters she was victimized by the sexism built into this traditional situation.

Both Pam's and Rhonda's parents exhibited goodness and care in their moral judgements. They showed self-control and degrees of artistry and love in their relationships with their daughters and others. These levels of moral and ethical maturity were, in turn, reflected by Pam and Rhonda in their relationships with their children. In terms of Gilligan's stages of moral development, Pam tended to operate at a "goodness" stage regressing to "survival" when she got pregnant and then building back up to goodness. As she faced up to her divorce, she moved from goodness to "caring," balancing care for others with care for herself.

Rhonda vacillated between survival and caring. Because of the continued care she received from her parents, she was able to go through a divorce and a custody suit without becoming bitter or resentful. Both Pam and Rhonda, in turn, have well-established "mature" relationships with their children.

Because of all of these qualities of their relationship with their parents, neither Pam nor Rhonda developed emotionally divided selves. To the contrary, they developed strong, integrated self-concepts. The emotions of these women were not intensely conflictual, although they did have a few childhood hauntings to exorcize.

Mature Becoming in Social Context _____ 10

Introduction

As a study of human becoming, this work runs parallel to that of developmental theorists. The term "development" carries with it a lot of baggage that does not fit the life experiences of the women as they described them. The idea of a stage-to-stage progression where one gets not only bigger but smarter, nicer, and wiser was not borne out in this study. Developmental theory tends to overlook the extent to which human becoming in childhood (and throughout life) may be marked by adverse experiences, such as abuse, neglect, incest, or poverty.

The life experiences of the women in this study are better captured by the terms "becoming mature." To Boelen, maturity is not something you achieve, but something that is always a possibility for any person. The mature person is one who is in dialogue with the child in herself, and with the ghosts and spirits of significant others who have become a part of her being. The ability to be mature is facilitated by circumstance, such as the degree of support offered by others, the kinds of stresses and time pressures one is placed under, the level of economic resources available and the kinds of work, educational, and religious organizations in which one must function.

Some persons do become mature regardless of unfortunate circumstances. Others remain immature in spite of advantages. The key factor necessary to attain maturity is either to have had mature parents or to redo one's own parenting. The process of becoming mature requires recognition of the "ghosts" of immature parents and others in one's life and replacing these with mature "spirits." This chapter summarizes and integrates the results of this research. First the process of the research as an interpretive spiral is described. Then the quantitative, systematic, and qualitative findings from the study are summarized. These findings are related to the theory of mature and immature parent–child relationships. Following this, the findings are discussed in relation to the ways social contexts either promote or hinder becoming mature.

Interpretive Spiral

Interpretive sociology viewed as hermeneutic phenomenology was used as the methodological approach. From start to finish, the research involved an interpretive spiral with four major turns. (See Fig 10.1 below.) A "turn" is a place in the hermeneutic spiral where a new direction is taken leading toward a deeper understanding. There were four such major turns in this interpretive process. Each "turn" (noted on the left side of the figure) leads to a looping back of findings or "results" (noted on the right side of the figure).

This study began with an interest in the development of self in childhood and how this effects adult life. Fifty-three women who met for 15 weeks in intensive support/research groups, participated in the study. All of them were involved in career development or change efforts in addition to their activities with family and friends. Writing the narratives (autobiographies, diaries, phenomenological time/memory studies, time schedules) and creating the other texts (tape recordings, dis-

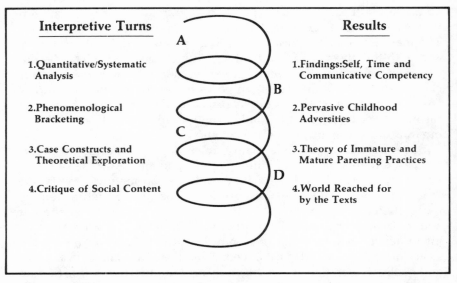

Figure 10.1. An interpretive spiral of the phenomenon of maturity. Drawing by Jeanne Broussard.

cussions) was the next step. The first interpretive turn occurred when
the narratives and other data were quantified and systematized and the
results analyzed in relation to the guiding theories. The analysis yielded
findings about the effect of significant others in childhood on the way
time was spent and experienced. The effect of the research process on
the participants was also assessed quantitatively (Fig. 10.1A)

The second turn was a phenomenological one (Fig 10.1B) The "scientific" results accomplished to this point were bracketed as were the normal assumptions about the subject at hand. The phenomenological analysis yielded the essential experience (eidos) of the effect of childhood
adversities on adult life. To arrive at this I had to realize that I could not
fully understand what was being communicated without looking at
what effect my own childhood was having on my understandings. Once
I accepted the blockages to understanding coming from my own consciousness, I returned to the "things themselves"—the narratives written by the women. Based on this second reading, I was able to grasp
the way in which childhood experiences impacted on adult life.

By writing the eleven case constructs in chapters 5 through 9, I was
able to illustrate how and why this occurred. Vestiges of childhood experiences were reconstructed on a daily basis by the women as internal
voices of significant others which inspire us (spirits) or haunt us
(ghosts). The third hermeneutic turn (Fig. 10.1C) was toward theory development beyond the scope of the sensitizing theories used initially.
This was necessary in order to theoretically integrate the grounded findings arising from case constructs. A theory of mature and immature parent–child relationships resulted. This theory was later related to the
texts of the case studies.

The final turn (Fig. 10.1D) is really a beginning. It cannot be completed in the scope of this book, but only suggested. This is the turn
toward the "world reached for by the text." To look in this direction
means looking at the social world in which the narratives were written
and experienced. One also looks for what was not there that needs to
be available for mature becoming. This interpretive turn suggests the
kinds of communities and organizations which must be promoted to
foster mature becoming.

Summary of Findings

This section will summarize the analysis of the quantitative, systematic, and qualitative data gathered for this study in relation to the theory
of mature becoming. The five small groups of women which were part
of this study were structured to facilitate unconstrained communication.

A scale was constructed using Habermas' four criteria for competent or constraint-free communication and each of the participants was rated accordingly. The scale included the criteria of truth, truthfulness, normative appropriateness, and understandability. The women were rated both for interaction with their families (based on audiotape recordings and transcripts) and in the groups (based on direct observation and videotapes).

The analysis of these ratings showed a higher degree of communicative competency in the groups than in the home. This indicated that our efforts were successful in alleviating power distortions in the communicative processes in the groups. A factor analysis showed that the communicative competency in the groups was consistent over time.

This finding was congruent with the results from coding the speech patterns and body language patterns displayed on the videotapes. These patterns indicated that as the groups became more cohesive, the role patterns crystallized between group members. The second tapings showed more open body language then the earlier tape indicating that there was trust established in the groups.

The research project stressed continued involvement and interpretation on the part of each participant. The effectiveness of the groups in providing therapeutic benefits to the women was supported by their assessments of the effects of each aspect of the project on their behaviors and understandings. Averaging together the various aspects of the study, 79% of the women said involvement in the study resulted in changes in their behaviors or understandings or both.

Coding the autobiographies and quantifying the resulting data yielded overwhelming support for Mead's argument that the self is built up from the internalization of the attitudes of significant others. Whether positive or negative, the women agreed with the attributions and expectations of these others. This held true whether they liked or disliked these others. The sex of significant others had some effect on how they were evaluated. For preschool age, males were evaluated higher than females. By the teenage years, this had reversed.

The ability to critically reflect upon the influence of significant others was stimulated in some cases by inconsistencies between the inputs of various significant others. For the most part, however, the women accepted both sides of such contradictions. For example, Gloria's mother thought she was "stupid and slow." Her teachers thought her "intelligent and fast." She accepted all of these evaluations and then managed them by segmenting areas of her life. She continued to perform well academically and on the job, and poorly in close relationships. The data thus show the roots of the emotionally divided self which is one of the characteristics of immaturity.

The time schedules showed that most of the women were involved in a stressful pace of life. The single parents and young married childless women slept less than single childless women or married women with children. Single parents in the group also had less leisure time.

Systematic analysis of the phenomenological time/memory studies showed that children live temporally in an extremely intense present. The past and future hardly exist for the child. This makes the effect of their primary caretakers as powerful significant others on them all the more clear. The sensory bracketing studies revealed that even bodily-sensory experiences are related to others. Memories of touch, smell, hearing, and sight from childhood and adulthood are usually associated with persons. Longer term temporal experience, both for the women as children and as adults, also was associated primarily with social events such as birthdays, holidays, and other family activities. Death was not an accepted reality for most of the women either as children or as adults. A few of the women had an authentic acceptance of their own mortality. Such acceptance is an important aspect of mature becoming.

The results from the quantitative and systematic analyses set the background for grasping the women's becoming mature, but did not reach the essence of what they had been saying and writing about most intensively for those several months—the effect of adverse childhood experiences on their adult lives. The case constructs illustrate how this occurs. Each case construct, which typifies a number of women in the study, was analyzed in relation to the theory of mature and immature parent–child relationships. In most of the case constructs, the parents related to their children in predominantly immature ways. "Pam's" and "Rhonda's" parents, although not perfect, exemplified mature parenting.

Overview of Theory of Parenting Practices

Table 10.1 below summarizes the parenting practices experienced by the women in the study according to some key dimensions of the theory of mature and immature parent—child relationships. (See Chapter 4 for an explication of the elements in the theory.) The analysis was done on the basis of the eleven cases, which were selected and constructed to typify certain kinds of experiences discussed by the women. The "Abuse" column is based on the case constructs of physical abuse and

Table 10.1. Abused, Deprived, and Happy Childhood and Mature and Immature Parenting Practices

	Abused	Deprived	Happy
Primary bond	Fractured	Fractured/stable	Stable
Mirroring	Inadequate	Inadequate	Adequate
Style of parenting	Double/project	Reversal/project	Empathic
Communicative stance	Blaming	Blam/irrel/objectiv	Congruent/bla
Attributions	Negative	Neg/mix/pos	Positive
Expectations	Positive/mixed	Negative/positive	Positive
Temporality	Stressful	Stressful/meaning	Meaningful
Defenses	Psyc/immature	Immature/neurotic	Neuro/mature
Dramatic form	Tragic	Tragic/comic	Comic/tragic
Moral development	Survival/goodness	Goodness/survival	Goodness/care
Ethical level	Resent/indulgence	Self-control/artistry	Artistry/love
Child's self-integration	Divided	Divided	Integrated

incest including Rebecca, Gloria, Greta, Janet, and Delores. The "Deprivation" column includes those case constructs involving the death of a parent and those involving poverty or neglect, namely Karen, Shelly, Barbara, and Michelle. The "Happy" column includes the case constructs of Pam and Rhonda who received "mature" parenting.

Those women who were physically and/or sexually abused as children reported behaviors and attitudes on the part of their parents that indicate immaturity in every dimension of the theoretical framework. In addition, they showed greater immaturity then did the parents of the women in the "deprived" category. Among the deprived, those who suffered from poverty and neglect described greater immaturity on the part of their parents then did the remaining single parents where one parent died. Those in the happy category described parental behavior and attitudes that were more mature overall then those in the abused or deprived categories. To explore further the theory of mature and immature parenting in relation to the varying types of childhood experiences described by the women, a comparison will be made over the various case constructs for each component of the theory. The kinds of immature parenting practices experienced by the women vary with the nature of the adversities they suffered.

All cases of physical abuse and sexual abuse experienced a ruptured primary bond to either mother or father or both. Michelle and Barbara, cases of poverty and neglect, seem to have experienced stable primary bonds. The cases of death of a parent necessarily involved a rupture of primary bonding, but at relatively later ages (Shelly at age 12 and Karen at age 11). Primary bonding was most stable in the mature parenting experienced by Pam and Rhonda.

Only among those experiencing mature parenting was there adequate mirroring. Rhonda benefited from this more than Pam. Pam's mother was too concerned with Pam being "perfect" to mirror her full range of feelings.

Those women who suffered physical or sexual abuse experienced double-image or projective parenting. Incest victims necessarily are victims of double-image parenting because they first are given the attributions of sex objects and then forced to meet the physical needs of the parent. Death of a parent resulted in reversal parenting for the Shelly and Karen. In these cases, the child took on the role of the deceased father or mother. The poverty and neglect cases (Michelle and Barbara) illustrated projective more than reversal parenting. Qualities of self-sufficiency beyond her years were projected onto Michelle—hence she was neglected. Barbara was neglected by her mother who criticized her as a hyperactive tomboy. Considering "happy" childhood, Pam's mother tended to put her in the role of sister. She was expected to take care of the mother's need for support and companionship and help with the younger siblings. Pam received some degree of empathic parenting, seemingly more from her father than her mother. Her time/memory studies contain vivid images of him. Rhonda's experience of both her parents was as empathic. They continually demonstrated sensitivity to her needs and feelings.

The cases of physical and sexual abuse experienced their parents primarily as blamers in their communicative stances. Michelle, a case of poverty and neglect with some hint of physical abuse by an alcoholic father, experienced her parents as noncommunicative. The "irrelevant" or distracted communicative stance fits this the best. Barbara saw her parents as either ignoring or blaming her. Those whose parents died when they were children did not seem to have benefit of congruent communication in their remaining single parents. Shelly's father was "objectivistic" or "computer-like" in his communicative style. Karen's mother seemed to dissociate in a somewhat irrelevant or distracted manner. Pam benefited from some degree of congruent communication on the part of her parents in combination with a blaming stance. Rhonda's parents were able to be direct about their thoughts, feelings and expectations. They seemed to be the most congruent communicators among the parents in the study.

The parents of the women who were physically and/or sexually abused tended to use "psychotic" or "immature" level defense mechanisms. At times, the mothers of both Janet and Delores seemed to be practicing the psychotic level mechanism of denial or distortion in relation to the activities of their husbands. Beating or sexually abusing a child are instances of "acting out," and "immature" or adolescent level defense mechanisms. Michelle's and Barbara's parents showed some immature and some neurotic level mechanisms. For example, Michelle's father's alcoholism and Barbara's father's verbal and physical abuse are forms of immature "acting out." Michelle's mother showed dissociation or displacement (neurotic) mechanisms in her noncommunicative relationship with her daughter. Neglect of a child's emotional and/or physical needs may also be a form of passive aggressive behavior (an immature defense mechanism.) Barbara's father showed signs of "reaction formation" toward her when she went into puberty. He changed at that point from being companionate to cold, possibly using this distance to displace aroused sexual feeling toward his daughter at this time.

Karen's and Shelly's remaining single parents tended to use neurotic defenses. Shelly's father's overinvolvement in work following his wife's death is a form of displacement. Karen does not present a strong image of her mother's defenses. Reading between the lines, she may have used a mature mechanism of sublimation, by a greater involvement in the church. Pam's and Rhonda's parents used neurotic to mature defenses. There was humor, altruism, and sublimation in these families.

All of the cases of abuse, physical and sexual, reported receiving negative attributions from their parents, coupled with positive expectations. In other words, their abusive parent places his or her child in a double bind. On the one hand, the parents expect them to fulfill familial responsibilities and achieve both at school and at work. However, these daughters did not receive support in the form of appreciative or positive attributions from their parents that would engender self-confidence. More importantly, the lack of positive attributions makes it difficult for them to feel good about themselves regardless of their achievements. Their sense of pleasing their parents would come primarily from achievements. To obey the ghosts of these parents they must succeed. Ironically, they must also have low self-esteem, if they are to meet their parents' expectations! Until these women change their childhood ghosts into spirits they will never be pleased with themselves and will tend to take a blaming attitude toward others.

The adversities of poverty and neglect experienced by Michelle and Barbara were accompanied by negative or mixed attributions and mixed expectations from their parents. The attributions and expectations of their parents seemed to be less contradictory then in the abuse cases. Those who suffered the death of a parent, Karen and Shelly, share similar positive attributions and expectations with Pam and Rhonda

("Happy"). Karen's and Shelly's memories of their deceased parents' attributions and expectations tended to be positive. Karen's father, however, limited his expectations of her because she was a girl.

All of those who suffered adversities of abuse and/or neglect also had a stressful experience of time. They did not highlight family holidays and special events as meaningful and enjoyable aspects of the experience of time's passage. To the contrary, these abused and neglected participants either did not mention holidays or they experienced them as stressful. Michelle, as a child, dreaded weekends and holidays when large family gatherings would occur. She found them hectic and chaotic and much preferred to be alone and read. The death of a parent, while it evoked memories, did not lesson the experience of holidays and family events as meaningful. The highest degree of joy expressed surrounding shared family holidays was that of Karen and Shelly, with happy childhoods. The whole family enjoyed anticipating, having, and remembering the event.

In all of the childhood homes of the women who were physically or sexually abused or neglected a dramatic atmosphere of tragedy prevailed. Blaming communicative stances kept these environments filled with anger. Rebecca, Gloria, Greta, Janet, Delores, Michelle, and Barbara were all victims and, at times, scapegoats in these tragic dramatic systems.

Karen's Shelly's, and Pam's home environments had elements of tragic and comic dramatic form. The death of a parent as a child is tragic and effects the rest of the child's maturation. Pam became a tragic victim of the dramatic action in her home when, as a high school senior, she became pregnant, married, and left her home town in "disgrace." Pam's home also had elements of the comic. Rhonda's experience of her home rings happy and secure. No scapegoats or tragic victims were necessary to her family. Her family dynamics seemed to fit the comic dramatic form the best.

The parents of each of those women who suffered from physical and/ or sexual abuse as children were described by their daughters as similar in ethical and moral development. In relation to Gilligan's stages of moral development, they were oriented toward either survival (when under stress) or goodness—being accepted. My discussion of the moral development aspects of the theory of immature and mature parenting will focus mostly on the mothers. The stages are based on Gilligan's study of moral development in women who moved from a survival orientation through a focus on sacrificial goodness, to care, where there is responsibility for self in balance with others.

Rebecca's mother was survival-oriented when remarried to a man who was abusive to her daughter. Gloria's mother was functioning according to morality of "goodness" in her desire to be thought of as a good person. She maintained extensive involvements in church, scouts, and other social activities. These activities bolstered her image as a good Christian at the same time that she was blaming and cruel toward her children. The mothers of Janet and Delores, whose spouses were sexually abusive to their daughters, were at "survival" or "goodness" levels in Gilligan's framework. The sense of "goodness" would have been toward their husbands, for whom they felt responsible. At a more basic level, there was some survival orientation. They must have desperately needed these relationships for them to overlook for so long their negative behavior in regard to their daughters. Janet's mother was an adult child of an alcoholic mother. As such, she was "co-dependent" (in current psychological jargon). The co-dependent ideally needs to take care of the dependent other. The "survival" aspect for Delores' mother was also economic.

Michelle's and Barbara's mothers similarly were survival-or goodness-oriented. Michelle's family was poor and dependent upon their alcoholic father's salary from the coal mines. Michelle's mother, as an abused spouse, was bitter and withdrawn, yet she showed aspects of goodness in her relationship with her husband and children. The primary quality experienced by Barbara in relation to her mother was rejection. A rejecting mother is not caring, or even "good." She is dealing with personal survival issues.

In the case constructs involving deprivation due to death of a parent, both remaining parents seemed motivated by goodness. They accepted their responsibility for their children. A hint of survival orientation was evident in their concern that Karen and Shelly do what was necessary for survival whether it be working, house cleaning, or getting married at the correct time.

Among the "happy" children, Pam's mother took a survival/goodness orientation toward Pam as she had several younger children and needed Pam's help in coping. Pam's father exhibited aspects of a mutually caring relationship with Pam. Rhonda's experience of both parents was as caring.

A progression can be seen in the experience of ethical aspects of parenting practice. Persons who are at the highest ethical level, according to Weinstein, have well-developed self-control, which provides the basis for artistry and then love. All of the case constructs of those who were abused had parents who had not achieved adequate self-control, and, consequently, had not moved on into developing artistry and love. The poverty and neglect cases showed some movement into self-control and possibly artistry. Karen's mother, after her father's death, and Shelly's father, after her mother's death, exhibited self-control, artistry, and aspects of love. Pam's and Rhonda's mature parents showed aspects of artistry and love in their ethical levels.

All of the women, except for Pam and Rhonda, described themselves in ways which fit Denzin's concept of the emotionally divided self. (See Table 10.2 below.) This finding is perhaps the strongest argument for the importance of becoming mature. It is painful to experience the self as emotionally divided. Such inner conflict saps one's ability to express oneself artistically and to love. It also ensures that one is likely to project this unresolved tension upon one's children. Facing up to the ghosts of one's childhood and making them into spirits is the best way to overcome the divided self.

Interpretations: Future Directions

Parent–child relationships do not exist in a vacuum. The horizon of each family's experience looms unseen. Like the sky, it sets the scene for the dramatic picture of daily life. Whether sunny, rainy, polluted, or star-filled, the sky sets the tone of the landscape. Sky is not only horizon. It is the air we breathe. It makes our lives possible and is inside as well as outside of us.

Table 10.2 The Emotionally Divided Self

Physically abused	
Rebecca	Divided
Gloria	Divided
Greta	Divided
Sexually abused	
Janet	Divided
Delores	Divided
Poverty and Neglect	
Michelle	Divided
Barbara	Divided
Death of a Parent	
Shelly	Divided
Karen	Divided
Happy Childhood	
Pam	Integrated
Rhonda	Integrated

The social and cultural context is this sky and air that framed and infused the daily existence of the women in the study. The social, economic, and political aspects of life influenced and set the climate for family interaction. Parents may be "mature" or "immature" in good and bad social contexts. High resource contexts facilitate and sustain becoming mature.

Paul Ricoeur (1976) contends that any interpretation is not complete until the "world reached for by the text" is explored. This world was but vaguely grasped by most of the women, but experienced to a considerable extent by Pam and Rhonda, who were fortunate enough to have parents who were more mature than immature. The world reached for by adult survivors of neglect, poverty, physical and psychological abuse, incest, or the death of a parent is a world in which they would be cared for and appreciated. It is one where there would be empathic understanding and where power "trips"would be undermined by shared laughter.

What kind of a social world is it where so many do not become mature and where these many, as parents, cause pain and foster immaturity in their offspring as they haunt them throughout their lives? The exploration of the social horizons of mature and immature becoming is the final hermeneutic turn taken in this text.

To stop at this point in the interpretive process would amount to blaming the victim. It is not enough to say what kind of parent–child relationship and what kind of family environments are necessary for adequate maturation. One must look underneath for the reasons why so many live this way, and why some escape into authentic caring. Is the historical continuity of immaturity a force within certain family lines? Does it follow from generation to generation like alcoholism? Or are such families a part of a larger socioeconomic and cultural network that fosters their continued immaturity? Here the hermeneutic process must be extended, following Droysen's important leads, (see Burger, 1976) beyond the social psychological to the level of cultural, historical analysis, and then beyond that to cultural criticism and to a vision of a better way of life hidden in the documents.

Caring Relationships and Becoming Mature

To become ethically and emotionally mature, parents must at some time in their lives, and again at points of stress, experience directly and closely personal caring relationships. Even in a context that facilitates caring, parents will not always act maturely because they may not have been raised to maturity by their parents, or they may face unavoidable vicissitudes, such as illness or death of a loved one. The resources available in the community, such as support networks and institutional supports greatly effect the nature of parent–child relationships.

Henry S. Maas (1986) discusses the effects of the social environment on child development and family life. He emphasizes that social context can either foster or inhibit parent–child attachment (p. 15). Garbarino (1982) similarly contextualizes the structure of family life. He found that the number of reported cases of child abuse decreases as more jobs are available in a community. Other factors that put a community at "sociocultural risk" for child abuse include sexism, racism, acceptance of violence as a mechanism for control, and an individualistic ethics and mythology (pp. 52–53). As Garbarino states, socially and culturally rich environments, such as exist in cohesive urban neighborhoods or small towns of about 500, are ideal for fostering child development. Such neighborhoods provide networks of persons who know about each other and share similar concerns. Such community contexts must not be repressive, or cult-like, as the negative case of Jonestown will illustrates (see Wooden, 1981).

The effect of social context is evident in the cases where there was physical or sexual abuse, poverty, neglect, or death of a parent. The lives of the women in this study sharply reveal the way the social context may fail to provide adequate supports for the needs of both parents and children. Even in the case of mature parents and happy family life, social contextual factors had some negative impact on the girls' lives.

This section of the text briefly discusses the following aspects of poor social and cultural supports: inadequate or nonexistent economic opportunities; lack of social networks; repressive, rigid, and unresponsive church, work, and educational organizations; and sexism in families, schools, churches, work, and social environments.

The impact of economic conditions was evident in the life of each woman in the study. Inadequate economic resources dramatically impacted the lives of Rebecca, Greta, Delores, Karen, Shelly, and Michelle. Rebecca's life was made insecure from early childhood due to her parent's divorce when she was 3 years old. Not only did she lose a relationship that she remembered fondly, but she lost a secure physical base. She had to move from boarding house to boarding house with her mother as she found work. Frequently, she was not even able to stay in the same home with her mother.

The combined negative forces of poor economic opportunities and racism polluted the social worlds of Greta and Delores. Like many young black women in the lower socioeconomic brackets, Greta became pregnant while a young teenager, only to compound her problems. Greta and her family have been unable to sustain the economic resources required to send Greta to college and care for Greta's daughter. In spite of her strong determination, being a young single mother with little economic support made it impossible for Greta to continue at college. Delores managed to do better, but she did not become a mother until after she completed one college degree. In Delores' case, however, the horizon of poverty experienced as a child looms large as a force in her continued inner turmoil in caring for her child and relating to her husband.

The economic depression of the 1930s impacted heavily on Shelly's life. This was compounded by the death of her mother. The shock of her father's death was heightened for Karen by an immediate economic fall from an upper-middle-class life to near poverty. Michelle also felt the effect of the coldness of spirit in the stark economic conditions for coal miners in the 1930s–1940s. In such a situation, her father's turn to alcohol, and her mother's emotional withdrawal, were understandable.

The impact of the death of a parent as a child, as in the cases of Shelly and Karen, brings the lack of adequate community and social supports into sharp relief. There were not sufficient resources available to help these families fill the vacuum in their lives created by death. Both Shelly and Karen fell into these chasms as children, forced to play adult roles. Greta's family situation tragically illustrates such a lack of needed help. Inadequate child care and personal networks for Greta while in school precipitated her early withdrawal from college. This focus on the impact of social factors on the women's lives must be linked to the theory of mature and immature parent–child relationships.

The quality of life is intertwined with the kinds of organizational structures in which we work, worship, conduct community affairs and play. Gloria's and Delores' lives were marked by their father's employment by the military. Several forced family moves initiated by the military took Gloria away from her beloved grandmother who was her only source of responsive mirroring and positive attributions and expectations. The inability of Gloria and Delores' fathers to be "mature," providing nurturance, understanding, and warmth must have been intensified by their work lives.

The military is the most rigid hierarchy in human society, except perhaps for the prison. In rigid hierarchies, communication is limited to the "chain of command"—the exact opposite of what is needed to establish "competent communication" in Habermas' sense. One is trained not to understand, but to obey. Emotions are not to be felt and appropriately expressed, but repressed. The military is a social institution that trains those charged with the legitimate use of violence. It condones a viewpoint that the assertion of force is a necessary and desirable means to maintain social order. No wonder there is a high incidence of violence in military families.

Rest and recreation are also formally and informally channelled to allow for what Marcuse (1964) aptly labeled "repressive desublimation." The military man is encouraged to find immediate and meaningless sexual gratification. The true maturity of the military person is assaulted because he does not actively participate in determining his own ends and means: "Ours is not to wonder why, ours is but to do and die." In work life, the military person is infantilized. Thus the "infantry" is an ironically appropriate word for a military unit.

For many of the women in the study, religious organizations were and are major sources of personal and social support. They were also sources of unhappiness. Barbara, Pam, and Rhonda, three of the most mature women in the study, each maintained a meaningful participation in the church throughout their lives. In Pam's life, the church also had the effect of binding her to a life of duty and obedience, even at times when greater independence of spirit may have served her better. She may not have chosen to have as many children as she did, as young as she was. She may not have remained tied, duty-bound, to her husband for so long, in an unsatisfactory marriage. Nor may she have felt quite so obliged not only to marry at a young age due to her pregnancy, but to leave her home town in a "state of disgrace" because the word was out that she and her husband "had to" get married.

A church which holds to the "religiocentric" doctrine that they possess the *only* way to the truth is socially harmful in a world of many religions. The negative force of such doctrines impacted heavily in Michelle's life. Her parents disowned her and her husband for years because they joined another Christian church! Similarly, Rebecca suffered from the strictures of her church in two ways. In the first place, it established an overriding sense of guilt in her for any infraction of the many rules. Second, the church rejected her socially because they did not approve of her marriage to a widowed church member.

Gloria reacted to her church through a rejection of hypocrisy. First, she could not fully accept the literal meaning of some of the beliefs. Such a literalist approach to meanings defeats the intellect and mitigates against an authentic sense of "wonder" that Beolen found essential to mature becoming. The sensitive and intelligent mind, such as Gloria's, will rebel at dogmatic interpretations of great mysteries of being. Second, Gloria was personally troubled by the inconsistency she observed between professed principles, such as love and charity, and the cruelty she experienced at home.

In the area of sexual behavior, repressive religious institutions may have reverse side effects from what they intend. Foucault (1976) pointed out that an intense cultural focus on sexual behavior has the consequence of reinforcing sexual interests. Janet's strict, church-going father was not above sexually exploiting her sister, and Janet as well. Greta's mother and her church strongly forbade dancing and feared and negatively sanctioned sexual attachments between teenagers. Yet her mother also encouraged her early courtship which resulted in her pregnancy.

The scepter of sexism pierced the lives of each of the women in the study. None of them escaped unscathed. The impact of sexism in the families, churches, schools, and economic sectors is evident throughout the case studies presented.

Rhonda was faced with men trying to date her who assumed that because she was divorced she would be willing to sleep with them on the first date. Barbara was told by her divorce attorney that she should beg her husband to reconcile, since there was little "demand" in the marriage or job market for women of her age. His language portrayed a deep sexism in that he obviously viewed women as a product to be bought, bartered, and sold on the marketplace of sexuality.

Shelly has had to be a servant to father, brothers, husband, and sons her entire life. She could not fulfill many of her ambitions, from playing basketball competitively in high school to a dedicated pursuit of her career throughout most of her life. Although brilliant, Karen's ambitions were directed at an early age to marriage as a career, even though she found housework and child care duties boring. Karen's middle-aged mother, a trained nurse, could not get a job following her husband's death because she was thought too old to begin her career. This showed the tremendous force of the combined impact of sexism and ageism on the middle-aged woman.

Betty and Delores were raised in families where daughters were viewed and used by their fathers as potential sex objects. Our culture intensifies incest desires because of the sexist glorification of young women and the devaluation of older women as sexually desirable. Because of the cultural association between sex and power, those weaker are seen as even more sexually appealing. When wives and daughters are viewed as male property, they are already "set up" as objects to be used.

Janet was beaten by her husband to the point of requiring emergency hospitalization. Fourteen of the women in the study (25%) admitted to having been physically abused by husbands, father, or boyfriends either in the group discussion or in the narratives.

Each woman, except perhaps Pam, chose a typical woman's occupation such as nurse, teacher, therapist, social worker, and librarian. The low value placed on "female" careers will ensure that throughout their lives (short of major political change) they are not likely to attain the economic security of their male counterparts.

Theory of Required Structure For Maturity

The impact of social factors on the women's lives must be linked to the theory of mature and immature parent–child relationships. Mature becoming requires a social structure consisting of community, ethical communication, and authenticity.

The accelerated tempo of life and the number of responses and interactions required has a negative effect on well-being and the quality of relationships (see also Simmel, 1950; Engelmann, 1966). The difficulty of maintaining the "pedal point" of ties to primary others is evident in the situations of geographic mobility, where parents are frequently located across the country from their children and grandchildren.

Huertas-Jorda (1979) treats the cultural level as the realm of the "proto-symbolic." This includes ideals, myths, legends, beliefs, values, and the practices that give them form. Relatedness to the "proto-symbolic" is essential for any adequately developed self. Many persons do not attend church or do so ritualistically. Even for the ardent church goer, the awe and majesty of religious symbols is difficult to maintain against the onslaught of scientific materialism, on the one hand, and a demystifying realism within religious institutions, on the other. When religion takes the same format as most television programs, complete with commercials, it is questionable whether it can meet the need for rich meaning and connectedness. Among the other social institutions to which one may look for "proto-symbolic" ties are the arts, politics, education, and sports. Each of these institutions in modern society has been criticized for depersonalization, bureaucratization, and domination by the market.

Communities in which meaningful cultural identities may be generated and maintained are threatened in modern mass society. According to Huertas-Jorda, ethnic neighborhoods should be fostered and encouraged because persons can feel most at home and centered in such communities. Huertas-Jorda favors a pluralistic rather then "melting pot" approach to social organization.

George Herbert Mead hypothesized that in playing organized games, the child recognizes the existence of the "they," an abstract other who makes the rules by which games are played. Mead saw the great importance of an expanded generalized other as a source for an improved moral order and for the development of ever more ethical selves (Broyer, 1973). The existence of a generalized other, as hypothesized by Mead for many persons, is questionable. In a study of the development of self of 300 college students, I found that most of them did not possess a "generalized other" in Mead's sense. Rather, they thought of their actions in relation to their immediate friends and other reference groups (Malhotra, 1977).

Habermas' theory of communicative competency and the necessary assumptions underlying it of truth, truthfulness, understandability, and comprehensibility provides an additional critique of social context. For these norms are violated in a pervasive manner in everyday life. Advertising is an art of deception where school glue is used in place of milk to make cereal bounce and where products which are supposed to nourish you are harmful. Strategic communication which is a means to an end abounds and replaces symbolic interaction. Persons no longer participate in conversations where they discover mutual interests. Rather, they are divided into two groups: managers and clients of "total institutions" (Habermas, 1973).

Duncan's concept of "I–It" communication provides a model for how the self relates to society. In "I–It" communication one addresses God, "Humanity," "Nation," "Motherhood" or some other abstract principle of social order. In prayer, religious ritual, meditation, or exhortation, one attempts to communicate with the gods in suitable linguistic form. As Jim Jones and the Jonestown tragedy so well illustrated, such attempts may easily become distorted and used to justify terrors (Wooden, 1981). Duncan contended that religion was a source of mystification. He scorned "revelations" which cannot be answered, where edicts are issued, and where no dialogue is possible—for this justifies scapegoating, repression, and terror "in the name of" whatever god or other "scared" principle is evoked.

Duncan's dramatistic sociology (1962) provides a critique of the context of institutions and organizations. Social organization in the tragic mode is rigidly hierarchical. The rules of those in power cannot be broken without guilt and victimage to restore the balance of power. To repair the damage without changing the rules and hence the hierarchy, a scapegoat must be found, vilified, and punished or persecuted. The victim may be an aspect of the self or projected outward, as in persecutions of homosexuals and welfare recipients.

Repressive work organizations abound and place their employees or inmates under stringent controls. Such environments fit a tragic communications model. They make persons less likely to be able to be altruistic (Vaillant, 1977) and more likely to blame, placate, project, or be objectivistic (Satir, 1983) in their way of communicating. Persons working in such organizations will tend to repress their emotions or express them through acting out, denial, or physical illnesses.[1] They will be less likely to be able to provide an ethically and emotionally mature home environment for their children since they must work all week and worship on Sundays in contexts that mitigate against emotional and ethical maturation.

Organizations structured along the lines of comedy, according to Duncan, will still have rules and hierarchies, but they will be subject to negotiation and change. All will be seen as humanly imperfect, and mistakes and foibles will be matters for gentle shared laughter, and then agreed upon change. The comic scapegoat is the clown, who is not tortured and killed but is laughed *with*, as a source of enlightened joy. Comedy is shared laughter at our common imperfections.

Applying Weinstein's (1985) guidelines to ethical becoming in organizations reveals many of them to inhibit ethical growth. Most organizations do not provide for the cultivation of self-control, for controls are externally imposed. They do not appreciate and reward artistry, but conformity. Many work organizations view their employees as objects to be manipulated or controlled. This attitude rules out love in Weinstein's ethical schematic. Persons are thus forced to act in such organizations according to an ethic of survival, or perhaps "goodness" but are not encouraged to achieve a balance of care for self and others in Gilligan's sense. As a result, defenses commonly practiced in these organizational environments will run the gambit from the psychotic to the immature to the neurotic in Vaillant's sense, rarely reaching the mature level where altruism and sublimation will be common.

Intersocietal and international relations reflect this on a macrocosmic level. The nuclear arms "race," and undercover wars to "protect" perceived interests of the power elite are outstanding examples. Fears and aggressions are channelled outside of the system, reinforcing paranoia internally. Denial is used on a massive level so that daily life may continue under the threat of total annihilation of all life.

For Heidegger, the Meadian "generalized other," society, is not benign, but a source of inauthenticity. "They," "Das Man" swallows one

---

[1] Elgin (1980) twisted Satir's communications model into a strategic technique for verbal self-defense on the job by using "objectivistic" communication.

up in pettiness, gossip, and curiosity about matters of no real consequence (Malhotra, 1987a). Children are particularly vulnerable, under conditions of rampant television usage, to being absorbed in such inauthenticity. Television, computers, machines, plastic toys, and gadgets all fill in the gaps where awareness may have flowered. Death is denied. The mass media and the supermarket mitigate against the child's appreciation of objects and beings in relation to Heidegger's "fourfold" of earth, sky, mortals, and immortals. To Heidegger, all things manifest the essence of being if they are truly understood in relation to the fourfold. For example, an object as simple as a cup of coffee can be so appreciated. The coffee beans grow between earth and sky and are harvested, roasted, brewed, and enjoyed by mortals. The meaning of a shared cup of coffee reflects the entire past and future of a culture in which cups of coffee are enjoyed in various social settings (see Zimmerman, 1981: 235–236). A person seen as an object is viewed inauthentically as a means to an end and a player of roles. The person as a being in the world must be seen in relation to a particular part of the earth from which she came, in relation to the sun and stars and the air, which bring cycles of life and meaning. She[2] must exist in conscious and solicitous relation to others who live in the present as well as to historical predecessors. The technologizing of all objects and persons as objects reduces all to their instrumental value.

Heidegger's "deep ecology" (see Zimmerman, 1986) provides a critique of the social context in which technology reigns supreme. The essence of modern technology is "Das Gestell" the "standing reserve" (Heidegger, 1977) All objects, nature, and persons are viewed and used by technology as resources for exploitation. Forests are not wonderlands filled with mystery, beauty, and awe and are not respected as homes for millions of wondrous creatures. Rather, they are lumber reserves. Persons are not beings to be enlightened, but bodies to fill slots in the technological system through appropriate occupational training. Objects are only objects for use.

The child, in the technologized society, is viewed from the prenatal stage onward as part of "Das Gestell." The amniotic sack is penetrated to detect early malformations. Sound wave graphs and photo-x rays are made of the fetus. Labor is often induced or a Cesearian section performed if the birth does not fit the desired clock schedule. Contractions

[2]In order to provide a sense of flow and versimilitude, female or male pronouns are used at various points in the texts. This avoids the sexism of using consistently male pronouns and the awkwardness of using "he/she" constructions.

are counted. Medications are measured. At birth, the child is measured and weighed against the standards. Movements become "developmental tasks" and records are kept about the first smiles, crawls, and walks.

The medical institution commands the center stage in the early life of the infant. This concern is transferred for those certified to be medically "normal": to the day care center, nursery school, and then the educational system. Once in school, SAT and ACT scores mark progress and determine futures. Children are not "cultivated" to grow according to their own internal needs and dictates, but are prefabricated to become suitable members of the "standing reserve." In such a state of "fallenness" it is the rare child who is allowed to own herself—to be authentic.

Denzin, (1984) aptly describes the fact that the "they-other" contributes to the divided self:

> The self becomes indistinguishable from the "they-self." These others are indefinite. They haunt the subject with their presence in the world. The "they-other" is given the qualities of emotional docility, calmness, serenity, security, and a sense of superiority that makes him feel inferior to it. The subject attempts to take on the moods of the other and fails. This failure places a double wedge between the subject and himself and between the subject and the others of the world. He is driven, in his own eyes, which are the appropriated eyes of the other, further into the empty interiority of the self. Acts of violence draw him out into the world. The use of chemical substances such as prescription drugs and alcohol is sought as a source of strength. Elevated moods fill the emptiness the subject feels on the inner sides of his self. Resentment is an overwhelming emotional attitude toward the other. (p. 207)

The child learns to imitate the "they" to be accepted as a "good" self in terms of "they." But he inevitably fails, and in any case resents not being accepted "for what he really is." But when he looks for what he is he can only find the terror of emptiness. An enormous cultural and personal defense system is erected to help persons avoid these realizations. Nevertheless, the defenses are always penetrable.

The Dialectics between Social Context and Personal Maturity

The grounded findings relate to the theoretical framework of adequate and inadequate parent–child relationships (see Chapter 4). This relates directly to the theory of social context (see Table 10.3 below). In an adequate social context, parents will have greater chance of being able to act maturely, communicate congruently, mirror their child's behavior empathically, provide intellectual and artistic stimulations and

Table 10.3. The Social Context of Caring

Low-resource contexts	High-resource contexts
Das Man (the rule of anonymous power)	Authentic caring
Das Gestell (the world as the standing reserve for technological use)	The world as appreciated in the fourfold of earth, sky, mortals and immortals
Rational-purposive action	Symbolic interaction
Power saturated communication and strategic communication	Competent communication (truth, truthfulness, understandability comprehensibility)
Material resources inadequate	Material resources plentiful
Fractured and/or routinized relationships	Social relationships stable and stimulating
Relationships between organizations ruthless	Fair and just interorganizational relationships
Projective, reversal, and double-image relationship between societies and institutions and toward nature	Caring relationship between societies and institutions and toward nature
Vicious cycle of contempt in institutional/intercultural relations	Empathic understanding between cultures
Organization communication: blaming, irrelevant, objectivistic	Organizational communication: placating, congruent
Tragic model of social organization	Comic model of social organization
Survival and/or goodness primary ethical grounds for organizations	"Caring" ethics between organizations
Acting out encouraged politically and economically	Altruism encouraged and practiced
Time pressured, clocked	Flow of rich shared temporal experiences
Release from time constraints artificially induced	Festivals as community
Religious institutions repressive hierarchical, restrictive, foster defensive reaction formations divided selves, splits	Religions foster communities appreciative relationships, integrated selves
Educational institutions foster manipulation and control	Educational institutions foster self-control, artistry, and love
Sexism	Mutuality between men and women

rich emotional bonding, and use sublimation and altruism as primary defenses, appropriately suppressing negative affects.

The relationship between social context and adequate parenting is a dialectical one, not a simple one-way causation. This is because bitter, frustrated, and hassled parents also make uncaring citizens, administrators, managers, and employers. The dynamics of state-capitalism and a war-readiness economy foster uncaring policies and procedures throughout the society. Exploitative industries and manipulative advertising abound. Child pornography, sadomasochistic sex, drugs, and alcohol all cater to immature, dissatisfied parents and adults and are run and operated by unethical persons. Such harsh political and economic realities provide ample outlets for hostilities and fearful projections of immature persons.

The World Reached For—A Caring Community

A caring community would be one in which the mutuality between persons and the natural environment was respected and appreciated. Contrary to the exploitation and plunder promoted by a "homocentric" view of the world, the caring community would protect all living creatures of whatever species as rightful co-travelers on spaceship earth. There would be an end to inhumane laboratory and commercial exploitation of animals. The earth's form and elements and all other objects, animate and inanimate, would be appreciated. Each would be properly understood in its relations to the fourfold: earth, sky, mortals, and immortals (see Zimmerman, 1981: 235–236). In this context, the natural cycle of change, from birth through death, would be accepted, not artificially resisted. There would then be adequate resources to meet basic needs for all creatures. Within this ecological setting, communities could build systems of stable, revered cultural histories. Here rich and artistically and emotionally satisfying festivals, rituals, and other shared activities would tie persons to higher spiritual concerns. Organizations in which one works would be continually renewed from the grass roots level. Here, in egalitarian, competent, and congruent communication with one another, structures for work, play, and family activities would emerge, flourish, and be transformed or ended as best meeting the interests of all creatures involved. Persons would thus be active participants in determining the course of work, family, play, and community life. The clock and the watch would be abandoned or kept as cultural curiosities from a pressured and insane past when human beings did little else but count their time, their money, their birthdays, and each other.

A caring community was present in glimpses in the lives of each of the women in the study. Even in the darkest moments, the hope and vision of a better life was implied by its absence. Each person can imagine what such a community of care would be like. Some theorists, such as Proudhon, Diderot, Marx, Ghandi, Martin Luther King, August Comte, and Jessie Bernard have presented powerful images of community. To formulate a plan for a community of caring is beyond the scope of this work. More importantly, it is counter to the purpose and findings of this book for a writer in isolation to come up with such a plan, for a caring community must be participatory. Therefore, I will only briefly sketch out here some suggestions based on the findings of this study that such planning could use as starting points:

The *planning* for such a community must be *participatory*. The groups discussing the plans must be structured along the lines of Habermas' "ideal speech situation." The norms of "competent communication" (truth, truthfulness, understandability, and comprehensibility) must be fostered. Strategic and manipulative communication must be ruled out. In this way communities of persons could uncover their actual "interests" and needs.

Social organizations must be *small in scale*. Social theorists such as Toennies, (1957) Weber, (1958) Ghandi, Schumacher (1973), and Munch arrived at the same conclusion—human social organization becomes more dehumanizing the larger it gets. Schools, work places, and governmental structures, all must be established at smaller levels. Communities that share geographical locations of living, work, and play should be fostered. As Ghandi tried to impress on the people of India, the movement toward urbanization and away from village life was not in the interests of most persons. The economist Schumacher stressed a similar point through his concept of decentralizing production under the rubric of "small is beautiful." Nation-state and global coordination should occur along the lines of federations of self-sufficient communities. Within such a system, individuals would be able to reassociate with different communities.

The *spirit of comedy* as opposed to tragedy should prevail in communities and organizations. Heidegger reaches for this in his writings on the "anarchic" community. By this Heidegger meant that an overconcern for order and control must be overcome. The great artists, such as Beethoven, have provided such an image. In his 9th symphony, Beethoven celebrates the community of human beings.

Social and cultural forces set the context and allow the probability of family relationships, which, in turn, foster either the maturity or immaturity of members of all ages. In this study it was not anticipated that most of the women would have suffered the effects of what is recognized as a result of the study as immature family relationships. The amazing amount of child abuse and neglect found unexpectedly in these cases was an important result of the study. This discovery led me to look deeply into the documents, notes, and my memories of the processes for the kinds of parent–child relationships remembered by the women.

The ghosts and spirits of childhood haunt and inspire us throughout our lives. In order to become mature, it is important that we rid ourselves of the ghosts of immature parents and others. The women in this study have broken significant ground in doing this in their own lives. They found that by remembering their childhood, and by writing about it and discussing it with others they could catch up with some of these ghosts and exorcize them or change them into spirits. It is vitally important that each of us do this in order that unnecessary suffering be alleviated. As members of communities, it is equally important that we develop institutions that provide adequate resources for becoming mature.

Bibliography

American Psychiatric Association. (1980). *Diagnostic and Statistical Manual of Mental Disorders*. Washington, D.C.

Astin, Helen. (1976). *Some Action of Her Own*. Lexington, Ma.: D.C. Heath.

Bateson, Gregory. (1958). Language and psychotherapy: Frieda Fromm-Reichmann's last project. *Psychohistory* 21: 96–100.

Becker, Ernest, (1973). *The Denial of Death*. New York: Free Press.

Boelen, Bernard J. (1978). *Personal Maturity: The Existiential Dimension*. New York: Seabury Press.

Bowen, Murray A. (1960). A family concept of schizophrenia. *In* D. Johnson (ed.), *The Etiology of Schizophrenia*. New York: Basic Books.

Broyer, John. (1973). Mead's ethical theory. *In* Walter Robert Corti (ed.), *The Philosophy of George Herbert Mead*. Winterthur, Switzerland: Amriswiler Bucherie.

Burger Thomas (1976). *Max Weber's Theory of Concept Formation: History, Law and Ideal Types*. Durham, NC: Duke University Press.

Chodorow, Nancy, (1978). The Reproduction of Mothering. Berkeley: University of California Press.

Christian Science Monitor (1985). November, vol. 25.

Cicourel, Aaron. (1973). *Cognitive Sociology*. London: Longman.

Cohen, Joan, Coburn, Karen L., and Pearlman, Joan C. (1980). *Hitting Our Stride: Good News about Women in Their Middle Years*. New York: Delacorte.

Cortese, Anthony. (1984). The sociology of moral judgment: Social and ethnic factors. Paper presented at the American Sociological Association Annual Meetings, San Antonio, Texas, August.

Denzin, Norman K. (1978). *The Research Act*. (2nd. ed.). New York: McGraw Hill.

Denzin, Norman K. (1984). *On Understanding Emotion*. San Francisco: Jossey Bass.

deMause, Lloyd. (ed.) (1974). *The History of Childhood*. New York: Harper and Row.

Derrida, Jacques. (1978). *Writing and Difference*. (Trans. Alan Bass). Chicago: University of Chicago Press.

Duncan, Hugh Dalziel. (1962). *Communication and Social Order*. New York: Oxford University Press.

Elgin. Suzette Hayden. (1980). *The Gentle Art of Verbal Self Defense*. New York: Dorset Press.

Engelmann, Hugo O. (1966). *Essays in Social Theory and Social Organization*. Dubuque, Iowa: Wm. C. Brown.

Erikson, Erik. H. (1950). *Childhood and Society*. New York: Norton.

Foucault, Michelle. (1976). *The History of Sexuality*, vol. I. (Trans. Robert Hurley). New York: Random House.

Freud, Sigmund. (1960). *The Ego and the Id*. (Trans. J. Riviere; J. Strachey, ed.). New York: Norton.

French, Marilyn (1977). *The Women's Room*. New York: Jove.

Garbarino, James. (1982). *Children and Families in the Social Environment*. New York. Aldine.

Gibbs, Laura. (1987). Marital and career adjustment among mid-life female graduate students. Thesis. Texas Woman's University, Texas.

Gilligan, Carol. (1982). *In a Different Voice: Psychological Theory and Women's Development*. Cambridge: Harvard Univ. Press.

Glaser, Barney, and Strauss, Anselm. (1967). *The Discovery of Grounded Theory*. Chicago: Aldine.

Glass, James M. (1985). *Delusion*. Chicago: University of Chicago Press.

Godamer, Hans George. (1975). *Truth and Method*. New York: Seabury Press.

Guajardo, Hope. (1980). The phenomenology of time consciousness in the life cycle of a Mexican-American woman. Professional Paper. Texas Woman's University, Texas.

Habermas, Jurgen (1970). *Toward a Rational Society*. Boston: Beacon.

Habermas, Jurgen. (1973). *Knowledge and Human Interests*. Boston: Beacon.

Habermas, Jurgen. (1979). *Communication and the Evolution of Society*. Boston: Beacon.

Heidegger, Martin. (1962). *Being and Time*. (Trans. John MacQuarrie and Edward Robinson). New York: Harper and Row.

Heidegger, Martin. (1977). *The Question Concerning Technology and Other Essays*. (Trans. William Lovitt). New York: Harper and Row.

Herman, Judith (1982). *Father-Daughter Incest*. Cambridge: Harvard University Press.

Horney, Karen. (1950). *Neurosis and Human Growth*. New York: Norton.

Huertas-Jourda, Jose. (1979). The phenomenology of living presence. Department of Philosophy, Ohio University, Athens. Photocopy.

Husserl, Edmund, (1970). *The Crisis of the European Sciences and Transcendental Phenomenology*. Evanston, Illinois: Northwestern University Press.

Justice, Blair and Justice, Rita. (1979). *The Broken Taboo: Sex in the Family*. New York: Human Sciences Press.

Justice, Blair and Justice, Rita (ND). *The Abusing Family*. New York: Human Sciences Press.

Karp, David A. and Yoels, William C. (1982). *Experiencing the Life Cycle: A Social Psychology of Aging*. Springfield, Illinois: Charles Thomas.

Kelman, E., and Stanley, Bonnie. (1974). The returning student: Needs of an important minority group. *Eric Ed*. 103–747:1–21.

Kohlberg, Lawrence (1981). *The Philosophy of Moral Development*. San Francisco: Harper.

Lacan, Jacques. (1977). *Ecrits: A Selection*. New York: Norton.

Lakoff, George, and Johnson, Mark. (1980). *Metaphors We Live By*. Chicago: University of Chicago Press.

Langs, Robert. (1982). *Psychotherapy: A Basic Text*. New York: Aronson.

Langs, Robert (1985). *Madness and Cure*. New Jersey: Newconcept Press, Inc.

Langs, Robert (1986). The denial of death in the psychotherapeutic process. Lecture presented at the Institute for Communication and Mental Health Studies. Denton, Texas.

Levinson, D., Darrow, C. M., Klein, E. B., Levinson, M. H., and McKee, B. (1978). *The Seasons of a Man's Life*. New York: Alfred Knopf.

Luquet. J. (1964). *Bulletin de Psychologie*. No. 236: Tome XVIII, 3–6, November: 112–13, 176–185; 199; 204–10, 216

Maas, Henry S. (1984). *People and Contexts: Social Development from Birth to Old Age*. New York: Prentice-Hall.

Maas, Henry S. (1986). From crib to crypt: Social development and responsive environments as professional focus. Boehm Memorial Lecture. Rutgers, New Jersey: Rutgers The State University, School of Social Work.

Malhotra, Valerie A. (1976). Critical dimensions in social psychology: Habermas and Mead. In T. R. Young (ed.), *Current Directions in American Social Psychology*. Ft. Collins, Co.: Institute for Advanced Studies in Sociology.

Malhotra, Valerie A. (1977). Relating Mead's model of self and phenomenology: An empirical analysis: *The Wisconsin Sociologist* 14 (Winter): 8–24.

Malhotra, Valerie A. (1979a). Critical dimensions in symbolic interaction: On pseudo-communication. Paper presented at the Midwest Sociological Association Annual Meetings, Minneapolis, Minnesota, April.

Malhotra, Valerie A. (1979b). Multiple triangulation in the study of a halfway house. Paper presented at the Southwestern Sociological Association Annual Meetings, Ft. Worth, Texas, March.

Malhotra, Valeria A. (1980). Power and communication: An outline of a critical symbolic interactionism. Paper presented at the American Sociological Association Annual Meeting, August, Boston, MA.

Malhotra, Valerie A. (1982). Power-saturated vs. appreciative communication among children and between children and adults. Paper presented at the Tenth World Congress of Sociology, Mexico City, August.

Malhotra, Valerie A. (1983). The social construction of self as formulated in Meadian autobiographies. Paper presented at the Annual Meetings of the Society for the Study of Symbolic Interaction, Detroit, Michigan, August.

Malhotra, Valerie A. (1984a). Lifestyles and time schedules of women students. Paper presented at the Midwest Sociological Society Annual Meetings, Chicago, Illinois, April.

Malhotra, Valerie A. (1984b). Research as critical reflection: A study of self, time and communicative competency. *Humanity and Society* 8, (no. 4 November): 468–477 [Also *In* Nebraska Feminist Collective (ed.), *Feminist Ethics and Social Science Research*, (1987) by B. Harting Lewsiton, N.Y.: Edwin Mellen Press.]

Malhotra, Valerie A. (1985a). Child development from a Heideggerian perspective. Paper presented at the Fifth Annual Heidegger Symposium, North Texas State University, Denton, Texas, June.

Malhotra, Valerie A. (1985b). A critical-symbolic interactionist approach to group therapy with women. Paper presented at the annual meetings of the Texas State Chapter of the National Association of Social Workers, Dallas, Texas, October.

Malhotra, Valerie A. (1986b). Notes on the integration of sociological theory with practice, research and teaching. *The Practicing Sociologist* 8 (no.4) (Winter):5–6.

Malhotra, Valerie A. (1987a). A comparison of Mead's "self" and Heidegger's "Dasein": Toward a regrounding of social psychology. *Human Studies* 10:357–382.

Malhotra, Valerie A. (1987b). From "self" to "Dasein": (*In* Norman K. Denzin (ed.), *Critique and Renewal in Social Psychology. Studies in Symbolic Interaction*, Vol. 8, pp. 23–42. Greenwich CN.: J. A. I. Press,.

Malhotra, Valerie A. (1987c). Habermas sociological theory and clinical practice with small groups. *Clinical Sociology Review* 5:181–192.

Malhotra, Valerie A. (1987d). Review of "Finite perfection: reflections on virtue" by Michael A. Weinstein. *Journal of Political Theory*, August, pp. 443–449.

Malhotra, Valerie A. (1988). Time and memory: A social psychological etude inspired by Alfred Schutz. In L. Embree (ed.), *Worldly Phenomenology: The Continuing Influence of Alfred Schutz on North American Social Science*, pp. 101–123. Washington D.C.: University Press of America.

Malhotra, Valerie and Deegan, Mary Jo. (1978). Comment on Perinbanayagam's The significance of "Others" in the thought of Alfred Schutz, G. H. Mead and C. H. Cooley. *Sociological Quarterly* 19 (Winter): 141–145.

Malhotra, Valerie, and Deneen, Jeffrey. (1983). Habermas' communicative competency: A statistical analysis within a hermeneutical context. Paper presented at the Midwest Sociological Association Annual Meetings, Kansas City, Kansas, April.

Marcuse, Herbert. (1964). *One Dimensional Man*. Boston: Beacon.

Mead, George Herbert. (1934). *Mind, Self, and Society*. Chicago: University of Chicago Press.

Mead, George Herbert. (1938). *The Philosophy of the Act*. Chicago: University of Chicago Press.

Mead, George Herbert. (1959). *The Philosophy of the Present*. LaSalle, Illinois: Open Court Press.

Merleau-Ponty, Maurice. (1964). *Signs*. (Trans. Richard C. McCleary). Evanston, Illinois: Northwestern University Press.

Miller, Alice. (1984). *The drama of the Gifted Child: How Narcissistic Parents Form and Deform the Emotional Lives of Their Talented Children*. New York: Basic Books, Inc.

Miller, David L. (1973). *George Herbert Mead: Self, Language and the Social World*. Austin: University of Texas Press.

Mills, C. Wright. (1959). *The Sociological Imagination*. New York: Oxford University Press.

National Center on Child Abuse and Neglect. (1985). "Research in Brief." Washington, D.C.

Munch, Peter (1971). *Crisis in Utopia*. New York: Crowell.

Owens, Lorrie. (1981). Doing nothing: The effects of keeping time schedules on research participants. Paper presented at the fall sociological research symposium, East Texas State University, Commerce, Texas.

Perlman, Helen Harris (1986). Unfinished business of childhood. Lecture presented at the National Association of Social Workers, Annual Conference, Chicago, IL.

Piaget, Jean. (1965). *The Moral Judgment of the Child*. (Trans. M. Gabain). New York: The Free Press.

Postman, Neil. (1982). *The Disappearance of Childhood*. New York: Delacourt Press.

Rappaport, Judith. (1984). Mid-life women at social work school: A comparative study. *Dissertation Abstracts International* 45:6.

Rasmussen. Davie (1982). Communicative action and philosophy: Reflections on Habermas theorie des kommunication Handelus. *Philosophy and Social Critisism* 9(1):1–29.

Ricoeur, Paul. (1974). *The Conflict of Interpretations: Essays in Hermeneutics*. Evanston, IL: Northwestern University Press.

Ricoeur, Paul. (1976). *Interpretation Theory: Discourse and the Surplus of Meaning*. Ft. Worth: Texas Christian University Press.

Ricoeur, Paul. (1981). *Hermeneutics and the Human Sciences* (Trans. and ed. by John G. Thompson). Cambridge: Cambridge University Press.

Ricoeur, Paul (1984). *Time and Narrative*, Vol I (Trans. by K. McLaughlin and D. Pellauer). Chicago: University of Chicago Press.

Roach, Rose Marie. (1976). Honey, won't you please stay home? *Personnel and Guidance Journal* 55(2):491–497.

Rogers, Carl R. (1961). *On Becoming a Person*. Boston: Houghton Mifflin.

Russell, Diane. (1984). *Sexual Exploitation*. New York: Russsell Sage.

Satir, Virginia. (1983). *Conjoint Family Therapy*. Palo Alto: Science and Behavior Books, Inc.

Schumacher, Ernest Frederick. (1973). *Small Is Beautiful*. New York: Harper and Row.

Schürmann, Reiner (1987). *Heidegger on Being and Acting: From Principles to Anarchy*. Bloomington, IN: Indiana University Press.

Schutz, Alfred. (1970). *In* Helmut Wagner (ed.), *On Phenomenology and Social Relations*. Chicago: University of Chicago Press.

Schutz, Alfred. (1973). *Collected papers, Vol I., The Hague: Martinus Nijhoff*.

Schutz, Alfred (1975). *Collected Papers*, Vol. II. The Hague: Martinus Nijhoff.

Schutz, Alfred (1976). *Collected Papers*, Vol. II The Hague: Martinus Nijhoff.

Schutz, Alfred (1982). *Life Forms and Meaning Structures*. London: Routledge & Kegan Paul.

Schutz, Alfred, and Luckmann, Thomas. (1973). *The Structures of the Lifeworld*. Evanston: Northwestern University Press.

Selfe, Lorna. (1977). *Nadia: A Case of Extraordinary Drawing Ability in an Autistic Child.* New York: Academic Press.

Simmel, George. (1950). The metropolis and mental life. *In* Kurt Wolff (ed.), *The Sociology of George Simmel* Glencoe, Illinois: The Free Press.

Smith, Dorothy (1987). *The Everyday World as Problematic:* Toronto: University of Toronto Press.

Sorokin, Pitirim. (1956). *Fads and Foibles of Modern Sociology.* Chicago: Henry Regnery.

Speier, Matthew. (1973). *How to Analyze Everyday Conversation.* Pacific Palisades: Goodyear Press.

Stabel, Carol. (1981). An analysis of the effects of writing daily journals. Paper presented at the Fall Sociological Research Symposium: East Texas State University, Commerce, Texas.

Tittle, Carol K., and Denker, Elenor. (1977). Kuder occupational interest survey profiles of re-entry women. *Journal of Counseling Psychology* 24:293–300.

Toennies, Ferdinand (1957). *Community and Society.* New York: Harper & Row.

United States Department of Commerce (1974–1975). *Population Bulletin.*

Vaillant, George E (1977). *Adaptation to Life: How the Best and the Brightest. Came of Age.* Boston: Little, Brown.

Wagner, Helmut. (1983). *Phenomenology of Consciousness and Sociology of the Lifeworld.* Edmunton: University of Alberta Press.

Weber, Max (1958). (*In* Hans Gerth and C. Wright mills (eds.), *From Max Weber: Essays in Sociology.* New York: Oxford University Press. *Webster's New Twentieth Century Unabridged Dictionary.* (1979). New York. William Collins, Inc.

Weinstein, Michael. (1985). *Finite Perfection: Reflections on Virtue.* Amherst, MA.: Univ. of Massachusetts Press.

Wooden, Kenneth. (1981). *Children of Jonestown.* New York: McGraw-Hill.

Young, T. R. (1978). *Some Theses on the Structure of the Self.* Boulder: Institute for Advanced Studies in Sociology.

Zastrow, Charles and Kirst-Ashman, Karen K. (1987). *Understanding Human Behavior and the Social Environment.* Chicago: Nelson Hall.

Zimmerman, Michael E. (1986). Toward a Heideggerean ethos for radical environmentalism. Paper presented at the 3rd Annual Heidegger Conference, University of North Texas.

Zimmerman, Michael E. (1981). *The Eclipse of Self: The Development of Heidegger's Concept of Authenticity.* Athens, Ohio: Ohio University Press.

Guidelines _____ Appendix I

Figure A1. Guidelines for Autobiographies

Select two or three significant others from each period of your past experience. Select those who have had an impact on your "self," that is recognizable today. The periods of your experience which need to be covered are the following:

a. preschool	e. ages 26–35
b. ages 6–12 (approximately)	f. ages 36–45
c. ages 13–18 (approximately)	g. ages 46–55
d. ages 19–25	h. 56 and over

SIGNIFICANT OTHERS

Remember that significant others may include the following:

a. persons you actually knew
b. persons you knew only indirectly
c. fictitious characters (TV, books)
d. authors, political figures, or other noteworthy persons
e. other (such as imaginary others)

For each age category complete the following:

a. Select two or three significant others.
b. State what your relationship to them was.
c. State what qualities or characteristics you think they attributed to you.
d. State what expectations you think they had (have) about you.
e. State how you reflectively evaluate these attributions and expectations. Do you accept or reject them? Why?

G<small>ENERALIZED</small> O<small>THER</small>

For each age category also suppy the following information:

    a. What was your conception of "society?"
    b. What groups (formal and informal), institutions, associations, etc., had an effect on you?
    c. What attributions and expectations do you think "society" and these groups, institutions, and associations had (have) in regard to your "self?"
    d. How do you reflectively evaluate these attributions and expectations?

Figure A2. Communicative Competency in Group Interaction Rating Sheet

Evaluate the performance of each participant both at the beginning and at the end of the project along the following dimensions:

P<small>ERFORMANCE AT THE</small> B<small>EGINNING OF THE</small> P<small>ROJECT</small> _____
P<small>ERFORMANCE AT THE</small> E<small>ND OF THE</small> P<small>ROJECT</small> _____
C<small>ODE</small> N<small>UMBER OF</small> P<small>ARTICIPANT</small> _____ I<small>NITIALS</small>
<small>OF</small> E<small>VALUATOR</small> _____

	Always	Most of the time	Some of the time	Very seldom	Never
1. Participant acted in a domineering manner	1	2	3	4	5
2. Participant tends to bore others in the group	1	2	3	4	5
3. Participant tended to stimulate others in the group	1	2	3	4	5
4. Participant acted in a supportive manner to others	1	2	3	4	5
5. Participant acted withdrawn or indifferent in the group	1	2	3	4	5
6. Participant said little, but was involved	1	2	3	4	5
7. Participant showed hostility to the group discussion	1	2	3	4	5
8. Comprehensibility: The participant exhibited the linguistic skills to make herself understood	1	2	3	4	5

Figure A2. (*cont.*)

9. Truth content (objective):
   Participant made objectively
   true statements   1   2   3   4   5
10. Normative appropriateness: The
    participants communication
    was appropriate within the
    norms of correctness
    governing the situation   1   2   3   4   5
11. Truthfulness (sincerity): The
    participants appeared to speak
    and react truthfully (sincerely)   1   2   3   4   5

Figure A3. Analysis of Conversational Transcripts

INITIALS OF CODER _____

NUMBER CODE OF PARTICIPANT _____

1. Count the total number of times the participant speaks _____
2. How many requests or demands are made by the speaker? _____
3. How many of these requests or demands are carried out by others? _____
4. Which of the following best characterizes the overall interaction?
   (*Check one*)
   _____ a. democratic
   _____ b. dominated by participant
   _____ c. dominated by spouse or friend of participant
   _____ d. dominated by child(ren) of participant
   _____ e. dominated by other (specify)

	Always	Most of the time	Some of the time	Very seldom	Never
5. The participant dominates over others in the conversation	1	2	3	4	5
6. The participant adequately but non-domineeringly expresses her needs and concerns	1	2	3	4	5
7. Overall, the participant adequately responds to the needs and concerns of others	1	2	3	4	5
8. Overall, the participant is dominated by others in the conversation	1	2	3	4	5

Figure A3 (*cont.*)

9. Comprehensibility: The participant exhibited the linguistic skills to make herself understood in the conversation	1	2	3	4	5
10. The participant made objectively true statements (*in your opinion*)	1	2	3	4	5
11. Understandability: The participant communicated within a frame of reference normatively appropriate to the situation	1	2	3	4	5
12. Truthfulness: The participant appeared to communicate truthfully (sincerely)	1	2	3	4	5

Characteristics of the Participants ——— Appendix II

Table A1. Age

Age	Absolute freq	Rel. freq. (%)	Adj. freq. (%)	Cum. freq. (%)
24 and below	14	26.4	31.1	31.1
25 and over	31	58.5	68.9	100.0
No answer	8	15.1	Misg	100.0
Total	53	100.0	100.0	

Table A2. Marital Status

Marital Status	Absolute Freq.	Rel. freq. (%)	Adj. freq. (%)	Cum. freq. (%)
Single	20	37.7	37.7	37.7
Married	25	47.2	47.2	84.9
	8	15.1	15.1	100.0
Total	53	100.0	100.0	

Table A3. Parental Status

Marital Status	Absolute freq.	Rel. freq. (%)	Adj. freq. (%)	Cum. freq. (%)
No children	27	50.9	50.9	50.9
Has children	26	49.1	49.1	100.0
Total	53	100.0	100.0	

Table A4. Number of Children

No. of Children	Absolute freq.	Rel. freq. (%)	Adj. freq. (%)	Cum. freq. (%)
0	27	50.9	50.9	50.9
1	5	9.4	9.4	9.4
2	15	28.4	28.4	60.3
3	4	7.5	7.5	88.7
4 or more	2	3.8	3.8	96.2
Total	53	100.0	100.0	100.0

Table A5. Race

Race	Absolute freq.	Rel. freq. (%)	Adj. freq. (%)	Cum. freq. (%)
Caucasian	41	77.3	77.3	77.3
Black	5	9.4	9.4	86.8
Mexican Amer.	3	5.7	5.7	92.5
Iranian	1	1.9	1.9	94.3
Other	3	5.7	5.7	100.0
Total	53	100.0	100.0	

Table A6. Grade Point Average

Grade point average	Absolute freq.	Rel. freq. (%)	Adj. freq. (%)	Cum. freq. (%)
1.00–1.99	9	17.0	17.0	17.0
2.00–2.99	8	15.1	15.1	32.1
3.00–4.00	36	67.9	67.9	100.0
Total	53	100.0	100.0	

Evaluation of Significant
Others _____ Appendix III

Table A7. Evaluation of Significant Others in Relation to Sex of Significant
Others (%)

Sex of significant other	Positive	Mixed	Negative	Other	Total
Female	52.5	37.5	7.5	2.5	100.0
Male	52.6	36.8	7.9	2.7	100.0

Table A8. Evaluation of Significant Others According to the Sex of Significant
Others and the Age of Participant (%)

Age of participant sex of significant others	Positive	Mixed	Negative	Other	Total
Pre-school					
Female	64.0	24.0	8.0	4.0	100.0
Male	73.9	13.0	8.7	4.4	100.0
Age 6–12					
Female	42.9	42.9	9.5	4.7	100.0
Male	41.2	41.2	11.8	5.8	100.0
Age 13–18					
Female	55.6	38.9	5.5	0.0	100.0
Male	42.9	52.4	4.7	0.0	100.0
Age 19–25					
Female	55.0	30.0	10.0	5.0	100.0
Male	55.2	31.0	3.4	10.4	100.0
Age 26 plus					
Female	71.4	14.3	0.0	14.3	100.0
Male	76.9	15.4	0.0	7.7	100.0

Table A9. Evaluation of Significant Others According to Age of Partidipants (%)

Age of participant	Positive	Mixed	Negative	Other	Total
Preschool	68.6	20.0	5.7	5.7	100.0
Age 6–12	42.4	42.4	12.1	3.1	100.0
Age 13–18	63.9	33.3	2.8	0.0	100.0
Age 19–25	58.5	29.3	4.9	7.3	100.0
Age 26 plus	71.5	19.0	9.5	0.0	100.0

Table A10. Acceptance of Attributions by Age of Participants (%)

Age of participant	Accepted	Mixed	Rejected	Other	Total
Preschool	88.9	3.7	0.0	7.4	100.0
Age 6–12	90.4	3.2	3.2	3.2	100.0
Age 13–18	90.0	10.0	0.0	0.0	100.0
Age 19–25	87.9	6.1	3.0	3.0	100.0
Age 26 plus	78.9	15.8	5.3	0.0	100.0

Table A11. Acceptance of Expectations by Age of Participants (%)

Age of participant	Accepted	Mixed	Rejected	Other	Total
Preschool	84.6	7.7	7.7	0.0	100.0
Age 6–12	74.1	14.8	11.1	0.0	100.0
Age 13–18	79.4	10.3	10.3	0.0	100.0
Age 19–25	55.5	26.0	14.8	3.7	100.0
Age 26 plus	78.7	7.1	7.1	7.1	100.0

Table A12. Evaluation of Significant Others by Participants (%)

Significant Others	Positive	Mixed	Negative	Other	Total
Mother	54.1	35.1	8.1	2.7	100.0
Father	50.0	40.0	6.7	3.3	100.0
Stepfather	50.0	50.0	0.0	0.0	100.0
Grandmother	64.7	35.3	0.0	0.0	100.0
Sister	50.0	50.0	0.0	0.0	100.0
Brother	59.9	30.0	10.1	0.0	100.0
Teacher	56.5	34.8	8.7	0.0	100.0
Friend	60.0	40.0	0.0	0.0	100.0
Girlfriend	55.6	33.2	5.6	5.6	100.0
Boyfriend	46.6	40.0	6.7	6.7	100.0
Aunt	50.0	50.0	0.0	0.0	100.0
Imaginary friend	50.0	33.3	0.0	16.7	100.0
Other friend	37.5	50.0	12.5	0.0	100.0
Husband	55.6	33.3	7.4	3.7	100.0
Male children	53.8	30.8	7.7	7.7	100.0
Female children	50.0	37.5	12.5	0.0	100.0
Church minister	100.0	0.0	0.0	0.0	100.0
God	20.0	40.0	40.0	0.0	100.0
Co-workers	0.0	0.0	100.0	0.0	100.0
Employer	0.0	0.0	100.0	0.0	100.0
Other	50.0	40.0	6.7	3.3	100.0
Uncle	100.0	0.0	0.0	0.0	100.0

Table A13. Attributions by Age of Participants and Acceptance of Attributions by Participants (%)

Age of participant/ Acceptance of attributions	Self-oriented	Other-oriented	Negative personality trait	Developed appreciation	Other
Preschool					
Accepted	88.9	0.0	0.0	0.0	0.0
Mixed	3.7	0.0	0.0	0.0	0.0
Rejected	7.4	0.0	0.0	0.0	0.0
Total	100.0	0.0	0.0	0.0	0.0
Grand total	100.0				
Aged 6–12					
Accepted	19.4	38.7	12.9	3.2	0.0
Mixed	3.2	9.7	3.2	0.0	3.2
Rejected	3.2	0.0	0.0	0.0	0.0
Total	25.8	48.4	16.1	3.2	3.2
Grand total	96.7				
Aged 13–18					
Accepted	30.0	36.7	16.7	1.7	0.0
Mixed	0.0	6.7	3.3	0.0	0.0
Rejected	0.0	0.0	0.0	0.0	0.0
Total	30.0	43.4	20.0	1.7	0.0
Grand total	95.1				
Aged 19–25					
Accepted	30.3	42.4	6.1	9.1	0.0
Mixed	0.0	3.0	3.0	0.0	0.0
Rejected	3.0	0.0	0.0	0.0	0.0
Total	33.3	45.4	9.1	9.1	0.0
Grand total	96.9				
Aged 26 plus					
Accepted	42.1	36.8	0.0	0.0	0.0
Mixed	5.3	3.3	0.0	0.0	0.0
Rejected	5.3	0.0	0.0	0.0	0.0
Total	52.7	40.1	0.0	0.0	0.0
Grand total	92.8				

Table A14. Effects of Research on Participants

Effect	N	%
Changed behavior and understandings	18	34.0
Changed understandings only	24	45.0
No effect reported	6	12.0
Not completed	5	9.0
Total	53	100.0

Table A15. Factor One—Coherency of
Communicative Competency

Item title	Factor loadings
Stimulating	.820
Withdrawn or hostile	−.600
Support	.578
Comprehensibility	.915
Truth content	.542
Normative appropriateness	.781
Truthfulness (Sincerity)	.694

Table A16. Factor Two—Sheltered Group Non/
Dominance and Home Dominance

Item title	Factor loadings
Early group	
Domineering	−.571
Boring	−.817
Said little but involved	.498
Late group	
Domineering	−.761
Boring	−.823
Home	
Domineering	.513

Table A17. Factor Four—Support/Hostility

Item title	Factor loadings
Early in term	
Support	− .634
Hostility	.916
Late in term	
Support	− .598
Hostility	.773

Table A18. Communicative Competency in the Home and Comprehensibility in Sheltered Groups

Item title	Factor loadings
Home	
Truth content (objective)	.476
Normative appropriateness	.721
Truthfulness (sincerity)	.598
Second group taping	
Comprehensibility	.420

Table A19. Power Distortion in Sheltered Groups and the Home

	Early group		Late group		Home	
	Frequency	%	Frequency	%	Frequency	%
Always	0	0.0	0	0.0	0	0.0
Most	3	6.7	3	7.7	8	28.6
Some	8	17.8	10	25.6	7	25.0
Seldom	16	34.6	13	33.3	10	35.7
Never	18	40.9	13	33.4	3	10.7
N^*	45	100.0	39	100.0	28	100.0

$^*N$'s are unequal because of the option that each participant could exercise with regard to any segment of data contribution.

Table A20. Comprehensibility in Sheltered Groups and Home

	Early group		Late group		Home	
	Frequency	%	Frequency	%	Frequency	%
High	19	42.2	14	35.9	0	0.0
Medium high	15	33.3	15	38.5	9	32.1
Medium	4	8.9	5	12.8	16	57.2
Medium low	4	8.9	2	5.1	2	7.1
Low	3	6.7	3	7.7	1	3.6
N^*	45	100.0	39	100.0	28	100.0

$^*N$'s are unequal because of the option that each participant could exercise with regard to any segment of data contribution.

Table A21. Normative Appropriateness in Sheltered Groups and Home

	Early group		Late group		Home	
	Frequency	%	Frequency	%	Frequency	%
High	16	36.4	14	35.9	0	0.0
Medium High	0	0.0	19	48.7	0	0.0
Medium	19	43.2	2	5.1	10	35.7
Medium low	6	13.6	3	7.7	14	50.0
Low	3	6.8	1	2.6	4	14.3
N^*	44	100.0	39	100.0	28	100.0

$^*N$'s are unequal because of the option that each participant could exercise with regard to any segment of data contribution.

Table A22. Truthfulness in Sheltered Groups and Home

	Early group		Late group		Home	
	Frequency	%	Frequency	%	Frequency	%
High	23	53.4	0	0.0	0	0.0
Medium High	0	0.0	19	48.7	0	0.0
Medium	14	32.0	16	41.0	13	46.4
Medium low	5	11.4	3	7.7	12	42.9
Low	2	4.6	1	2.6	3	10.7
N^*	44	100.0	39	100.0	28	100.0

$^*N$'s are unequal because of the option that each participant could exercise with regard to any segment of data contribution.

Table A23. Truth content in Sheltered Group and Home

	Early group		Late group		Home	
	Frequency	%	Frequency	%	Frequency	%
High	12	27.3	0	0.0	0	0.0
Medium High	0	0.0	9	23.1	12	44.4
Medium	21	47.7	23	59.0	11	40.8
Medium low	10	22.7	5	12.8	3	11.1
Low	1	2.3	2	5.1	1	3.7
N^*	44	100.0	39	100.0	27	100.0

$^*N$'s are unequal because of the option that each participant could exercise with regard to any segment of data contribution.

Table of Types of Expectations by Age of Participants and Acceptance of Expectations by Participants

	Family activies			School work			Personality traits		
	Positive	Negative	Future	Positive	Negative	Future	Positive	Negative	Other
Preschool									
Accepted	7.7	3.8	3.8	11.5	3.8	0.0	46.2	3.8	3.8
Mixed	0.0	0.0	0.0	0.0	0.0	3.8	3.8	0.0	0.0
Rejected	0.0	3.8	0.0	3.8	0.0	0.0	0.0	0.0	0.0
Total	7.7	7.7	3.8	15.4	3.8	3.8	50.0	3.8	3.8
Grand total	94.6								
Aged 6–12									
Accepted	7.4	11.1	3.7	29.6	11.1	11.1	0.0	0.0	0.0
Mixed	0.0	3.7	3.7	3.7	0.0	3.7	0.0	0.0	0.0
Rejected	0.0	0.0	3.7	0.0	3.7	0.0	3.7	0.0	0.0
Total	7.4	14.8	11.1	33.3	14.8	14.8	3.7	0.0	0.0
Grand total	99.9								
Aged 13–18									
Accepted	0.0	6.9	13.8	13.8	6.9	24.1	10.3	3.4	0.0
Mixed	0.0	6.9	0.0	3.4	0.0	0.0	0.0	0.0	0.0
Rejected	3.4	0.0	3.4	0.0	0.0	0.0	0.0	0.0	0.0
Total	3.4	13.8	17.2	17.2	6.9	24.1	10.3	3.4	0.0
Grand total	96.3								
Aged 19–25									
Accepted	7.1	10.7	7.1	10.7	0.0	14.3	3.6	0.0	0.0
Mixed	0.0	14.3	0.0	0.0	0.0	0.0	0.0	0.0	0.0
Rejected	0.0	0.0	0.0	0.0	0.0	0.0	0.0	0.0	0.0
Total	10.7	21.4	17.9	32.1	0.0	14.3	3.6	0.0	0.0
Grand total	100								
Aged 26									
Accepted	14.3	7.1	14.3	14.3	14.3	7.1	7.1	0.0	0.0
Mixed	0.0	14.3	0.0	0.0	0.0	0.0	0.0	0.0	0.0
Rejected	0.0	0.0	0.0	0.0	0.0	0.0	0.0	0.0	0.0
Total	14.3	21.4	14.3	14.3	14.3	7.1	7.1	0.0	0.0
Grand total	92.8								

Index